WICKED LIKE A WILDFIRE

LANA POPOVIĆ

WICKED LIKE A WILDFIRE

KATHERINE TEGEN BOOKS
An Imprint of HarperCollins Publishers

Katherine Tegen Books is an imprint of HarperCollins Publishers.

Library of Congress Control Number: 2016963757
ISBN 978-0-06-243683-2

Typography by Torborg Davern
This book is set in 11pt Adobe Garamond Pro.
17 18 19 20 21   PC/LSCH   10 9 8 7 6 5 4 3 2

First Edition

To my own Mama and Tata, for their boundless love and steadfast support. I couldn't have done this without you.

WICKED LIKE A WILDFIRE

ONE

Cattaro, Montenegro

MY SISTER AND I WERE BORN ALL TANGLED UP together, both tiny enough that our unruly descent just narrowly missed killing our mother. I liked to think there would have been a fair bit of screaming on Mama's part in the ruckus that followed, but that's just my wicked fancy. Maybe she was stoic and flawless as ever, Snow White giving birth under glass. Either way, tending to her, no one spared the time to note which of us had arrived first. And so although we weren't identical, by sheer bloody technicality we were always the same age, neither a minute older nor younger than each other.

Mama kept us in a single cradle, one that Čiča Jovan had carved for her from cherrywood before we were born. It was a whimsical thing fit for changeling children, wrought with mermaids trapped in ivy, open seashells with tiny apples growing in them instead of salty flesh. Sometimes I wondered if I'd have liked my own cradle as much as I would have liked having my own room once we were older. But Malina still liked to fall asleep by matching her breathing to mine, rubbing her feet together like a grasshopper.

The only real bedtime story Mama ever told us traced back to those early days, when we were both so little the tops of our skulls hadn't yet hardened into something that could withstand the world. The mother I knew might have been tempted by that fragility, the urge to press her thumbs into such yielding clay. To see what marks she could make.

She must have been so different, then.

Instead, when we were old enough for our pale eyes to focus, she brought an assortment of offerings on a milky sea-glass platter. From it, she plucked tiny slivers of fruit and brushed them over our lips, one by one. Apple, mango, strawberry, papaya, prickly pear, some so exotic she could only have gotten them from the cruise ships that docked in the bay, rather than the open-air market outside the Old Town walls. Each was at its peak, the perfect moment of ripeness before turning. Then she passed violet petals beneath our noses, followed by jasmine, orchid, and peony; small lumps of ambergris; splinters of oud wood and sandalwood and myrrh.

Waiting to see which would bring forth the gleam, the magic that ran through our blood.

For me, it was the hibiscus flower, the petal red and fleshy as our mother trailed it over the tip of my nose, before she let me gum it to release its tart flavor. For Malina, it was a gleaming, perfect cherry, which Mama crushed into a paste that she let my sister suck from her ring finger.

It was bad luck to name a daughter after the thing that first sparked the gleam, Mama said. So I was Iris, for a flower that wasn't hibiscus, and my sister was Malina, for a raspberry. They were placeholder names that didn't pin down our true nature, so nothing would ever be able to summon us. No demon or *vila* would ever reel us in by our real names.

Even caught up in the story, Mama could never quite explain what the gleam looked like once she found it. Maybe our cloudy baby eyes cleared, like a sky swept by a driving wind. Maybe our tiny hands clenched fistfuls of air, seeking the tools that we'd use to capture the gleam once we were older. She never said.

Listening to her tell it, I could have sworn that she'd loved the needy little creatures Malina and I had been. Even if the whole thing was just a story—who rubs flowers and fruit and whale vomit on babies, anyway? What if one of us had been allergic?—it was still beautifully spun. There was love in its very fabric.

Then again, all that was seventeen years ago. These days, had someone asked me if our mother loved us, any "yes" would have caught in my throat like a fish bone. And had someone asked me if I loved my mother, I thought I knew what I would say.

But then she died without dying, and I didn't know anything at all.

THAT WHOLE WEEK felt like a gathering storm. It was only the end of May, but already so stifling that just the effort of breathing made you mutinous. Malina and I worked split shifts at Café Tadić since school had let out for the summer, and that Tuesday I'd drawn the early straw, which I usually preferred. On my way out at six a.m., I'd see the sunrise over the mountains that Cattaro huddled against, the sky glowing like a forge before the craggy peaks above us lit with the first slice of the sun.

It reminded me of what my world had once looked like, brilliant and blazing and alive from every angle, back when I could make almost anything bloom.

But the sky was still a barely blushing dark as I trailed the side of our tiny house just before five, wincing as the courtyard pebbles dug into my soles. I'd taken my flip-flops off to minimize crunching in the predawn hush. Mama would already be at the café—she'd been asleep long before I snuck out the night before—but Mrs. Petrović next door was a nasty, busybody hag who could have been a KGB spy in another life, or possibly this one. Ratting me out to Mama made her downright gleeful, pointless as it was. Mama knew perfectly well she couldn't keep me inside when I wanted out. I only bothered with the skulking to avoid the fights—"What kind of mother do you make me look like, sneaking out like a thief in the night?"—and even that was mostly for Malina. She couldn't stand the sound of our mother's rage battering against mine.

I was still bobbing along on some mixture of high and tipsy as I hauled myself onto our window ledge and swung my legs over, the contentment lingering round and compact in my belly like a sun-warmed egg. That wouldn't last. Soon, it would crack into a slimy nausea, just in time for my arrival at the café.

A faint rumble of triumph echoed through me. Along with

most everything else that I did, Jasmina the Peerless *hated* it when I came to work hungover. And this morning I wouldn't even have time to wash the alcohol fumes from my skin and hair. A small—and smelly—victory, but I'd learned to take them as they came.

Malina was still sound asleep as I gingerly dropped both feet onto our splintered hardwood floor, toe to heel, bending over to deposit my flip-flops beside them. My stomach lurched; maybe that rumble hadn't been all triumph. I leaned my butt back against the sill, breathing deeply to settle my insides. We kept our window flung wide open in the summer, and the slight breeze stirred the multicolored Japanese parasols fanned out across our ceiling, stripped of their handles and overlapping one another.

This was one of my projects from years ago, before I graduated to proper glassblowing under Čiča Jovan's watchful eye. When my gleam began to wane, Mama had presented me with a consolation prize, an article about American artist Dale Chihuly's largest installation: the Fiori di Como, a garden of glass flowers blossoming on the ceiling of the grandest hotel in Las Vegas. Its steel armature alone weighed ten thousand pounds; it had to, to support the forty thousand pounds of glass that clung to it. It was the biggest glass sculpture in the world.

I had painted the parasols with a painstaking, delicate rendering of the wisteria flower tunnel in Kitakyushu, Japan, gridding out the slim ribbing of the tunnel's truss to create the optical illusion of dimensionality—so that whenever Malina and I looked up, it would feel like we stood in the Kawachi Fuji Garden, beneath a pink-and-violet, pastel rain of dripping wisteria. Mama hated it. She didn't have to say so, but I'd seen the tightening in the small muscles of her face so many times when she came in to fetch one of us and couldn't keep herself from looking up into the shower of flowers I had painted for Malina and me.

Maybe her distaste made me love it just that much more; I wouldn't have put that past me. But that was a fringe benefit, far beside the point. What I really loved was looking up and knowing that a place existed for me somewhere far away from here. A place that belonged to me at least in half.

But this morning, the sight of the paper petals gave me a flutter of unease. Passed out on Nevena's couch last night, I'd dreamed of flowers, fields of black roses that glistened wet beneath a sky hovering on the brink of storm. Each time I woke it had been gasping and sweaty, heart stuttering in my chest until the alcohol and weed dragged me back down. I hardly ever remembered my dreams, but I could still nearly smell those dark roses, taste the slippery dew on the petals as I tore them off their stems and placed them on my tongue.

Shaking off the sudden chill, I tripped over one of Malina's strappy sandals and banged into our vanity table, cursing under my breath as our perfumes rattled. Our room was so tiny that we could reach out and bridge the gap with touched palms when we sat on the edge of our beds. On cue, Malina flung herself over from her stomach to her back, like a breaching dolphin. She draped an arm over her face and mumbled thickly. I caught a drawn-out "Riss," followed by what sounded suspiciously like "calzone."

"Oh, I think not, milady," I told her. "Fetch your own lunch. You don't have to be at the café until one anyway, so just grab a sandwich on the way or something and we can have calzones from the Bastion for dinner, if you like."

She gave a disgruntled groan and rolled back over to face the wall. I shrugged and turned to our tarnished mirror. My black tank top from last night was at least three years old and too small, embossed with a pair of glossy red lips pursed around a sequined skull. With my low-slung denim cutoffs, it showed the canvas of lower belly pinned between my hip bones—and if there was one thing Mama couldn't stand, it was an unseemly amount of daughterflesh on display. My hair was too straight to tangle, but the eyeliner had smeared nicely in my sleep. The overall effect was a little like something wary, pale-eyed, and possibly bitey peering out from the overhang of a cave.

Perfect. Degenerate chic, at your service.

Before I slipped out, I darted over to kiss Lina's sleep-mussed temple. Her black curls—so dark they seemed nearly blue in certain light, but with the most surprising sable undertone where the sun caught their depths—were bird's-nest tangled, and she smelled warm and sleepy, Dove soap and the lingering patchouli that was the base of her favorite homemade perfume. Beneath it, I could smell her skin, and my stomach bucked with love. For a moment I had a pang of powerful longing, like a gong rung inside my belly, for the nights when we had slept cuddled together, our sweet baby breath whispering over each other's faces.

Lina stirred, scrunching up her face like a little girl. "Riss," she mumbled, "is there a reason you're sniffing me like a truffle pig?"

I dropped down onto my own bed as she propped herself up on her elbows, yawning hugely. "Maybe I just *relish* the scent of sister in the morning."

"That sounds purely wrong." She wrinkled her nose. "Can't say

I reciprocate, either. What were you doing at Nevena's, anyway, bobbing for apples in a tub of rakija? I don't know how you stand that stuff; you'd think they could make apricot brandy taste better than rat poison mixed with cheap perfume. Who else was there?"

"That is for us, the cool and popular, to know, and you to find out." I grimaced. "Or more like the cool and the popular and yours truly, Nev's impostor tagalong. No one else much worth talking to, really. But you should still come out with me sometime. Get all wild and free and such, for once."

She gave me a sleepy half smile, a glossy black curl sliding over her rounded cheek. My sister had the sweetest face, a gentler rendering of our mother's that drew from our father mostly in the slight slant of her gray eyes. Her full lower lip was cleft like a cherry, and it made all that beauty somehow both playful and kind. You could easily see the shared blood between us, and maybe on the surface, you might even mistake us for the same substance.

But like water and alcohol, the resemblance ended there.

"Maybe I like staying home?" she said. "Maybe I have better things to do with my nights than tag along to your spite parties?" It always got under my skin when Lina talked in questions; she'd picked it up from years of playing ambassador between me and Mama.

"Oh, like maybe walking on eggshells around Jasmina the Peerless while she plans the next day's menu and ignores you?" I mimicked. "And I don't go out just to spite her, you know. Not everything I do is about her."

"Seems like it is, these days," Lina said quietly. She dropped her eyes, black lashes fanning lush against her cheeks, her fingers twisting into the sheets. Her hands were the unloveliest part of her, wide palms and spidery violinist's fingers with cuticles run ragged from her nervous nibbling. My own had gathered a respectable collection of burns and nicks from glassblowing and working at the café, but they were still fine-boned and pretty, the nailbeds slim. I won when it came to hands. At least there was that.

"A little easy for you to say, isn't it? You can still sing like you used to, back when she still let us practice with her." I couldn't keep the bitterness from my voice, like one of Mama's orange rinds before she candied them. "I can't make anything bloom other than flowers anymore, and even then only I can see it."

Except for when I drink just enough, I didn't add. Or smoked so much that my thoughts sparked around each other like a school of minnows, slippery and silver, impossible to grasp.

You can sing like you always could, and still she doesn't even hate you.

"I'm sorry," Lina whispered, struggling to meet my eyes. I knew she could feel the roil of my emotions, that it chafed her not to sing it back at me or soothe me, but sometimes I couldn't curb myself just to ease her. "I know that's hard for you. But maybe it's better this way? I can sing, but that's all it is—weird, maybe, but just *song.* There's nothing for anyone to see. But you, it used to be like New Year's Eve when you made things bloom. And you know we can't be all flash and glitter like that. It's not safe for any of us."

I clenched my teeth until my jaw burned. Safety was Mama's eternal refrain. It was why we'd only eaten the moon together at nighttime in the tiny garden behind our house, hidden by the trellis of creeping roses and oleander, back when Lina and I were

9

little. "Only in the dark, *cvetiću*, and only with each other," Mama would whisper in my ear, holding my hands in her strong grip as I bloomed the starlight dappling through the canopy of leaves above. "That's the only place we're safe."

I couldn't remember the last time our mother had called me "little flower," or touched me with such tenderness. As if I had grown into a cactus instead of something softer, and she didn't want to risk my spines.

"The townsfolk with the pitchforks, I know," I said. "Lovers and neighbors and friends, all turning to burn the witches. But don't you wonder sometimes if it's worth it, giving up so much? When we still have to keep folding ourselves so small all the time?"

Lina looked away, a soft flush rising on her pale skin. "Of course it's worth it," she murmured. "Beauty's worth it even in the smallest scale. You have your glass, I have my violin. It's enough, like Mama always said."

Yet even as she said it, she began humming under her breath. The back of my neck prickled, and a wash of goose bumps spread down my arms. Even after all these years, hearing Lina harmonize with herself always gave me chills, the way it sounded like three voices in one. This melody was subtle, three layers of a bittersweet arpeggio that split and reflected my emotions like a prism: the anger, the loss, and the biting sense of injustice, along with a gentle apologetic undertow that was her own offering.

There was another hue to it, too, a tinge of guilt that didn't feel like mine. Even as the song melted my annoyance with her like spun sugar in water, I frowned, trying to place it.

She caught herself abruptly and cut off the melody.

"Sorry," she said, clenching both hands in her lap until her knuckles turned white. "I know you hate it when I do that. Do you—will you be going to the square after your shift today? If Nevena stays longer at the café, I could leave early and bring my violin, come keep you company?"

Coming from Lina, this was a fairly high-level peace offering. I sold my glasswork figurines to tourists in the Old Town's Arms Square, and Malina's singing and playing always meant I'd sell more that day. It made customers pliant, more willing to part with their money for a pretty piece of glass. Mama had no idea we ever did it, of course. And if it felt a little swindly to sway people like that, it only added to my thrill. Lina had never liked that part of it as much as I did, even if she was only making it easier for people to do what they already wanted. It baffled me how much this bothered her; what was the point of power at all, if she shrank back from it anytime it caught and flared?

Especially when hers still gleamed so brightly while mine guttered by the day.

"I thought you had a violin lesson with Natalija this afternoon."

"I can cancel that, if you want. I already saw her earlier this week."

"Don't worry about it," I said curtly, stepping back into my flip-flops. "I only have a few pieces left from the last batch, anyway. Not enough to show."

She sighed behind me. "Riss—"

"I'll see you later."

I could feel her eyes heavy on my back as I left.

TWO

OUTSIDE, THE MORNING WAS FRAGRANT WITH THE SPICE of the oleander drifting from the back garden. Our bicycles leaned together against the chain-link fence. Above them, a warm rainbow of bougainvillea clung to the links, fading like twilight from fuchsia to orange, yellow, and peach before nestling into the green of stems and leaves.

I paused for a moment as the flowers burst into their usual spectacle. Each separate blossom multiplied, over and over, until the tangle burgeoned into sparkling symmetry, a fractal sphere like a honeycomb. I saw these flowers every morning, fiercely grateful that their dazzle never dimmed. That was my gift, my variant of the gleam. I didn't just see flowers; I saw them to the nth degree. Each bloomed into a little galaxy that I could cup inside my palm, the sticky stars of its pollen caught between my fingers. Petal nested within petal, each level of the pattern cradling tiny versions of itself, stamen and pistil and vein and leaf swirling in concentric patterns like a nautilus shell.

It hadn't always been just flowers. When I was younger, the whole world had bloomed for me. Sunlight through summer leaves had spiraled into a blaze of gold and green, an infinite pillar of fireflies swarming into the sky. Pebbles and stones beneath my bare toes would whirlpool into cream and slate and gray. Even the cross-hatch of tanned skin on the back of my own hand would fractal for me, layering like dragon scales.

Back when Mama still let us practice the gleam together— *eating the moon*, she always called it, like something out of a fairy tale, like the three of us were strong enough to swallow the sky —I'd even been able to share what I saw with both of them. Even the memory of that happiness was painfully fierce, a bubble of vast joy that strained my lungs. In the summer dark of the garden, the sigh of leaves and crickets stirring the silence around us, Mama would let me bloom balls of tinsel or twine, hand-fuls of beach glass and jars filled with seashells, bowls clicking with tigereye marbles. When I made each explode into fractal fireworks between us, Mama would slip one of the moon-shaped truffles she made for those nights into my mouth—dark choco-late, sea salt, and a sweet curl of jasmine, the taste of the summer night dissolving on my tongue. Then Lina's song would settle over us, her triad of voices clear and lilting as a flute, the precise pitch of wonder.

We had been so beautiful together, reflecting one another like a family of mirrors.

The word for "witch," *veštica*, meant "deft one," and that was what we'd been: deft in beauty, versed in its tastes and sounds and textures as it wove like a ribbon through our fingers. It was an heirloom we carried in our blood, a legacy of magic passed down from womb to womb. All the women in our family had it.

Some had even died for it.

Lina and I had been seven when Mrs. Petrović next door saw one of my fractals bloom. Maybe our light laughter had woken her, quiet as we always tried to be, or maybe she'd caught a thread of Lina's song in her sleep and it had drawn her to the window. The next morning, Mama had trotted us next door and talked her down easily, with a basket of warm trifles from the café and her own cool and perfect poise. Lina and I had been playing with firecrackers, she lied smoothly, because we were young and silly and overly bold, too used to running free during the long hours she was gone. Yes, the colors were very unusual; she thought maybe that kind was called a snapdragon, wasn't that charming? No, of course, sweet names were no excuse for such a fire hazard, and her without a man to tame that unruly garden in the back. We should still have known better, and now we knew never to do it again.

It wasn't until she brought us back home that her hands began to shake. She had us kneel with her on her massive sleigh bed, its swooping wooden headboard polished to a honey gleam; Čiča Jovan had made it for her from reclaimed wood. She'd let us sleep in it with her on the nights we ate the moon together, and it had always felt to me like the safest place in our little house.

But now, the devastation that swept over her face when she turned to us made my stomach drop, Lina's clammy fingers curling into mine like a reflex.

"That was the *last* time," Mama said, running her tongue over her teeth. The movement pursed her lush mouth and bared the strong, Slavic bones of her face: a squared jaw and cheekbones that cleaved air, a bold but dainty falcon's nose. The large, thick-lashed gray eyes she shared with me and Malina sparkled oddly, and I suddenly realized what it was—she was trying not to cry. "No more eating the moon for us, not ever. I should have never—I've let you both practice for too long. A little longer, and I won't be able to hold on to you. There'll be no tamping you down."

"But why?" I demanded. "Who cares if she saw me? She looks like a shrunken head."

Malina smothered a snicker next to me. "Smells like one, too," she whispered.

"*Quiet*," Mama snapped. An electric eel of fear raced down my spine, leaving a hot flush in its wake. Lina dropped my hand in shock. Mama never spoke to us so sharply. Even when she was at her wits' end, her low, throaty voice only dipped lower, softening like a velvet warning.

Her gaze flicking between us, she knelt so we were face-level with her, gray eyes meeting gray. "You know we have no family," she said. "I've told you that much. The three of us, all alone in the world."

"And Čiča Jovan," Malina added. Only we got to call him "čiča,"

Old Man Jovan. From us, it was both affectionate and respectful, the next best thing to calling him our grandfather. "That's why you named the café after him. Because he's like our *deda*."

"Yes, as good as a grandfather—maybe even better—though he isn't blood. But before I had you, I had a twin sister of my own, and a mother, too. They would have been your blood, your aunt and your *baba*. If they had lived."

Lina's breathing went shallow beside me. I could see Mama's turmoil, but my sister could feel and hear its buzz. That's what our mother sounded like, Lina told me later. Like she'd swallowed a beehive, a high-pitched panic of wings and stingers.

"What happened to them?" Lina asked, and from the pained way she said it I knew she felt it already, and that it was terrible.

Mama was still young enough then that we could sometimes read her face, and I could see the splitting inside her, the battle between *tell* and *don't*.

"Ana and I were eighteen," she said, her voice colorless and thin like onionskin. "Ana fell in love that year, even though your grand-mother forbade it. Love makes us even brighter than we are, until the gleam grows into a roman candle, impossible to contain. Every-one can see us shine with it, then, and it's the nature of the human beast to fear what it doesn't understand."

I struggled to make the pieces clasp together. "But didn't our grandmother love our grandfather?"

"She never loved him," Mama said. Her face had smoothed out flat, until she looked just like she sounded. "That's why she thought it was safe to accept when he asked her to marry. And why she thought it would be safe to stay with him, once Ana and I were born. We lived in a mountain village many hours from here; Tata raised goats to make cheese, and Mama brewed medicines. And perfumes too, the prettiest you ever smelled, so fine they made you *feel* things."

"The way your treats make people think of places?" I asked. That was our mother's gleam: the sights of the world translated into flavor. "Was that Grandmother's gleam?"

"It was," she said. "Ana's was bigger, and much more wild. When she danced, it was like watching legends come to life, paintings that breathed and pulsed to the heartbeat of her steps. And when she fell in love . . ."

Mama's eyes grew distant with the memory, soft and diffuse like the fog that sometimes gathered above the slate waters of the bay. "She danced and danced. Love stoked her flame, and she showered the sparks of her gleam all over everything, until they spread to your grandmother and me. That's what it's like, when the women in our family eat the moon. We're bound to one another, braided together. And when we catch fire, we burn as one."

"And then what, Mama?" Malina said. Her hand had crept back into mine.

Mama's gaze sharpened back into focus. "Then, we all grew stronger. Your grandmother stopped blending her perfumes, but even still, the house was full of the most wonderful scents; they simply rolled off her, like sea spray from the water. I stopped baking, but your grandfather said he tasted sweet and savory things even when he'd eaten nothing for hours, tastes that made him think of places he had never been. As if ghosts were feeding him morsels. He muttered constantly about *vila* women and witches, and wore an evil-eye bracelet to fend off curses."

She worked her jaw back and forth, then drew her full lower lip, softer even than Malina's, through her strong white teeth. "And one day he walked in on Ana dancing. I was outside in the barn, but I saw him drag both of them out of the house, Ana by the hair, Mama by the arm. Mama had tried to come between them, to lull him with one of her quieting scents, but it only made him more furious. How long had we all been bewitching him, he wanted to know. Were Ana and I even his daughters, or children of demons?"

I barely understood what she meant, but bile welled in my throat all the same.

"Mama saw me cowering in the doorway, and screamed at me to run. And I did—but not until I saw him drag them to the precipice, the cliff's edge Ana and I had always been forbidden to go near. And he *threw* them over"—Lina and I both flinched hard—"like they were nothing. I stayed, frozen, until I couldn't hear them screaming anymore. I've never taken you up to the mountains, but they're terribly tall. It was a very long way down before the sound stopped carrying. Once I finally moved, I ran far and hard until I reached this little city. And here our Čiča Jovan found me, and took me in."

Malina pressed against my side, both of us trembling. The questions had blackened and curled up inside me, and all I wanted was for Mama to stop.

She fixed us in her feather-lashed gaze and put a light hand on each of our cheeks. Her fingers were so cold I could feel their chill leach beneath my skin. "Do you understand me? Ana fell in *love*, and then she was seen. If a father could kill his own child because she gleamed, what do you think a stranger would do to you? That's why you never let anyone see you. And that's why we take care to never, ever fall in love."

I found my voice again, a rusted wire in my throat. "But Mama, I don't want to stop," I said, digging my nails into my palms. Even then, the power to bloom was the one thing, the best thing I had. Where Lina was sweet-tempered and tender, I was stark and sharp, fashioned of edges. I wasn't already deft in Mama's kitchen like Lina was, school bored me to misery except when it came to poems and stories, and I didn't have a whisper of our mother's easy charm.

On top of it all I looked like a thing apart, some prickly off-shoot of my mother's and sister's languid beauty. What would I be without the gift? Would I even belong with them? "I could learn to be so careful, I promise I could, if you just *teach* me. Only ever in the dark, like you said. But please, Mama, don't make us stop."

"It's not just about you," she said, soft. "You're so bright, you'll make all of us too easy to see. Beauty is our birthright, but only as long as we do it safely. I'll find you some other way to bloom, something that won't show you for what you are."

She lifted a hand as if to touch my cheek again, and I flinched away from her fingers. Her hand stilled in midair; maybe that was the moment she first turned herself to winter.

IN THE TEN years since, I'd lost everything but the flowers, and I wasn't even sure why those hadn't faded. It had been like going color-blind, or growing scars inside my eyes. My world had gone so flat that sometimes, nothing but the magma roil of the glass furnace in Čiča Jovan's workshop felt even remotely real.

And yet here I still was, same as ever, stuck with Mama and the café. Because what else was there to do, for me? Where else was there to be?

I unlocked my bike from the fence and swung my leg over the rickety two-speed Schwinn, and the bougainvillea fractal faded away. Pressing my feet into the groaning pedals, I set off along the Škurda, the stagnant little river that trickled by our ramshackle, whitewashed old house. As I cut a left along the Adriatic Highway toward Cattaro's Old Town, I could already catch the brine of the bay, glimmering beneath the limestone cliffs across the water. Our city nestled in the deepest recess of the Gulf of Cattaro, a pool of the Adriatic two inlets removed from the open sea. The mountains circled the bay like hands cupping a palmful of water much deeper and more dazzling than the sky—a solid ring of verdant rock broken only by the narrow thread of the Verige Strait.

Past the bridge over the second leg of the Škurda River, the Venetian ramparts surrounding the Old Town came into view. Old Cattaro had been settled by the Romans around 160 BC, and a thousand years later the stone city still clustered behind the ancient walls, a mosaic of gray blocks and red roofs against the cliffs that soared above.

Outside the blackened walls, I slid off the bike to walk it beside me through the Sea Gate. *Tuđe nećemo, svoje ne damo*, proclaimed the inscription carved into the stone above: "What belongs to others, we do not want; what is ours, we will never surrender." The entrance opened into the Arms Square plaza, with its medieval clock tower and stone shops, cafés, and hotels with wrought-iron balconies and green shutters. Bike tucked tightly against my side, I navigated through the warrens of the streets, passing boutiques and bakeries and jewelry shops until I emerged into the sunlit square of the Cathedral of Saint Tryphon.

A vague pall of incense always hung over the square, even with the sweeter smells emanating from Café Tadić across the way. I secured my bike to the little post Čiča Jovan had nailed for me by the café door and found him already inside at the glass dessert display, in his neatly pressed slacks, matching waistcoat, and blinding white shirt. Not quite one of the vintage three-piece suits he still wore from his time as a man about town in Belgrade, but close; he was the only person I'd ever known who dressed formally for comfort. Even at seventy, he was still striking in a weathered, leonine way, his snowy hair thick and swept back like a wave crest from a bold forehead, blue eyes piercing beneath craggy, bushy white brows.

He was leaning heavily on his "battle cane," the dragon-headed, warrior-king's cane he'd carved for himself when his left hip gave out and he'd had to have it replaced four years ago. In his other hand he held one of my mother's specialty *burek*, a savory goat-cheese pastry studded with pine nuts and drizzled with honey. He bought one almost every morning, as much to see his honorary granddaughters as to sample Mama's flavors. "I only have so many days left," he always said. "And I'll be damned if I miss any opportunities to start them with my girls and the best *burek* in God's great world."

"But we're a European country," he was saying now to Mama, stoutly. "Still part of the European Union, part of the world, my girl. What the giants do affects us as much as anyone else. We *have* to care."

"Why?" my mother replied, leaning on the counter. Her dark hair was braided into a gleaming crown, and she wore one of her slim sheaths, dove gray beneath her stained apron. She propped her chin on her clenched fist, and I was surprised to see how white her knuckles were. "The rest of us should be so lucky to have that much strength, to do anything we wanted without being afraid. And look, instead, how small we are. What does it even matter what we think?"

I lingered in the doorway, intrigued by my mother's interest. She'd never shown any zeal for global affairs, and she was right about us; even by Southeastern European standards, Montenegro was such a tiny country, a little kingdom of mountains. All of five hundred thousand inhabitants hemmed in by Croatia, Bosnia and Herzegovina, Serbia, and Albania, with the Adriatic Sea lapping against our western coast.

My mother seemed to remember herself then, and the usual mantle of nonchalance settled back over her shoulders. Her face took on that lazy, indulgent look I knew so well, the one she used when men swaggered into her shop and bent over backward to pretend that she didn't fluster them. Some of them cursed too much, while others were so stilted and formal it was as if each time they met her was the first. Others plied her with current events, as if the doings of the world held enough mass to offset her gravity.

"I don't know, Jovan, really," she said with a languid shrug. "These mountains have kept us for thousands of years; even the Turks couldn't take them from us. What use do we have for the rest of the world? No matter what, my little café will still be here, won't it? And as long as I'm here, so will be your *burek*. What more can any of us ask?"

She gave him a sweet, close-lipped smile, and I could practically see his blood pressure spike. It infuriated me that she did this even to Čiča Jovan, who was almost family, as if she couldn't restrain herself from showing off. He didn't deserve to be plied with her tricks just for sport.

Jovan cleared his throat. "True enough, true enough." He backed away from her reluctantly, clutching the little package so tightly grease began to seep through the waxed paper, and nearly ran into me. "Ah, Iris, good morning! Didn't mean to trample you, sweetheart."

I smiled at him, giving him a quick, tight hug before tucking myself into the corner to let him by. "All limbs intact, old man. And make sure to eat that while it's hot." I gestured to one of the two iron tables at the opposite corner, arranged beneath my little bougainvillea glasswork sculpture; our other four tables were outside in the square. "Maybe take a seat with us and enjoy it here today? We love the company so early in the morning, don't we, Mama? It'll be hours before anyone else comes by."

She gave me a quick, flicking appraisal, from toes to temples. I'd been getting the Arctic blast of her silent treatment for two weeks now, since I accidentally stirred salt rather than sugar into a meringue and ruined a whole batch of her snowdrop kiss cookies. It would have been only a day's worth of fury if Malina had done it, but Mama's deep freezes were traditionally reserved for me. An offense was the best defense, as they say—whoever "they" were, I felt like we understood each other well—and I could see by the pretty flush rising along her cheekbones how deeply my clothing choices offended her.

My insides turned over with the queasy, ambivalent sense of victory I felt every time I scored a point.

"I could make you some of my white coffee to go with it, Jovan," she finally said, face warming as she shifted her gaze to him. "Only a dash of coffee and sugar in the milk, exactly as you like."

As if inviting him to stay was her idea. As if I hadn't even spoken.

Watching her, I felt a flutter from the weak, shameful part of me that never stopped straining toward her. I clenched my teeth and stamped the longing down, grinding it like a cigarette butt beneath my heel. There was no room for it here. There was no room for it anywhere.

THREE

JOVAN GLANCED FROM ONE OF US TO THE OTHER, SIGHING heavily. Better than anyone, he knew how things were between Mama and me, and knowing how it pained him only made it that much worse for me. "Who can say no to such a pair of beauties?" he finally said, lowering himself carefully onto one of the little chairs. His arthritis was flaring up, I could tell by the overly cautious movements, the strain in his jaw, the entire air of indignation at old age daring to befall him. "Iris, will I see you later today at the studio?"

"Maybe, but if not, tomorrow for sure." Patting his shoulder, I squeezed by him to slide behind the counter and into the kitchen, making sure I didn't accidentally brush Mama in passing. In the back, macarons were rising in one of the ovens, their delicate shells bright yellow. Dandelion clocks today, then. I could tell just by looking that they were still too soft to be taken out, so I joined Mama's pastry apprentice, Nevena, at one of the stainless steel counters, perching my chin on her shoulder as she whipped the creamy white base that would become the macaron filling.

She nudged her cheek against mine in greeting, smiling in profile.

"Morning, sunshine," I said to her. "How do you look so damn sprightly? Watching you take body shots off Filip might be the last thing I actually remember from last night."

Nev was two years older than Lina and me, bright and appealing as a freshly cut marigold—tall and lanky like so many Montenegrin women were, and blue-eyed and blond as a Scandinavian. Her fine hair was cut into a chin-length bob, one side tucked behind a neat little ear. Today she wore a pale-green, pin-up halter dress with gold unicorns prancing around the billowy hem, the neckline dipping low over her freckled cleavage. The shimmer of the fabric nearly made me drool with envy; none of my clothes even threatened to be that gorgeous. Nev was a councilman's daughter, and so sweetly gracious about coming from money it'd have made my teeth ache if I hadn't liked her so much.

"By God, I really committed to those," she agreed, flourishing her wooden spoon with such flair that creamy droplets splattered on the wall. Out of reflex, both of us glanced back at the front of the shop to see if we'd been caught—baking was like prayer to Jasmina, meant to be hushed and holy as a ceremony—but there was no sign of her. "I didn't have any of that lethal weed that new boy brought, though, maybe that's it. Speaking of which, come closer. You kind of reek, dollface. Maybe I'll catch a contact high."

"So I've heard. What new boy?"

Nev arched a wispy eyebrow and whistled low. "You really don't remember him? I'd never seen him at Filip's before, and he didn't look like a local. No idea who he knew. He was fucking gorgeous, though, I mean, *damn*. You were passing his joint back and forth, and saying something about how you could make a galaxy out of the ceiling for him if you had just enough." She snorted. "The way he was looking at you, I think he thought *some* kind of big bang was nigh, for sure. Whatever you were talking about, wanna teach me your ways? Always room for more boy-finagling tricks in the lady arsenal."

For a moment, I almost did remember something: the Christmas lights on Nevena's ceiling swirling like a nebula at the behest of my own twirling finger, and a tattooed arm alongside mine as we traced the whirlpools together.

But that was impossible. I wasn't strong enough anymore to make the bloom visible to anyone else, and it had been years since anything but flowers fractaled for me. It must have been a dream, the last wishful moments of waking tiding over into sleep.

I finally shrugged. "Wish I could help, but alas. No idea what I said. Filip's rotgut rakija slayed me as usual, it's like I never learn. Serves me right, forgetting a shiny new boy."

"Well, he knows where you work. You definitely mentioned"—she lowered her voice—"'Mistress Mean' out there, I heard *that* much. It was quite the shrill moment."

A cold hand gripped my stomach. Had I told him about the gleam? Could I have been that careless and stupid? "Did you hear—did I say anything else to him? Besides promising him the universe, apparently?"

Nev shrugged, jutting out her lower lip to blow a wayward strand out of her eyes. Another faint almost-memory flared, like the afterimage of the sun—a strand of someone else's hair tickly across my mouth. A warm finger brushing it off for me, before tracing the outline of my face and the hollows beneath my eyes.

"No clue," she said. "I was busy licking Frangelico off Filip, and you were kind of mumbly by then. I'm not sure when he left, but you were alone by the time everyone else cleared out. He'd tucked you in with a quilt and everything. Maximum cute."

I wasn't sure how I felt about that. Strangers didn't usually make it their business to talk to me, much less to coddle me with blankets. But even if it had been a dream, the memory of that fingertip following the curve of my chin—and a light stroke at the tender flesh beneath—made me flush warm underneath my skin.

I stepped back from Nev, rubbing my arms. "Did you need any help here? I'm not sure what to do, given that Jasmina still isn't deigning to speak to me. Must be Tuesday."

Nev rolled her eyes. She enjoyed such a smooth, sunny relationship with Mama that it seemed to me like a magic all its own. The permafrost between the two of us baffled her completely. "I think she'll want to start another batch of the dandelions soon, so you could get a jump on those. We're making at least eight other desserts today, too, so really just cut up whatever and I guarantee something will happen with it. I think we're running low on lemonade, too."

Café Tadić wasn't actually anything so simple as one of the Old Town's real cafés, which served cappuccinos and thick Turkish coffee, peach nectar and Pepsi, sandwiches and desserts that gathered dust for days in their tiered displays. My mother's café was a confectionery more than anything else. Some days she baked doe's back cake, a roulade of airy hazelnut dough and chocolate ganache dusted with ground hazelnuts, yet there was always an element of surprise—a sprig of mint that should have soured the cake, but that instead put you in mind of a glen in the woods. And with the next bite, a speck of wild strawberry, the kind that grew alongside forest trails, until you felt you walked them yourself with the liquid gleam of a fawn's eyes fixed on you from the bush.

Mama's desserts were nothing if not suspenseful.

Other days, she made floating islands, fluffy lumps of spongy, unset meringue bobbing in creamy zabaglione and laced with orange syrup, violet preserves, and a powder she ground from bee pollen, so that every bite tasted exactly like late spring sunshine. She churned her own gelato too, but her chocolate *stracciatella* was always streaked like a sunset with other things, marmalade and rose hip jelly and crystallized chips of honey, and somehow it put you in mind of the sky—the held breath of twilight, the sanctity of dusk, and the final slippage into night. And you knew that when she looked at the sky, this was the taste that bloomed in her mouth. Like me with my glasswork, Mama lived and breathed for the alchemy that went on in her kitchen. Her ingredients were so exquisite that most of our profit funneled back into buying more raw material. Sometimes I thought she would keep baking macarons that tasted like dandelion clocks drifting on a summer wind long after we ran out of money for bread and bologna and Carnex vegetable pâté.

"So what is it you're going for today?"

I whirled around, trying not to upset the mixing bowl I'd been cracking eggs into for fresh batter. Nev caught her breath in the corner, loud enough that Mama turned to her, absently tucking a stray strand behind her ear. She did that often, patting Nev's shoulder or stroking her flyaway doll's hair when they worked beside each other. It wasn't Nev's fault—she was naturally pettable—but no matter how many times I saw it, the knife never stopped twisting.

"Nevena, sweet, please go see to the storefront, would you?" she said, her tone meticulously even. "I'd like to speak with Iris for a moment."

Nev lingered briefly, raising her eyebrows at me over Mama's shoulder. I gave her a tiny nod. She wasn't going to help me now, no matter how much Mama liked her.

Mama cocked her head to the side, tendons cording down the slender but sturdy bow of her neck. Her eyes were glittering, bright and dangerous. They were palest gray, like mine; near transparent, with a darker line around the iris. Wolf eyes. "Tell me, is it gutter-trash whore today?" she mused. "It's hard to discern your fashion nuances, sometimes. Might be they're beyond me."

My stomach knotted. I always yearned for the battle, because it was so much better than nothing, but still it hurt every time she picked up the gauntlet.

"'Whore'?" I echoed softly. "I'm not sure what you mean, Jasmina, unless you're talking about getting knocked up by a sailor at nineteen. In which case, *astonishment*, Mother does know best! The gutter-trash element is still up for debate, though. I'll check back in when I'm old enough to breed my own bastards."

The gas-leak hiss of her gasp should have tipped me off, but she didn't hit me often and hadn't for a long time, long enough that I wasn't prepared for the meaty smack of her palm against my cheek. My head snapped back and my sinuses buzzed with an electric zing. Tears sprang to my eyes. The urge to sob was so strong it nearly doubled me over.

Every time, I hoped it would be different. That instead of rising to the challenge she would understand what I was doing and meet me halfway, on some neutral ground.

But she never did.

Instead she stepped close to me and gripped me by the chin, angling my face up to hers. Neither Malina nor I were quite as tall as she was. Her fingertips were rough from cooking, and smelled like lavender and spring onions. The scent reminded me of long-ago times when she'd touched me more, and I bit my lip as I met her gaze.

"One day you'll understand," she whispered, "what it's like to see your eyes in someone else's face. To see yourself reflected back, and simply not know how to tame it." She shuddered, lips tightening. "Or maybe you won't ever have to see that. And if you're lucky enough, you'll never have to do the things I do for you."

"And what things are those?" I shot back, my voice breaking as the tears ran hot down my cheeks. "Ignoring me? Making me feel dirty? Keeping me from the one thing I'm good at, the one thing that's best in this stupid, tiny fishbowl life? Thanks so much for all that care, Jasmina, but I could really do without."

She dropped my chin and stepped away from me, swiping a hand over her mouth. Her back straightened as if the stays had been drawn tight on some invisible corset.

"Pull yourself together, and then get back out there," she ordered. "We have a customer waiting outside. And send Nevena back in on your way out." She elbowed me away from the eggs and almond flour, not roughly but none too gently either, adding, "I hope you enjoy putting yourself on display like that. Certainly the men who see you will have a treasure trove of thoughts to tide them over once they're home tonight. Seems unfair that they should have all the fun."

"That's a bit rich, coming from you," I said, my voice still wavering. "You flirt with *everyone*."

Her shoulders twitched, but she didn't turn. "It's not the same. None of them could ever have me, and they know it. They wouldn't dare touch me. Unlike you."

"Are you telling me to go home and change?" I hated myself as soon as the words were out. I didn't want to do it—didn't want to pander to her—but now I actually felt as good as naked.

"Oh, no," she replied. The fire had been tamped down, and we were back to our usual purgatory. Just cold and ashes, with only the lingering tang of smoke to show that there'd ever been a spark at all. "Don't go to the trouble on my account. Who knows? Maybe you'll even draw us a bigger crowd today. Dessert and a show—it could be our new calling card. Now go see what they want. And at least try not to walk like you belong in those clothes."

FOUR

IT DOESN'T MATTER.

You hate her, too.

She only hurts you if you let her.

I looped the mantra in my mind like a prayer wheel. If I told myself these things enough, they all might become true. Still, fresh tears welled in my eyes, and I blinked furiously as I edged by Mama to go see to the customer outside. I found myself locking my knees as I walked, trying to suppress the slight, natural sway of my hips. As soon as I noticed it, I forced myself to stop. I wasn't going to let her change the way I walked, on top of everything else.

Nev caught my hand as I pressed by her, pulling me back. She made a little moue of sadness at how cold it was, and clasped it against her chest. The wealth of sympathy in her eyes, much warmer than blue eyes had any right to be, made me feel like I'd swallowed a mouthful of glass. I nearly pitched myself into her arms just for a second, to steal that one breath of comfort. To let someone else hold me, for once.

But that would have been weak. And moments of weakness grew into habit too quickly.

"Are you okay?" she whispered. "That was . . . even for her . . . I just don't understand it."

"It's fine," I said, swallowing hard. "I'm fine."

"Are you sure? I could talk to her, I could—"

"No, please. That'll only make it worse. She'll hate that you even heard that, and she's not going to let up on me, not even for you." I gave her a wobbly smile. "I just need a minute, and there's someone waiting at the tables. She needs you back inside, she said. You should go."

Nev let me loose uncertainly, stealing a last concerned look over her shoulder as she disappeared back into the kitchen. My hands were still shaking as I approached the one occupied table beneath our awning. I took a deep breath and stilled my fingers, so that our one-sheet menu wouldn't tremble as I laid it down in front of the old woman who sat at the table.

"Good morning, ma'am," I said, my voice sludgy with tears. I cleared my throat, eyes fixed on the table. "We don't have everything that's on the menu, but what do we have is marked off with the little stars. And I can tell you about all the other—"

"No need," the woman said, and I glanced up at her in surprise. Her voice had no trace of age to it, but was low and smooth, startlingly sweet. What I could see of her face was young, too. A large and sleek pair of sunglasses hid her eyes, against the bolt of sunshine that slanted over her even beneath the awning, but her delicate jawline was taut, her mouth pillowy and upturned. No crow's-feet or sagging jowls; even the skin on her neck was clear as a mirror.

It was the hair that had fooled me, pure white and almost dazzling in the sunlight. I had never seen white hair that seemed lush and healthy as snow-fox pelt. Twisted back from her temples, the rest of it fell loose, draped over one shoulder like a stole. She was stroking it as she watched me, and I couldn't blame her; I practically had to curl my fingers into fists to keep from reaching out and touching it myself. It was even brighter against her blouse, which was the exact azure of the water in the bay.

"You have really pretty hair," I said stupidly. "Is it dyed?" Of course it wasn't, idiot. No bleach in the world turned your hair into white silk.

"It isn't, and thank you," she said. "Yours is beautiful, too. And you have a very exceptional face to go with it, has anyone ever told you that?" She smiled at me, and to the surprise of no one, her teeth all but sparkled. I couldn't help smiling back, even though my insides still wobbled. "No, don't answer that. I'm sure you're sick of hearing it."

I wasn't, actually. Our father was Japanese, Mama had told me and Malina once in a rare, raw moment of softness. A sailor, on a week's leave in Cattaro, long gone by the time our mother even realized she was pregnant. Our black hair and the tilt of our eyes came from him, though where on Malina it came across as

Eastern European, on me it was unmistakably Asian, at startling odds with my gray irises. My high, round cheekbones were his too, prominent as apple halves beneath my skin. Because of my face, I'd heard "alien" and "geisha" and "*Japanka*," which simply meant "Japanese woman" but could be whetted into a slur sharp like a fishing hook.

But I definitely hadn't heard "exceptional."

Maybe that was why Mama's prohibition on love had never felt all that difficult to bear. Who was ever going to look at me here, anyway, in this sea of faces that looked not even a drop like mine, and see anything but strangeness?

"Just like a *vila*," the woman continued. "A Montenegrin fairy queen in the flesh."

I wondered whether she would consider adopting me, whoever she was. If she liked the look of me this much, she might like Malina even better. She could have us as a matched set.

Under my scrutiny she stopped touching her hair, and then began turning her own hand over back and forth, as if she'd forgotten it belonged to her. "Strange light here," she murmured. "Grainy, almost? Or much too bright?" She glanced back up at me, quirking her head to the side like a sparrow. "Does it look strange to you? The caliber of the light?"

"Ah, no?" I made a show of looking around as if I had some actual method for gauging light. "Seems like a pretty standard-issue early-morning gradient, to me. But I've never really, uh, examined light all that closely. I don't think."

"Gradient!" She clasped her hands together, delighted.

"Excellent word. Clever, too, then, and not just so lovely to look at. No wonder . . ."

She murmured that last bit low, like a secret to herself, but I could catch the pain behind it.

"I'm sorry," she said, mistaking my baffled silence for embarrassment. "I'm babbling like an idiot. It just feels so odd to be back here again, after so long. It all seems so *slovenly*, somehow. And the smells . . ." She took a deep breath, her nostrils flaring. They were absurdly perfect, precise as blown glass. It seemed like such a silly thing to notice, yet there I was, admiring them. "I'm not sure if I even like it here, anymore."

"Are you from around here, then?" I asked, curious. She had a touch of the lazy Montenegrin drawl to her accent, though nowhere near as strong as mine. Compared to the Serbs' crisp speech, we all sounded like we were talking around a mouthful of honey.

"Not exactly here, but close enough. Much closer than where I've been, anyway, and all this looks more familiar than not."

It occurred to me that this woman might be at least three-quarters batshit. Talking to her was kind of like riding a Tilt-a-Whirl, but I'd always liked those. "Maybe you know my mother, then? Jasmina. She owns this café."

The woman's lips twitched. The table rattled between us, so loudly I looked down to see if she had jostled it with her knees. But both her feet were on the ground, in dainty silver thong sandals. In contrast to the slender straps, her feet were roped with veins and knotted with bone spurs, the nails thick and unpolished. The table gave another solid rattle. Maybe a column of trucks lugging produce from Turkey was rumbling down the highway outside the city walls. Sometimes the stones carried the vibrations from the road.

She took another long breath and set both hands on the table, wrists crossed, a languorous movement that vaguely reminded me of someone, but that I couldn't quite pin down. "As it happens, I do know her a bit," she said. "I wonder if she remembers me. Do you think she might be free to say hello?"

"I can go take a look," I offered. The chances of my mother prying herself away from her kitchen to chat with a near stranger were hilariously slim—and I would bear the brunt of her irritation, to boot—but I found that for this woman, I was willing to take the risk. "Who should I say is asking for her?"

"Tell her it's Dunja."

"Dunja . . . ?" I coaxed, eyebrows raised.

"Just Dunja. If she remembers, she'll know."

I could feel her gaze still on me as I slipped back into the café, but I didn't mind. Despite the sunglasses, I hadn't caught anything but kindness in the way she watched me, and something even deeper, something I couldn't quite put my finger on. It felt almost like familiarity, but it couldn't have been that. We'd never met before; I wouldn't have forgotten someone like her.

Mama was rolling out phyllo dough in the back room, muscles coiling serpentine down her bare arms as she pressed her weight into the rolling pin. Nev wasn't there; she'd probably fled out back for a cigarette, like she did whenever she saw us snarling at each other. There was a dusting of flour high on one of Mama's cheeks, and her short, square fingernails were outlined in white.

Watching her, I imagined my heart encased with ice, like I always did when I had to deal with her after one of our flash-pan fights. Sometimes it was suspended in a laser-edged block, a perfect, transparent cube of clear and red. Other times I thought of a murkier slab, with just a smear of crimson behind dense whorls and eddies. I liked thinking about the shape that sheltered my raw heart, kept it safe.

She caught sight of me from the corner of her eye and straightened. "Where have you been?" she demanded. "Are you serving a four-course meal out there? Filling out an application for our Michelin stars? I need you to start slicing strawberries."

"Someone's asking for you outside," I replied, grateful that my voice didn't even tremble.

"If it's Marijana, the rent isn't due for another week, so she can go straight to hell until then. And stay there, too, if possible," she added sourly. "Humanity would rejoice as one."

"It isn't anyone we know. Some woman named Dunja. She wouldn't give me her last name."

Mama went so still I took a reflexive step back from her. It was uncanny, the way a snake freezes the split second before it strikes. She turned so pale that even her lips drained of color, and with her eyes wide and unfocused she was somehow even more beautiful, like a silent-movie heroine in a grayscale world.

For a moment, neither of us moved. It was so quiet I could have sworn I heard both our hearts thundering.

I broke the silence first. "You . . . you have flour on your face."

She blinked, her eyes clearing as she focused on me. Moving

like a marionette, she swiped a jerky hand over her face, missing the chalky patch.

"Let me get it." I approached her warily. She still held the rolling pin in one hand, her knuckles white with the force of her grip. But she wet her lips and gave a single nod, so I reached up and brushed it away with my thumb. When she still didn't stir, I moved to tuck back a stray curl that had come free of her braid. She caught my wrist with her free hand, and I choked back a yelp; her hands had always been steel-strong from her work in the kitchen.

"Leave it, Iris," she commanded. "And stay back here. I had better not see you come out."

"Why? Who is she? What—"

"No questions. This has nothing to do with you. *She* has nothing to do with you." Mama looked through me, as if I had no business existing with her in this moment. "She *can't* be here, and if she is—" She cut herself off, dragging her hand down her face until the iron mask of composure settled back over it. "You stay in here, Iris, if you know what's good for you."

Dropping the rolling pin, she swept out into the front room. I didn't follow her, but I pressed myself against the doorjamb of the kitchen, peeking out until my line of sight aligned with the front door and the tables outside. From there, I could see my mother advance on Dunja, and the tremble in Dunja's fingers as she laid them over her lips.

In the next instant, Dunja sprang out of her chair and they practically lunged into each other's arms. I clapped my hand over my own mouth; I had *never* seen Mama hug anyone so ferociously, her head tucked into the smaller woman's shoulder, Dunja stroking my mother's crown of braids and whispering into her ear.

Then my mother wrenched herself free and began shaking her head.

"You have to go back!" I pressed my cheek against the door-jamb, straining to hear my mother's fierce whisper. "Please. I know I promised, and I know I did it wrong, and I'm so sorry for it all. But you promised, too. So keep your end, *please*."

I couldn't hear Dunja's low reply, but I saw her shake her head and reach slowly into the pocket of her silken white harem pants, cuffed at the ankle, and withdraw something that glinted in her grip. She offered it to my mother, who shook her head again, tucking both hands behind her back like a child about to have her palms striped with a cane.

Dunja tilted her head to the side, beseeching, hand still extended. Finally, Mama took a single, furious step forward and snatched whatever it was off Dunja's palm, dropping it into her dress pocket. Then she spread her empty hands—*are you happy now?*—and whirled on her heel to march back toward the café. In between the bouts of rage and defiance strobing across her face, it was the well-deep sadness that threw me most.

Whatever had just passed between them, it had left my mother devastated.

FIVE

MAMA DIDN'T SPEAK MORE THAN TEN WORDS TO ME AFTER that. She'd disappeared deeply into herself, but it was a dangerous, time-bomb kind of stillness, like a very long lit fuse. I was full to bursting with curiosity, but it wasn't like I could ask her what had happened between her and this odd and beautiful stranger she clearly knew.

By the time Malina arrived for her shift, Nev had mangled some half-assed excuse for leaving early, and I'd have happily molted out of my own skin just to get away from Mama. I could see Malina assess our moods in her instinctive manner, her eyes flicking back and forth between us. She began to sing quietly, as if she couldn't help it, a skirling, eerie melody I recognized as a new variation on her theme for danger.

This one had the distinctive three-note refrain that tied it to our mother's mood. I'd heard it hundreds of times before: when Mama smelled smoke on me as I sat down next to her for dinner; when she caught me stealing nips of the expensive brandy from her larder so Malina and I could have birthday shots when we turned sixteen; when I brought home one piebald kitten after another and begged her to let us keep it.

But this melody had a new overtone, a counterpoint that captured my own tangled reaction, my discomfort and curiosity and deep desire to get the hell out of the café. And something below it, too, a subterranean thrum like shifting tectonic plates, something ancient and feral clawing its way through widening cracks.

It sounded like our mother was trapped, somehow, and very, very much afraid.

Malina kept humming even as she plucked an apron off its rusty hook and tied it around her waist, over a floor-length skirt splashed with marigolds and peonies like a watercolor. The flowing, lacy white peasant top she wore over it bared her creamy shoulders, and a kitschy little vial hung around her neck, tiny bass and treble clefs floating in sparkling water. In my opinion, most of Lina's outfits made her look like she spent her free time twirling in meadows and saluting the sunshine with her face, but then there were the shoes. While I wandered around in flats and flip-flops and generally didn't dwell much on my feet, Lina gleefully lost her mind over anything strappy and high-heeled and sassy-bright.

"Stop it," I hissed to her as she sidled up next to me and reached for a scrap of sweet dough in her usual scavenging way. I tried to eat as little as I possibly could at our mother's café, but Lina's fingers wandered freely into pie fillings and frosting, as if staging a silent protest against Mama meant nothing in the face of something sweet. "It's just making things worse."

"*What* things, Riss?" she whispered back. "It feels terrible in here. What's been—"

"If you're going to mumble like schoolchildren behind my back, at least call your sister by her proper name, Malina," Mama snapped, slapping her spatula against a cutting board. We both flinched. "She's not an animal, much as she does look like a cat in heat today."

Ris meant "bobcat," and out of all of Malina's nicknames for me, Mama hated that one with an especially concentrated passion. Maybe it cut too close to home, reminded her of all the things that pissed her off about me. The feline temperament, the defiance, some sort of invisible dander that Mama was particularly allergic to.

Malina gave my outfit a once-over, eyebrow quirking and one shoulder rising as if to say, *eh, she's not wrong.*

Traitor, I mouthed at her.

Slut, she mouthed back.

She already said that, I traced into the spill of flour in front of me, then smoothed it out again. *Get new material.*

Her eyes softening with sympathy, Malina dropped a little kiss on my shoulder before I twitched away from her. She frowned at me, hurt, but hers wasn't the comfort I needed now.

"So, I'm leaving, since Lina's here," I announced.

"Go ahead." Mama's voice was so distant and dim she may as well have been miles away. *Or at the bottom of a deep ditch*, the hate side of my brain whispered.

I snagged my little backpack and zipped outside, taking a deep breath of sunlit stone as soon as I was out the door, the tension in my shoulders easing a notch. I hadn't seen Luka since he'd come back from Belgrade last week to help at his father's nargileh café for the summer, but he'd texted me earlier to let me know he'd be waiting at our spot for lunch. Seeing him was the only thing I could think of that might possibly salvage the day.

It was too steep to take my bike up to the fortress with me, so I left it locked at the café and set out on foot. The street that led to the back entrance of the Old Town veered right, onto the path that would bring me outside the walls. There, I found the stone steps that wound up the mountain to the still-watchful ruins of Saint John's Fortress. It brooded above us like some crumbling, stolid sentry, built by the Illyrians and reinforced in the sixth century by Emperor Justinian to keep guard over the Old Town below.

My thighs burned by the time I reached the first level of the ruins. The secluded little bit of rampart that Luka and I had claimed years ago was several levels farther up, though below the castle tower itself. I was almost out of breath as I reached the last bit of trail I'd have to take, so hair-raisingly narrow that tourists never thought it led to anything, and locals had more sense than to attempt. I'd flattened my back against the cliff wall and edged there so many times over the years that the sheer drop beneath me barely even registered in the pit of my stomach.

Luka was already there as I inched my way into the little aerie of crumbling stone we'd discovered together, lounging on the rampart. "Lithe" wasn't a word I'd ever thought to use for any other boy, especially one as tall as he was, but it fit him, the way he draped himself over things as if they were his just because he was touching them.

I barely had time to set my backpack down before he swung himself off the wall and folded me into a bone-grinding hug. "Miss Iris," he murmured into my hair. He smelled different than I remembered, amber and pine resin, a warm and spicy soap I might have liked if it hadn't been so foreign. "So good to see you. They don't provide cliffside service like this in the Belgrade restaurants, let me tell you. And the Serbs say *we're* the peasants."

"Oof," I squeaked. "Let go, or you're going to crush me and there won't be any such service in your childhood home, either."

"Good point." I could hear him smile. "Can't kill the fair maidens of my childhood home. Otherwise, why would I come back?"

He gave me another squeeze before letting go, and we unpacked the food I'd snuck into my backpack for a makeshift picnic. I was beginning to think he'd forgotten when he carefully plucked a little package wrapped in tinfoil from his back pocket and offered it to me, one lean cheek creasing as he smiled. He always brought me a new flower when we met. Jade vine, ghost orchids, sprigs of fuzzy bottlebrush, and once even something called a chocolate cosmos. Rare, exotic flowers that couldn't possibly grow in the region, that I had no idea where he found.

He didn't know what they meant to me—I hadn't shared the

gleam even with him, as much as I'd sometimes yearned to have him see the best of me—but he knew I loved them, and it was enough.

I unwrapped it carefully, peeling back the layers until I found a perfect, still-living blossom inside, its petals moist with the water trapped beneath the foil. It was some kind of lily, creamy yellow that deepened into red as if dipped on the ends, and tiger-speckled along the inside with red flecks. As soon as my gaze softened it fractured into a starburst, a miniature firework of yellow upon yellow, a whirlpool of crimson flecks swirling around the minuscule black hole that was the flower's deepest inner point.

"What is it?" I breathed, like anything over a whisper might disturb the churning bloom. "Where did you find it?"

"It's an Italia Asiatic lily, and like I'd ever tell. I love when you see a new one for the first time," he added softly. "It's like a baby looking at something it's never seen before. I don't think you ever look at anything else like that."

"I'm glad you choose to find it endearing," I murmured back, still caught up with the contained, gorgeous explosion on my palm. "As opposed to strange and unnerving. That's the consensus around these parts."

"Nah. They just think that about your face."

I set the flower gently back into its foil cradle, then reached out and smacked him on the back of the head.

"Don't beat me, woman." He caught my hand and twisted it until I yelped. "At least not until after the food."

I sat back against the dusty stone, watching him as he ate in his fastidious, starving way, both of us cross-legged on the sun-warmed floor of the aerie. He was wearing city clothes, fitted jeans and a Lacoste shirt with something that actually looked like an alligator emblazoned above the breast pocket, instead of a black-market knockoff like everyone around here wore. His dark hair was much shorter than it had been the previous summer, before he left for college, and his face more angular than I remembered.

He'd been lean-faced and handsome even as a little boy, with those same watchful eyes, a startling light hazel beneath black lashes and the thick, dark eagle wings of his brows. He was eleven and I was nine when we met, the day he punched our most notorious mouth breather in the face for calling Luka's mother a child-stealing Roma. Later, I crept up to Luka and wiped the scrapes on his knuckles with a corner of my T-shirt while he watched me with solemn eyes.

After that, Lina and I had become inseparable from Luka and his sister, Nikoleta, who was a grade below us. We formed our own little group of half castes, an island of bright color. When we got older, the girls who'd once whispered about his Romany mother began to notice very actively how handsome Luka was.

But even if there wasn't so much as a kiss between us—and there never was—I was still the girl who'd touched him first.

"Hey," he said, startling me out of my thoughts. "Why you being so quiet, Missy? And you're not eating anything."

"Even the culinary treatings of Jasmina the Peerless get old, believe it or not," I said, shrugging a shoulder. "Unlike her spectacular bitchery. She likes to keep that fresh for me."

He snorted in sympathy. "She hasn't eased up, huh?"

"I don't think she knows how. It was even worse than usual

today, there was this . . ." The white flame of Dunja's hair blazed through my thoughts, followed by my mother's devastation and her fear. It felt so out of place here in the sunshine, and with pragmatic Luka right in front of me, like a swarm of moths where there should have been only butterflies. I could tell him about it later, once the strangeness had the time to fade. "But anyway, old news. Tell me about Belgrade."

He whistled low. "I didn't think I was going to like it, you know? So much space, so many variables, too easy to get lost in. But it's amazing, Iris, all these sleek modern buildings." He gave a light laugh. "Even their older ones are fancier than ours—the biggest theater has this glass covering over the neoclassical facade, like a museum exhibit. It's gorgeous, you'd love it. And they have stands where you can get a hot dog the size of your forearm, and you eat it with kefir."

I rolled my eyes. "Understood, pretty buildings and delicious food that lends itself perfectly to dick jokes, if I wasn't such a lady. Tell me about school."

He gave me a lazy smile, his eyes narrowing. "Well, as we know, the mathematics are inherently sensual when done by me," he began, and I cracked up despite myself. "But seriously, some of those kids are beyond brilliant. It's an American international college, so it's not even just homegrown math geniuses. My second week, one of the study-abroad students corrected the professor as he was writing out a proof, while he was still scratching it out on the blackboard." He shook his head admiringly. "Jolie's from Miami, but she thinks *I'm* exotic. And you should see her—"

"And stop," I ordered, giving him a mock shudder. "No need to regale me with your exploits. I'm familiar with the basic concept."

"You know," he continued, in the fake-casual tone that always raised my hackles, "you could come visit me sometime. There are so many galleries, and sometimes I go in just to see. None of them have anything like what you make."

"So what?"

"*So*, you only have one more year of school, and you can't tell me you want to be stuck here for the rest of your life after that." He glanced across the bay, resettling himself. "Even if sometimes it does seem like the most beautiful place in the world."

I followed his gaze to the water, like rippled blown glass from this high up, the mountains across the bay from us looming jagged. The usual ache rose up in my throat when the blue and white refused to form a shimmering mosaic like they once had. I swallowed it back down.

"Exactly," I said stiffly. "Why would I want to leave all this?"

"How many flowers in the world are you never going to see if you stay here?" he retorted. "And how many techniques are you never going to learn, because Jovan just dabbles in glassblowing and he's the only game in town? How are you even going to live off that here, anyway? You know Jovan can only afford to run the gallery because he sold his real one in Belgrade to retire here, and he makes those baubles to keep himself busy."

Anger rose up in me, tiny fizzy pockets like seed bubbles in glass. Those *baubles* were the only thing I had left of the gleam. And for all that I loved Cattaro, I'd spent so much of my life burning to leave this gorgeous prison, to see the places I'd only seen in books. It made me feel guilty sometimes, how badly I wanted to abandon all this beauty when other people were born trapped in deserts or slums. But our magic wasn't the Midas touch kind. And even if I somehow scrounged up enough money to spring me free, who would protect my sister from our mother once I was gone?

I began gathering up the remains of the food, crumpling foil and snapping the tops back onto containers. "You know I can't go anywhere," I mumbled, my throat aching. "Mama can't run the café without our help, and Malina won't leave her."

"Lina's a pure sweetheart, but you're not Siamese twins. Don't you think Niko and Tata needed me after Mama died? But I still left when I had to, Riss. Because I want to be an engineer, not the future owner of a nargileh café. They understood that."

"That is *not* the same!" I shot back. "I can't leave Lina to handle Mama by herself, and even if I could, you're forgetting that we. Have. No. Money. The café barely supports us as it is."

"You could get another job, and then you can save up and travel. There's backpacking, and hostels." He fixed his bright gaze on me, eyes earnest, and I felt my usual, dumb little twinge at how symmetrical his face was, that fine, straight nose and sculpted lips, the cheekbones sharp as arrowheads. It made him annoyingly persuasive—you agreed to things just so you could keep looking. "You could see the tree, Iris."

He meant the wisteria in the Ashikaga Flower Park in Tochigi, Japan, the one I'd told him about so many times. It was 144 years old, not the oldest in the world, but the book I'd read had called it the most beautiful. The central trunk twisted around itself like a helix, and held pink and purple blossoms that hung like waterfalls from a slim, steel framework around the trunk—half an acre of flowers above your head, like the sky itself was burning with the palest, most delicate fire. I could only imagine what it would look like to me, a riotous supernova of bloom and color.

And it was in Japan, so it came from the same earth that had made half of me.

I had never admitted to Luka how much it rubbed me raw, chafed at me like rope bound around my wrists, that I couldn't lay any physical claim to a country that was as much mine as Montenegro. A country in which I might have real family—a father, grandparents, cousins, maybe even other siblings. Half sisters or brothers with my eyes or chin or stock-straight hair just like my own.

But even if I wanted to find them, the crumbs Mama had ever let drop were far too few to form any kind of trail. I could never tell whether it was really that she only knew so much herself, after barely a week with our father, or that she couldn't stand the notion of losing control by letting us know too much. Our father's name was Naoki; that, she had been willing to cede. He came from Shimoda, one of the smallest port cities, its population only about twice that of Cattaro. I hadn't known whether to laugh or cry when I scoured the internet for it, only to find that it looked a bit like some much lusher version of Cattaro from a parallel universe, with rolling dunes of mountains steaming with hot springs.

Just like I hadn't known what to do when Mama told us his favorite food had been *uni*, sea urchin sushi. Something I couldn't imagine I would ever have the chance to taste. Since the idea of a Japanese restaurant opening in Cattaro—anywhere in Montenegro, really—was about as likely as actual teleportation to Japan, I talked Lina into hand-making a roll with me once, just to see if we could do it. I'd known we wouldn't be able to find avocados or nori sheets for rolling, but I hadn't been prepared for the mess of rice that crumbled pitifully apart instead of sticking, fish that sat rank in the mouth because it wasn't meant to be eaten raw, the lack of any savory sauce to mimic the umami taste of soy.

The worst of the burn was knowing that even if it had been as delicious as anything Mama made, we still wouldn't have had any idea how it was really supposed to taste.

"I'm sure the tree will be just fine without me," I said, shoving the last of the picnic litter into the backpack. "A lot like you in Belgrade, actually. I've heard from you, what, three times since you left?"

A tiny muscle in his cheek twitched. "That's not true, or fair. I had classes and a job and—"

I stood abruptly. "Anyway, it was nice to see you. I need to get back to the café."

That was a lie, and he knew it. But he was quiet as I left, seething with the silent frustration I knew so well in him. Luka wasn't one to throw a tantrum, not when he could creep up on you silently with logic. This particular argument gnawed at him especially because he could sense that, on some level, I knew he was right. I'd never know who I could be away from here until I gritted my teeth and left.

What he didn't know was how deeply it cut every time he brought it up. Because I always wondered: Was what I wanted exactly what my mother had wanted, before Malina and I chained her to this place?

SIX

I PICKED MY WAY BACK DOWN THE MOUNTAINSIDE carefully, wondering what to do with myself. I'd been planning on spending the rest of the day with Luka, lounging on the beach and then walking down the waterfront *riva* once the sun set, past the lanky rows of palm trees and the vendors who sold crepes, salty roasted corn, and oily cones of French fries drizzled with ketchup. No chance of that now. Čiča Jovan's studio, maybe, though he'd sniff out my off-kilter mood as soon as he laid eyes on me.

Back at the Cathedral Square, I went to unchain my bike, only to falter midstep when I realized the café door was closed—not even a flicker of movement inside. The doorknob wouldn't budge beneath my hand. Stifling a flare of panic, I cupped my hands around my face and peered in against the glare. Two crumb-crusted plates sat on the counter, alongside a slice of Spanish wind cake with frosting melting around the yellow dough and a mound of dried-out macarons.

My stomach knotted. The store was never empty at this time of day. We were open from seven in the morning until whenever we ran out of food at night, which was never earlier than six. I couldn't remember a single time when at least one of us wasn't behind the counter, a counter that should have been impeccable. Those abandoned desserts, wilting and far from beautiful, worried me more than anything else.

"Lina!" I called, rapping sharply against the glass. "Jasmina!"

Neither of them answered.

My heart pounding, I swung my leg over the bike and launched myself through the streets. Some of the alleys were so narrow that, had I been walking, I could have brushed both walls with only slightly lifted hands. I'd been navigating this polished stone maze since I was little, and this time of day there was barely anyone around to slow my headlong hurtle.

By the time I skidded to a stop in front of our flowered fence, I was so afraid I was gulping back tears, panic clogging my throat. When I found Malina in the yard on the creaking porch swing, with her legs tucked beneath her and Nikoleta curled against her side, fury burst through me like a flushed-out pipe.

"What the fuck is going on, Lina?" I demanded, flinging my bike against the fence so hard the chain links rattled. "Why is the café closed? I thought—" I rested my hands on my thighs and took a shaky breath. "I thought something happened to you and

Jasmina. Why the hell are you even out here? Where's Jasmina?"

Niko leaped up like a shot, moving to stand half in front of Lina, small hands planted on her hips. I would have laughed if I hadn't been almost hysterical; Niko had a face like a doe, heart-shaped and fine-featured as Luka's, her silky hair parted far from the left and sweeping above sloe eyes. She was petite and dark as their Bosnian Romany mother had been, and with her head tilted and jaw jutting, she looked like a fierce, tiny lapdog defending her mistress.

"Stop it, Iris," she snapped at me. Her voice sometimes still caught me by surprise, so much deeper and scratchier than it should have been. All that grit and smoke from such a pixie of a girl. "Can't you see she's already upset? Does this look like the time to terrorize?"

"I didn't mean—"

She chopped the air with one hand. "You *never* do. So maybe shut up first, and give Malina the chance to use her words. They're just as perfectly good as yours, I'm sure you know."

"Niko," Lina admonished quietly. "Maybe don't?"

"Fine." Niko dropped back down to the swing, crossing her tanned legs so that the bell charm strung on her anklet sang out a deceptively sweet little chime, but her torso thrummed with ten-sion. If I still wanted to fight, Nikoleta Damjanac would surely proceed to bring it. "Do your snappy thing before you say anything else, go on. It'll help."

I ground my teeth—Niko was even more impossible than Luka sometimes, all his logic and double the fire, minus the steely restraint—and wormed my finger beneath the elastic around my left wrist, snapping it three times until the sting pierced through the panic and rage. Once I'd remembered how to breathe I turned back to Lina, and now I could see that she'd been crying, and hard.

"Mama's inside," she said thickly. "I tried to stay in with her—to clean her up a little—but I couldn't take it, I'm sorry. I just couldn't listen to it."

"Did someone hurt her? What's wrong with her?"

Lina gave a hoarse laugh. "She's drunk, Riss. Stinking drunk. Like Mihajlo the Widower on a Saturday night."

I shook my head. "She can't be. You know Mama never drinks."

Lina shrugged one shoulder listlessly. "Well, she smells like she's been spending quality time with you, and threw up on herself at least once. So, there's that?"

"I'm happy to offer a second opinion," Niko said. "Based on the sample size of my brother and father, I can confidently concur that Jasmina's drunk as shit."

Malina gave a little hiccupping giggle through her tears, and Niko nudged her gently in the side. "See, that's better, pie," she murmured. "More of that, less of the salt."

Despite everything, I felt a sharp gnaw of jealousy at the two of them. We'd all grown up together and I enjoyed Niko when we weren't at each other's throats, but Malina had always been better friends with her. Watching them, I could never tell which one I was even jealous of: Malina for having a best friend who wasn't her own twin, or Niko for being able to both calm and warm my sister like I never could, like some sort of tiger balm.

I chewed on the inside of my lip, my mind racing in an effort to wrest everything back under control. "Tell me what happened after I left."

"Mama left the café right after you did, maybe five minutes after," Lina replied. "Said she had an appointment, but wouldn't tell me what. Since when does Mama have *appointments*, Riss? She never leaves the café during the day!"

Her voice rose, and Niko patted her thigh, making the low bear-cub rumble that meant annoyance or concern. Lina leaned against her for a moment, taking a deep breath and releasing it in a shuddering rush. My insides folded against each other; I wouldn't be able to tell her about Dunja yet. She needed to know, and I needed her thoughts, but she was too delicate right now. I'd have to hold that on my own for at least a little longer.

"I'm fine, really," she said to Niko, scooching away slightly. "I've got it now. Anyway, Riss, she came back maybe an hour or so later, and she just looked—I don't know. Beside herself, but all hollow. Like someone had *died* or something. So then she went into the larder and poured herself a glass—"

"Not a shot glass, but a glass-glass?"

"An actual glass. Two-thirds of the way up, like she was pouring water, and then she just drank it down in one go. I swear, she barely even flinched." She giggled wetly. "After that she just swiped the whole rakija bottle, like, to hell with *this*. It was actually pretty funny. I told her she was embarrassing us in front of the customers and then made her come home with me."

"You told her—you *made* her come home with you?"

"It wasn't so hard. She was getting a bit weirdly lovey by then." Her lips trembled. "It's all dissonance, like she . . . like she doesn't know her own mind?"

"Okay, then." I gritted my teeth. "I'm going to go see her. Why don't you stay with Niko, bunny."

She shook her head. "I'm coming with you. It's bad enough I just left her in there in the first place."

"Are you sure?" Niko murmured. "Iris can handle this, whatever it is. You could come home with me, sleep over tonight if you wanted."

"No, you go on, I'll see you tomorrow?" She looked back at me, teeth sinking into the notches of her lower lip. "You're not some conquering hero, Riss. It shouldn't always be just you when things get ugly, you know?"

THE PUNGENT BLISTER of liquor struck me as soon as we crossed our threshold. It was rakija, for sure; nothing else smelled both so sharp and foul. I assumed there were expensive brands that were probably smoother than anything I'd ever sampled, but from the smell of it, Mama hadn't been indulging in anything particularly top-shelf. Beside me, Malina nearly gagged, pressing the back of her hand against her mouth.

"See?" she choked out. "It's like you this morning. If all the air *everywhere* was made of your breath."

I ignored her. "Mama?" I called out, peering into the kitchen. Empty.

"Iris? That you?"

A wave of chills swept down my spine; I almost didn't recognize her voice. Underneath the slur, there was something else, a note of pleading I'd never heard from Mama before.

Another "Iris?" floated out, followed by a genuinely pitiful little moan. Lina and I exchanged a wide-eyed "oh shit" look before I laced my fingers with hers and followed Mama's voice to her bedroom, Lina trailing behind me.

I gently pushed the door open, peering around it. Mama's room was bigger than ours, but not by much, dominated by her sleigh bed. I lifted my gaze to the nook beneath her window, and my heart gave a hiccup—there she was, back against the wall and knees drawn up to her chin, her gray sheath ridden up so high I could see the long, tempered muscle of her thigh.

I let go of Lina's hand and slid between the footboard and the armoire, perching on the edge of the bed. Mama looked up at me wide-eyed, her face pale and salty-streaked with tears. She seemed so achingly young that I found myself suddenly overwhelmed with sympathy, a corkscrew twisting in my center. With her hair tangled and undone, dark as baker's chocolate and so long it nearly reached her waist, I suddenly remembered that Mama—the villain and the wicked witch, the stepmother who'd had the misfortune of actually bearing her unwanted offspring—was barely thirty-six years old.

"How are you doing?" I said, trying to remember the last time I'd spoken to her so gently. "I think maybe you need some water."

She shook her head once, like a decisive toddler. "No water." Squinting one eye shut, she reached down and groped around the floor beneath the alcove. "Was a bottle there . . ."

"I think that's all gone now. Why don't we—"

I went rigid as she wrapped her fingers around my wrist, tugging at me until I stood from the bed, practically looming above her. Her face turned so soft as it tilted up toward mine that I barely recognized my own mother.

"Iris . . . ," she murmured, stroking the inside of my wrist. Her eyes filled with tears, like water rushing over a frozen pond, and her face crumpled. "My hibiscus daughter. Why . . ." She shook her head and swallowed. "Why did you have to grow up so strong? Why did you have to make it so *hard*?"

With that, her arms circled me, locking around my waist, and she buried her cheek against my middle. I was so shocked that for a moment I stood stiff, arms lifted away from my sides.

"I don't know what to do," she whispered against my belly. "It wasn't supposed to . . . it wasn't supposed to go like this."

"What do you mean?" I whispered, setting one hand cautiously on top of her head. Her hair was finer than mine, thick and silky, the crown of her head warm beneath my palm. I dug my fingertips into her scalp and rubbed, trying to ease her like I did with Malina sometimes. "What wasn't supposed to?"

She whimpered against my stomach, her shoulders hunching, and I felt such a tremendous, unfamiliar flood of love for her I almost began to cry myself as I met Lina's wide eyes above Mama's head. "Let's get you into bed," I said.

She let me hook my hands under her armpits and heave her bonelessly up against me, Lina pulling down the sheets and gently tugging her toward the middle of the mattress. As soon as I moved away she bolted upright, her face taut with panic. "Where are you going?"

"Just to bring you some water," I soothed. "I'll be back in a minute. Lina will stay with you."

Mama shot me a look halfway between pleading and suspicion, then sank back onto her elbows, letting her head fall against Lina's shoulder. "My cherry girl, you smell so sunny," I heard her mumble as I left. "Do *you* still love me? At least a little?"

In the bathroom, I filled a glass and ran a washcloth under the faucet, wringing it out. The girl in the mirror looked so much more in control than I felt. Her eyes stared back at me, water-pale, and in the dim light from the tiny window the bones in my face looked not just stark but beautiful, my lips fine and dainty as the negative space left behind by a paintbrush. I splashed water on my face, taking deep breaths until my hands stopped shaking. I could do this. I could always do whatever it took.

Back in the bedroom, I clambered carefully onto the bed, shuffling to Mama on my knees. I handed the glass to Lina, and she held it to our mother's lips and fed her tiny sips as I dabbed at her face and the ruined front of her dress.

"Can you turn around for me?"

I unzipped her, tugging the dress down while she wriggled against it like an eel in a bucket until it finally slipped off. She let me work a T-shirt over her head, then lay back down, cheek pillowed on her arm and eyes half closed. "Will you lie down with me? You haven't done that since you were so small . . . you so roly-poly, Lina, and you, Iris, such a scrappy thing . . ."

"Roly-poly?" Lina echoed, smoothing a strand off her forehead. "Are you calling me fat, Mama?"

Mama rubbed her cheek against Lina's shoulder. "Never. Though no Linzer cookie was ever safe from you."

I knew things hadn't torn quite as jaggedly between them as they had with Mama and me—there hadn't been that dangerous sense of rent iron between them—but I'd had no idea they still teased each other this way. They never did it in front of me.

"Riss," Mama whispered, reaching for me. "Will you come, too, just this once? Please?"

Maybe the nickname was why I gave in. As unfair as it was that even this should be on her terms just like everything else, it was also like water to a cactus, parched even by its own low standards. There was so much I needed to ask her—about Dunja, and about what had driven her to this weakness—but I hadn't even talked to Malina yet. And seeing her so vulnerable had bled off my fury, enough that I couldn't bring myself to prick the thin-skinned bubble of this moment.

"Do you remember," she murmured as I settled awkwardly against her back, jerking when she looped her legs over mine, "do you remember the cake I made you?"

I did. It was for Malina's and my fifteenth birthday, and it had been a Sacher torte in the form of a roulade. Where there should have been just one layer of raspberry jam filling, she'd lined it with layer after layer of fruit alternating with chocolate, apricot-chocolate-strawberry-chocolate-peach-chocolate, into such a tiny central spiral that the sheets separating the core layers must have been thinner than rice paper. She hadn't baked us a birthday cake in years by then, but that one must have taken hours.

"I do. It was incredible." I hesitated. "You never told us why you did that."

"Because that's what your bougainvillea tasted like. I wanted you to know."

She meant the glass sculpture I'd blown, of the twilight bougainvillea that grew in our yard. My fractal masterpiece, the smallest and most precise glasswork depiction I'd ever managed—barely two feet long, yet as close as I'd ever come to conveying that honeycomb sense of infinity. I'd given it to her for her own birthday, that same year. No matter how things curdled between us, I'd never stopped giving her gifts. I told myself it was out of the sweetest spite, killing her with kindness. But it wasn't, and had never been that.

"Why *did* you hang it up at the café?" I asked her. "You always used to say the desserts were enough decoration."

She turned to look at me over her shoulder, until we were nearly nose to nose. Even heavy-lidded and sickly pale, she was magnificent in the slanting afternoon light. When I was little, I'd imagined her as one of the Montenegrin queens I read about in my storybooks—like Queen Jevrosima, ethereal mother of Crown Prince Marko, the hero of so many of our folktales. Prince Marko was a dauntless, vengeful protector of the weak, and I'd loved him with a child's fierce adoration until I read the story in which he tricked a Moorish princess into marrying him, then stole off with her gold while she slept because her dark skin startled him in the night.

After that, I'd always wondered what he'd have to say about my own angled bones and eyes.

But in all the stories his mother had been wise and kind, and unfailingly devoted.

And the way my mother watched me now was exactly as I'd thought Queen Jevrosima must have looked at her own son.

Her eyes fluttered closed, and she sighed. "Because, my flower girl. Because you made it for me."

SEVEN

MALINA AND I SPENT THE REST OF THE AFTERNOON AND evening taking turns watching over Mama while she snored, making sure she didn't throw up in her sleep. I must have fallen asleep myself during one of my later shifts; it was the unfamiliar expanse of Mama's empty bed that woke me. It felt like too much room without her and Lina in it.

I let myself laze for a few more moments, the events of the past night washing over me. Beneath the lingering shock, I felt a warm, new kernel of happiness, as if the years of frustration and fury rubbing me raw inside had finally grown a grain of sand into a pearl. I'd spent the night sleeping next to my mother, pressed back to back; she'd looked at me like she might learn to love me again. Maybe everything would be different now, somehow.

I propped myself up and peeked outside. The sky was still peachy and golden with trails of dawn, which meant Mama had probably already wrung herself out and left for the café. Stretching my arms above my head, I swung my feet over the side and headed to check on Malina and change out of the clothes I'd slept in.

My reflection in the armoire mirror froze me in my steps.

My hair was so straight it barely tangled even after sleep, and goose bumps stippled my skin as my fingers slid easily down its length, slipping over the colorful ribbons woven through it. They were arranged in asymmetrical sprays, and the effect was oddly striking, like fireworks bursting against a night sky. Each was barely thicker than a thread, slipknotted into place around the root of the hair, and every time I tilted my head they released faint wafts of leather, carnation, plum, and some sort of warm Arabian musk. I recognized the component scents—Mama used essential and fragrance oils in her cooking all the time, and Malina liked wearing them—but I couldn't remember having smelled this combination on either of them before.

My scalp turned taut and prickly as I imagined Mama hunched over me for hours as I slept, still drunk yet braiding ribbons into my hair with a touch so deft she didn't wake me once.

In Malina's and my room, I found Malina sleeping on top of her sheets, curled tightly on her side; ribbons twined through her curls, too, and I felt a ridiculous twinge of envy that of course, *of course* even this would look prettier on her. I leaned over her and wound a few carefully around my finger, separating them from her hair so I could sniff at them—hers smelled different from mine, a top note of sweet pea over a rich vanilla base, pierced with a sharp and surprising nip of verbena.

Turning away from her, I shucked my stale clothes and rummaged in our cluttered closet for my favorite sundress: deep violet patterned with iridescent beetles, a treasure I'd found at the flea market. Then I threaded my favorite silver hoops through my ears, feeling the comfortable drag of their weight on my lobes, and winged my eyes with liner. Unnerved as I was by the image of Jasmina blank-faced and intent in the dark, her fingers flitting through my hair like an animal preening its young, I wanted to look nice for her today. Maybe the ribbons were some kind of apology for . . . for everything. Maybe they were her way of opening the door again.

By the time I arrived at the café, I'd decided I liked the ribbons. They'd fluttered in the breeze as I biked, and I'd caught myself straining to catch whiffs of that bright perfume, to separate it from the salty air and car fumes, the savory simmer of bean and sausage stew put early on the pot for lunch.

"Jasmina?" I called out as I stepped inside. "How are you feeling? And what are these ribbons—"

The door to the kitchen swung open so hard it thundered against the wall, and my mother simply dropped through it, like a rag doll tossed aside by a child.

Time shuddered, then slowed to a crawl. It seemed like hours that I watched her falling, the image of every moment sharp and hard like an insect caught in amber, each locking indelibly into my memory like the missing pieces of a terrible puzzle:

Her outstretched arms flung up above her head like a dancer's, the incidental grace.

The streaming banner of her hair, sluicing through the air.

The droplets of her blood on the walls, spattered so bright and vivid they were almost pretty.

And then the bone crunch of the back of her head as it met the tiles behind the counter, out of my sight.

Just before I screamed and time snapped back into place like one of the rubber bands around my wrist, I heard the boom of the back door slamming, the distant staccato of running footsteps. The electric instinct to chase after whoever had done—*this*—to my mother juddered through me as I fumbled my way weak-kneed around the counter, as if my nervous system had brushed a live wire and caught fire. But I couldn't run, I couldn't go. I couldn't leave her.

Once, years ago, I'd fallen off the chipped, rusting monkey bars in our schoolyard and knocked all the air out of my lungs. I remembered gasping desperately for breath, the air sparkling in front of my eyes as if I'd temporarily gained the ability to see oxygen molecules.

That feeling of breathlessness, of almost dying, couldn't compare to the sight of her body, pale and curled like a pistil in the spreading pool of her own blood. I dropped down to the floor next to her, hard, a brilliant bolt of pain shooting up from my knees.

"Mama," I managed, through the taste of iron in my mouth. "Mama, please . . ."

She couldn't move her head—her neck was probably snapped,

or her spine, or both—but her eyes slid sideways, unfocused, to meet mine. They were glazing over, jellied, and the lids twitched frantically with every slow blink, as if it was taking the last of her lifeblood to move even that much. Maybe it was; there was blood *everywhere*, the copper reek of it sickly sweet and overwhelming. I could hear it thick and gurgling in her throat as she tried to draw a drowning breath. It was sticky in her hair, and all over my hands where I touched her chest, to try to peel the sodden blouse away and see how she was hurt. For a moment, the way it had seeped through the fabric looked almost like a blossom, and my vision lurched, threatening to fracture the blood into something beautiful.

Then the impulse receded, because I couldn't find a bullet wound or a stab mark. Nothing so clean or relatively kind.

Instead, beneath the blouse, her chest was smashed, entirely staved in.

My gut collapsed—what did I need it for, anyway, what was I ever going to eat again—and my own lungs wicked in on themselves. I made a smothered, keening sound as I caught her by the shoulders, trying to shift her head onto my knees, as if that could make a hint of difference.

"Iris," she forced out, blood leaking between her lips. "Dunja . . . don't . . ."

Then she simply stopped trying to breathe. I'd always heard there was supposed to be a last breath, a death rattle, but she didn't even have the luxury of one. Her eyes slid shut, lashes curling over the hollows beneath. I could still see a sliver of white between her lids—and then they flickered like moth wings, lashes twitching. As if she were *dreaming*.

Frantically, I felt for her pulse at her throat—nothing. My insides clenching, I leaned in close to her parted lips, hoping fiercely that I'd feel even the faintest whisper of her breath against my cheek.

Still nothing. No heat. No heartbeat.

Just her eyes, still ticking back and forth beneath her lids like a metronome. Suddenly, all I could see was a shimmering net that had lowered in front of my own eyes. The last of my consciousness broke over me, and right before I went under, I looked up at the wall over the table and found it empty.

My glass bougainvillea was gone.

MALINA'S SCREAMS BROUGHT me back.

"*Iris!*" she was shrieking. "No, no, no, Riss, no!"

I thrashed my way back to her, sitting up so abruptly the world tilted and slid sideways. A rush of nausea swelled up my throat and I clamped my hand over my mouth, wrapping my other arm around my sister.

"Oh thank God, Riss, I thought you—I thought—" She buried her face into my neck, her shoulders heaving. "I thought you were gone too, there's so much blood. . . ."

I looked down at myself. My front looked as though I'd been dipped in it, patches still shining slick. I trailed my fingers over the drenched fabric, feeling as though my hand belonged to someone else. It was sticky and cool, tacky between my fingertips as I rubbed them together.

Malina was crying more quietly now, but steadily, her nose streaming. "You were bent over her, and I thought maybe someone had attacked you both, and . . ." Her voice trailed off into a whimper. "She's dead, Riss, she's *dead*, oh my God. . . ."

I squeezed her hard against me. "But she *isn't*. I know it looks like—it looks so bad—but she blinked earlier, and her eyes were moving—"

She shook her head once, a tight snap like a spasm, biting her lip. "She's not breathing, Riss. There's no pulse. I think . . ." Her voice broke. "I think she's really gone."

I shifted and folded my legs beneath me, but as soon as I tried to stand, the world grew blinding and trembly, as if I were inside a lightbulb filament. I let go of Lina and pressed both hands against my face until my cheekbones ached.

"I can't stand up yet," I told her. "Call an ambulance. If there's anything left, maybe they can still bring her back."

THEY TOOK MAMA away from us; we weren't allowed to go with her, not even as next of kin, no matter how much I fought the paramedics and the police.

Nev had arrived long before the police got there; I dimly remembered pressing my forehead against her freckled shoulder, her arms around me and Malina as they both shook with choking sobs. At some point, a detective had peeled her away from us and then walked Malina and me over to Čiča Jovan's house, refusing to answer any of our frantic questions along the way.

I calmed down incrementally as soon as we were inside. I'd

been in Jovan's apartment so many times, for his family's *slava* feast in November, other holidays, and my drawing lessons—the glass-blowing, we did in his studio next door—that it smelled like home to me, apples and resin and aged wood. In the meantime, Čiča Jovan had seized control of the situation with the deft entitlement of someone who'd been at the household helm for a very long time, long enough to outlive everyone else. At his urging, Lina and I changed out of our clothes and into his late wife's fine cotton night-gowns and cashmere sweaters. For one stupid moment, I mourned the loss of my lovely dress, the tiny insects drowned in Mama's blood.

"What are we going to do about these?" Malina asked, finger-ing a strand of ribbons in her hair. "Should we take them out? Since Mama—since she put them in for us last night, maybe they're evi-dence?"

"You can do what you want, bunny, but I'm keeping mine," I said. "She might have meant them as a gift. I'm not letting anyone take them out."

By the time Jovan came to check on us, Malina had lapsed back into tears while I stayed dry as a stone. He coaxed us into drinking some brandy-laced tea, followed by a slug of straight brandy for good measure, then led us back to the mahogany table in the living room to speak with the detective. We sat side by side across from him, our arms brushing. Malina knotted her fingers in her lap until they turned white, and I curled mine underneath the table's lip, gripping it as if it could hold me. All I wanted was to feel tethered to the ground, and I was beyond grateful for Čiča Jovan's strong, gnarled hands heavy on our shoulders.

"What's wrong with you, Mirko?" he said in his quiet rumble. "I know all three of your grandparents living—and Petar too, God rest his soul—and what would they think of you refusing to let these children follow their own mother to the hospital?"

The detective shifted uneasily. He was an older man, with a pitted face and dark, hangdog eyes, and he looked almost as exhausted as I felt. "With all respect, Jovan, this is . . . an unusual situation. We can't allow them there until the doctors have gleaned a better understanding of the, uh, the parameters of her condition."

"Her *condition?* What are you even on about, boy?" Jovan rasped. "Jasmina was healthy as a plow horse, always has been. She's been good as a daughter to me for seventeen years, and she didn't have any *condition* I knew of. Why don't you just get on with it and tell us how she is? If these children are about to be orphans, they have a right to know."

The detective cleared his throat, a muscle ticcing in his jaw. "It's, well. The problem is that we're not sure."

"Sure about what?" I lashed out. "You haven't told us anything yet! There was so much blood, and I saw . . ." My mind flashed back to the mulched mass of Mama's chest, and I couldn't finish, my gorge rising. "What *happened* to her?"

"It's not that we don't know what happened, miss," he said quietly. "We do. Your mother's heart was crushed, by something slender but blunt, about like this." He held up his hairy hand, palm down, so the bony side of it faced us. "Obviously, it would take a huge amount of force to strike the sternum hard enough to pulverize the heart and most of the lungs. And it's still unclear what sort of weapon was used to exert this force in such a concentrated way."

I dug my fingertips into the table until I felt a splinter bite into the soft flesh of my thumb. Malina let out a choked sound and shoved away from the table, her chair squealing against the floor as she sprinted toward the bathroom. We could hear her retching, and Jovan lumbered after her, shooting the detective a poison-ivy look over his shoulder.

I swallowed, forcing down bile. "So what are you saying? Is she dead? I thought I saw—I thought she might not have been all the way gone. . . ."

Mirko dragged one hand wearily over his face, his pitted features distorting. "I know how it sounds. I'm sorry to even have to describe it to you, but . . ." He glanced up as Malina slid back in next to me, still breathing hard and wiping at her mouth, Jovan's hand landing firmly back on my shoulder. "The problem is that we're still not sure whether to treat this as an assault or a murder investigation, or if the distinction even matters. Your mother—the doctors don't understand what's happening to her. None of them have seen anything like this before."

A surge of static buzzed through my head. My tongue went dead and heavy in my mouth. "What do you mean?" Malina said, voice wavering. "What's wrong with her?"

He steepled his stubby fingers, looking at us over them. "She is dead, miss. Or she should be—she has no vital signs, no heartbeat, no blood pressure. Yet she also *isn't* dead. She opened her eyes several times in the ambulance, and she has detectable brain activity, that of a living person in a coma. It's as if . . ."

He worked his jaw a few times, as if trying to release pressure with a click. "Listen, *sine*. I'm not a religious man."

Sine. Son, a pet name for a younger person, boy or girl. Somehow hearing it made me feel even worse, the boundless sense of how baffled and sorry for us he was, this man who was supposed to solve things and protect us and neaten the world. Behind us, Čiča Jovan let go of my shoulder to cross himself.

The detective's bloodshot eyes snagged mine. "And I haven't been since I was younger than you both. But if I still were, and if I believed in such a thing as the soul, I would say that your mother's was trapped, tied to a broken body that simply can't sustain life. I don't understand how that's possible; none of the doctors do, either. They forbid us from even telling you about it for fear that it would get out, start a religious panic, people mobbing the hospital and shouting miracles and sainthood. But you girls go to school with my Goran. I couldn't keep a thing like this from you, not about your own mother."

He rubbed the back of his neck and worked his jaw again, and I could see again how much this pained him. "But she's quarantined now, and until they have a theory of it—what kind of disease might mimic life this way, maybe, some genetic defect your mother might have—they can't run the risk of letting you near her."

I could feel myself expand with rage, boiling from me like a solar flare. "*No.*"

His eyebrows shot up. "Excuse me?"

The chair legs screeched as I pushed away from the table, my palms slick on the varnished wood, knees locked to keep me upright. "You can't keep us away from her, not if she's still alive. Or whatever she is. Even if she were . . . fully dead"—everything was *insane*—"you'd still let us see her one more time, have her body for a funeral at least. So you'll take us to her. Now."

His mouth tightened into a grim line. "I can't do that, miss. I shouldn't even have told you to begin with. As far as the police are concerned, your mother *is* dead. I can't bring you to the quarantine, much less let you loose after."

Certainty flooded over me, pounded against my insides like a rain-swollen tide. I could do this for us, for me and my sister. "You *can*. Because if you don't, we'll tell everyone what you just told us. Our friend Nevena Stefanović—she was our mother's apprentice. She's also the councilman's daughter. Even if you detain all of us, you can't lock *her* away somewhere. And she'll do it for us, she'll tell everyone, and whatever happens then will fall on you."

I bit off the last of the words, forced them through chattering teeth. My entire body was trembling with just the effort it took to keep myself standing. Beside me, Malina rose and slid her arm around my waist, letting me lean invisibly against her.

"You wouldn't have said anything in the first place, would you, Detective?" she asked softly, her voice warm as a hand to the nape of the neck. "If you hadn't meant for us to force you to take us to her. You know what the best thing to do is, the kindest thing. I can tell you do. So just do it for us, will you? *Please.*"

He watched her silently, a hint of something like awestruck fear glinting deep in his pouched eyes. Finally he rubbed his chin with one hand, fingers rasping over the bristle of his stubble, and gave a single nod.

"Just the two of you, then."

Jovan heaved a harsh-edged sigh. "Mirko . . ."

"No, sir. Not even for you. Even this could ruin me, end my entire career. I have Kristina to think of, and my boy. I'm sorry, but it's the best I can do. It'll have to be just the two of them."

ALL THE HOSPITALS I'd ever seen had been grim, communist affairs, reeking of antiseptic and floored with curling linoleum or chipped tile. Like Mama, Lina and I had always been healthy enough to avoid everything but vaccines when we were little, so hospitals made us both nervous with the memory of the childhood fear of needles sliding under skin and the surrounding miasma of illness swampy in the air.

But this one seemed somehow worse than most, though it could have been the gloom of the rain-soaked night outside. The detective had insisted on taking us in late, long after hours, when the hospital depended on an underpaid and exhausted skeleton staff. In the dim, dreary hallway, we could hear the water beating on the roof like the rattle of dice in a cup, and even at this hour a few stragglers waited for attention in the seats that lined the corridor: a withered grandmother with mottled skin and scabs around her mouth, a little boy with a wracking donkey's cough who buried his face in his mother's lap when each bout got the best of him.

And then there was the moaning. It was faint but relentless, like the sound of the whistling witch-winds that sometimes stole through cracks in the walls in high summer, and it made all the fine hairs on my neck and arms stand on end.

After a brief conversation with a sallow-faced, tight-lipped nurse in crisp whites—I could see his hand brush hers, and wondered if he'd paid her to look the other way—the detective led us down the hallway, cutting a right into a massive room lined with cots separated only by thin curtains. The distant moaning we'd been able to hear even from the hallway was much louder here. I had thought it might be the cumulative hum of the sick, but most here were asleep and silent, save for snatches of mumbling and phlegmy snores.

We followed the sound down two sets of stairs, until we were well underground, and Mirko unlocked a padlocked door and shouldered it open with a grinding metal screech, bringing us to a stop in front of a room encased in glass. There was a set of clear double doors set into the glass, the vestibule between for decontamination, I guessed.

And beyond, our mother lay like a deathbed princess under fluorescent lights.

It was the ugliest sort of light, the kind that usually made anyone beneath it look like a riverbank corpse recently fished out of the water. But with her ravaged chest covered by thin sheets, and all that bloodied, knotted hair tucked away into a surgical hat, Mama was gorgeous as ever, so transparently pale I could practically see the finesse of the facial bones straining beneath her skin. Her eyes strobed, unseeing—closed, then half open, then closed—and she emitted a keening, unceasing moan like a deflating bagpipe, both too high-pitched and too soft to be so pervasive.

The moaning never flagged, not even for a moment. It sounded like the quietest torture, something so drawn out and tormented that only sheer fatigue kept it tamped down.

"I'll be at the stairs," Mirko said tightly, "when you're ready to leave." His footsteps clicked down the hall, then faded.

Once we were alone with Mama, I could hear Malina's breathing speed up beside me, and my heart began to pound in answer. "Riss," she choked out, stumbling against my side. "I can't stay here. I—I can't listen to her."

I wrapped an arm around her, clenching my other hand into a fist until my nails sank into my palms good and hard, slicing sharp. "Why?" I whispered, wanting and not wanting to know in equal and opposite force. "What does she sound like?"

Lina closed her eyes, her lips trembling, and the fine blue capillaries on her quivering lids reminded me so much of Mama when I'd found her that I wanted to thrust my own sister away from me, to cauterize the image from my mind. "She just wants it to *stop*. It all hurts so much, and she wants it to stop, and she's fighting and fighting with nowhere to go. There's nothing else, I can't hear *her* like I usually can, I can't even find her. It's like something feral's trapped inside her skin, Riss. Like a dying animal that just wants to finally die."

It was too much to take. I could feel steel slipping in, my blood turning to mercury. I had to be both stable and fluid, made solely of strength. There couldn't be anything warm or yielding to get in the way.

We had to find her, the woman who had done this to Mama. Wherever Mama's mind and soul were stranded, she was the one who had ferried them there.

EIGHT

MIRKO DROVE US BACK TO THE OLD TOWN, AND ČIČA JOVAN insisted we spend the night with him; neither of us could face going back to our empty house with the pall of Mama's absence, her death or undeath or whatever it was, hanging over it. And there was the horrible possibility that whoever had hurt our mother might be lurking somewhere near, waiting for the chance to strike at us too. It seemed ridiculous that anyone would want to hurt us, here where we knew everyone, but nothing was certain anymore.

Still reeling, I'd told the detective about Dunja, and my missing bougainvillea sculpture—he'd asked for anything we could think of that might help in the investigation, which he meant to begin no matter what was happening to Mama—and then assured us that officers were posted around the house to keep watch.

None of us knew what to do with ourselves after that. My insides felt clammy and numb, as if I'd been floating in icy water from the inside out. Jovan made sure we were comfortable in his guest room, but after we were settled I could hear him pacing the living room beyond our cracked-open door, murmuring "God, Jasmina, God, *kuku lele*" to himself, followed by a quiet rasping so low and terrible I didn't immediately recognize it as tears. I closed the door with a soft click, pressing my cheek against the warped surface.

Malina showered first, so she was already tucked up beneath the quilts in the guest-room bed by the time I padded out of the bathroom. I slid in next to her, folding myself around her curled body, and she tucked her feet against my calves. We lay together in silence for a long moment, listening to the rise and dip of each other's breathing until we finally matched up.

"What do you think is happening, Riss?" she whispered. "It has to be something like the gleam. Not exactly like it—nothing we do has ever been anything as terrible as that—but the same sort of thing. Some kind of magic. I mean, what else could it be?"

We'd hardly ever called it that before. "Magic" sounded like something out of one of my books, vast and impossible to reconcile with our world, gods and demons and creatures made from daylight or darkness but decidedly inhuman. The gleam felt more like a talent, a skill we'd been born with, if crafting beauty could be a genetic trait like the color of our eyes.

But it *was* magic. Mama had called us witches since we were little, to make sure we understood the danger and the secrecy we practiced, and witches worked with magic—that was their material, the fabric of their loom. And I remembered the sheer intensity of my fractals when I'd been at the height of my gleam. That girl hadn't just been beautiful; she had been so strong. And Malina still was, no matter how she tried to spare me by hiding the fullness of her gleam.

"It must be," I agreed. "But being alive when she should be dead . . . that's an infinity apart from eating the moon."

"And you think that woman you saw fighting with Mama has something to do with it?"

"Mama said her name right before she . . . stopped. She said, 'Dunja.' And then, 'don't.' And that woman was so strange when I talked to her. The way she spoke, the things she chose to say. Why would Mama have said her name if she hadn't been the one to do it?"

Malina let out a quavering sigh. "It's all so impossible, you know? My brain just doesn't want it. And either way—I don't think we're getting her back, Riss, not from whatever or wherever she is now. I guess it's really just you and me. Like you always said."

"But if it is magic, maybe it isn't permanent," I argued. "Maybe there's some way to undo it, if we can find Dunja."

"Maybe." I could hear the anguished doubt in her voice. We'd both seen Mama; I couldn't really imagine a magic that would bring her back from that, either, even if one existed that wouldn't let her go.

"I just keep thinking . . . ," I started.

"What?"

"I keep thinking, if she's well and truly gone, now I'll never get to ask her why. Why she was so hard on us, or on me, at least. No, don't deny it, I know she wasn't all cherry preserves and sugar water for you, either. But you know it was always so much worse for me."

"I do," she said softly. "I know. I think it might be because you kept stepping between us? Even when she wanted to take it out on me, you wouldn't let her."

"But still, it was always different with you. It never felt like she was sharpening herself on you just for the hell of it, like you were her whetstone." The memory of last night, the almost playful banter between them, drilled deeper inside me. "It's almost easier to think she never loved me at all, but then I have these memories of her taking us to the beach at Prčanj when we were little. We had swimsuits that matched hers, white with strawberries on them, and she'd tow us around in our floaties and pretend to nip our cheeks like snacks. Do you remember that?"

She nodded, her hair tickling my nose. I buried my face in her curls, inhaling her complicated scent—the sweet and oddly biting perfume of the ribbons, above the white musk, cedar, and patchouli from the little tinctures she and Niko blended together.

"I used to think it was because having us kept her from things she wanted for herself. She could have been a famous chef anywhere she wanted, instead of raising us with no one but Čiča Jovan to help." It was so hard to say this, even to her. "But then I wonder if that wasn't it at all. If it was maybe just raising *me* that did it."

She stiffened against me. "What do you mean?"

I bit down on the inside of my cheek until I tasted blood,

enough iron that I was sure my voice wouldn't break. "I know I'm not easy to love, sometimes. I hated her so much for taking the gleam away from me—I threw it in her face so many times—and I know I'm not very much without it."

Not like you, I didn't add. *You who'd still be so sweet and perfect even if you couldn't sing.*

"So I wonder if maybe she loved me at first, but then . . . couldn't anymore. Because I'm all harsh and sort of scabby, and I can be terribly mean. And I know how much she values—valued—beauty, and I'm not beautiful like you—"

"How dare you say that?" The outrage in her voice took me aback. "You think you *made* her stop loving you, like you weren't good enough for her to love? I'm not going to lie—I've seen you taunt her even when you didn't have to, and so maybe there was a circle you both fell into and then there was no way out. You haven't called her 'Mama' in years and years; you did that on purpose just to bait her, you know she hated that. And the way you always talk about Japan . . ."

My shoulders tensed like a stitch drawn tight. "What do you mean?"

"Japanese flowers, Japanese food. Trying to learn to write *kanji*. Like you're so desperate to get away from here—from me and Mama—that you'd latch onto anything and ride it as far away as it could take you."

"That's not fair." Except, it was, at least in part. "Or true." That, too. "Those things belong to us. And you're the one who found the patterns for the kimono online, remember? You're the one who bought fabric and snuck her sewing machine to Jovan's studio to sew them for us."

I could hear her swallow. "But I don't call relatives we might have in Japan—if they even exist—*real* family, like you do. As if Mama and I are fake to you."

"That's not how I mean that," I whispered. "I didn't mean to hurt her. Or you. I just meant, maybe there I would be someone. Someone real, not just a poor-man's version of the two of you."

Lina brought her thumb to her mouth and chewed furiously at it. "Please, please never say that to me again. There's no world in which I'm whatever it is you think I am. Prettier, easier to love, somehow *better* than you. I can't stand knowing that you think that. That's—that's such *bullshit*, Riss."

She spat the word out like it hurt, like she'd been holding tacks on her tongue. I knew how much she hated swearing, and somehow that one word in the whole un-Malina-like tirade comforted me more than anything else she'd said. I stayed silent but I tightened my arm around her waist. In turn, she curled her fingers around my wrist, her ragged cuticles scratchy against my skin. Then she snapped my hair band for me once, as if she knew I needed it. A warm breeze stole over both of us through the cracked-open window, bringing with it the smell of night-blooming jasmine and the sea.

"Are you going to say something?" she whispered.

"It's just, I can't feel anything properly. Other than that one feeling. I haven't even cried since we got here."

"That's not all you feel," Lina murmured. "That's just the top." She shifted against me, reaching up to knot my fingers with hers.

"Do you want me to sing it for you? It would be better with the violin, but I can do it if I use all three."

I hesitated. Malina's polyphonic songs could be overwhelming when she didn't hold back, not just echoing emotions but stealing inside you through the cracks—and whatever lurked below my frozen surface, the trapped minnows and monsters underneath, I wasn't sure that I wanted to meet it face-to-face.

But the mother who had nibbled on our cheeks—the mother who'd looked at me like Queen Jevrosima at her beloved son—she deserved my tears.

"Go ahead," I said.

She sang softly, just loud enough for me to hear, the hum of the fundamental joined by one overtone and then the other. At first the song was peaceful, gentle dips and falls like seawater rippling under a night sky scattered with dim stars, but then I caught the refrain, and it was us—two girls adrift on a raft big enough for three, an endless sea lapping against the edges. We were together, but so alone, far from any welcoming shore. And the space between us, mother-shaped, ached with every note that formed its contours.

We'd had a mother, wrapped in barbed wire more often than not, but still alive and ours.

And now we didn't. Whatever was happening to her, she was gone. We had only each other, and it wasn't nearly enough.

I felt my tears before I even knew I was crying, sliding silent but scalding down my cheeks. I wept into Malina's hair until my body quaked, my ribs aching with the sobs I swallowed. I'd thought nothing could be worse than when Mama's eyes chilled, or when she flamed into sudden rage like a phoenix, but I'd been wrong. This was worse, so much worse—especially when I remembered imagining her dead a thousand times over, after she slapped me, ignored me, or gutted me with a single word.

And worse yet when I acknowledged the faintest tinge of relief beneath it all.

"I saw it happen, Lina," I whispered through the tears. "I saw it—I saw her *dying*. I can't . . . it keeps playing in my head, on loop. I can't think about anything else." I could hear her shuddering breath jostle between the notes of the melody. "And sometimes . . . sometimes I *wanted* her to die. Do you think . . . ?"

"No," she said firmly, breaking off the song. "Of course you thought about it, sometimes. So did I. So do kids whose mothers don't ignore them for two weeks because they accidentally put salt instead of sugar in the meringue. It doesn't mean we wished her dead, you know?"

WE BOTH GREW quiet after that. I turned away from Malina, my spine notching into hers like clockwork gears. Drained of everything, I fell asleep in a lurching, heavy drop, as if I'd been heaved into water with stones tied to my feet.

And then the bed was gone and I was cold, colder than I'd ever been inside a dream. The night sky above me was both black and bright, feathered with a vast, milky tapestry of stars and a sickle moon. I stood on a sweeping mountain plateau, circled by peaks looming darker than the night above. Frosted pines surrounded the clearing, and at its very center, a naked woman knelt with her face turned up to the sky.

I followed the spill of moonlight on her dark hair, so long it swept over her shoulders and covered her breasts, its ends brushing the thick, curved muscle of her thighs. I could see the wisps of breath pluming from her flared nostrils; she was so much warmer than the air that the snow had melted beneath her folded legs, all the way down to the brittle, dead grass and earth beneath. Even from where I stood, I thought I could smell her, something sweet and stirring that pierced me to my core.

It was too dark and she was too far for me to make out the features of her face, but I could see the liquid glitter of her eyes. And when she met mine, there was nothing else. Only her and me, two fixed points in a universe that wheeled furiously around us.

I loved this woman, I realized. I *adored* her. I wanted her to hold me, to own me, to chain me to her side with a collar made of silver links. Because nothing more was needed—I would never run from her.

There were things scattered in a circle around her, too, wickedly sharpened stones, little sigils shaped from sprinkled powders, and flowers so perfectly dried they looked like sketches against the snow. They burst into fractals when I looked at them, multiplying into a spiraling infinity around her. Together with the powder sigils, they made a complex design that shifted and blurred every time I looked at it head on—a geometric ring around her like the rapid spread of ice crystals under a microscope.

The powder was made of ground and colored bone, I knew somehow, from the skeletons of things she had killed with her own hands. Little things, rodents and hatchlings and baby snakes; bigger things, foxes and wolves and sinuous ermines; and biggest things, that she'd had to strike with spears and slash with knives, peeling back glistening hanks of muscle to reveal the bleach of bone beneath.

Even the dye was made from murdered life, the shells of glossy insects she'd smashed with her own fists, flower petals bled of color in her grip.

There was also a brilliant little heap right in front of her knees, as if she'd shaped it into a pyramid with her hands, and though I wasn't close enough to tell what it was, I could see it glittering madly beneath the moonlight.

One of the sigils kept catching my eye, because I knew—I felt—this one had been made of something small, something fuzzy-haired and squalling as it swung little fists in search of a missing mother. Because that was what it would have taken, to summon the attention and favor of the old gods who would let her do what must be done. To give body to that which had none.

And yet as soon as I thought it—*she killed a child for this*—the certainty was gone.

She watched me, humming a tune that dipped low before soaring high, the warmth of her rising off her silhouette in an icy halo. This dark flower of a woman, this sacred lady, would never have done a thing like that. I couldn't have loved her if she had, and love for her was the only thing I knew.

Without breaking the lock of our gaze, she reached out and delicately plucked up one of the stone blades, her fingers fine and dark against the snow. Slowly, she drew it along the inside of her arm, and I winced as I saw it bite into skin, the well and sluice of her blood down to her palms. She let it drip over the flowers and patterned powders, then gathered them all up and crushed them between her hands. With splayed fingers, she smeared the paste over her face, and throat, and chest, until her eyes blazed between the whorls and streaks, her hair like water dappled with moonlight.

The song she hummed grew louder, and I loved her so much I wanted to die. If she would let me be her daughter—if she would deign to be my mother—I would fling myself off mountains, let river water fill my lungs until they burst. But only if my death was what she wanted.

Then she rose up in a fluid movement, rocking back onto her heels. The love inside me eddied like whirlpools, tinged with a dash of panic, a hint of terror. She made her way to me with slow, deliberate steps, each fine-boned foot searing an imprint into the snow below her soles. A light, feathery snow began to fall, and it gathered in my lashes even as it barely glanced her skin before melting.

Her fingers were so hot when she trailed them over my face that I would have flinched away from her, if her humming hadn't held me fast.

"*Mara*," she whispered, the sound of it so alien I wondered if it was a word in some other tongue. She bared her teeth in a smile, and they flashed white in the dark.

"*Mara*," she said again, her tongue flicking behind her teeth. She ran her fingers through my hair. The snow had turned to flurries that whipped around us, and still she stroked my hair, from its roots to its ends, until I nearly swooned at her touch. Even in the dream, ribbons were threaded through its length. *"Marzanna. More. Moréna."*

It wasn't a word, I realized. It was *her*. It was her name, and she had many.

"Maržena," she continued through gritted teeth. A flood of pure terror flushed through me, until she gripped my face in one strong, bloodied hand and I went slack, gasping with fear and adoration. I could smell her fully now, the iron reek of blood, the dry salt of bone, and an overwhelming wave of sandalwood. *"Morana, Mora, MARMORA!"*

The last she shrieked into my face, her voice blending with the gale, and I tore myself awake like a bandage off a wound. I was still screaming her names as I sat up in bed, my entire body shuddering. Beside me, Malina sat stone-faced, her jaw clenched so hard I could see the tendons in her throat twitching.

I folded over until my head lay in her lap, pressing my fists against my face.

"Did you see her?" she whispered, in a cold, uncanny dual voice that sounded nothing like her. I'd never heard her just speak in polyphony before. "Did you?"

"Yes." I bit back a whimper. "I saw her."

It felt like a long time until she laid her hand on my head.

NINE

I WOKE AT DAWN, AS IF MY INTERNAL ALARM CLOCK hadn't come dislodged in spite of everything that had happened. It seemed impossible that either of us had managed to get back to sleep after a dream like that—a dream that we'd somehow shared, something we'd never done before—but Malina was still resolutely asleep, curled tightly like a mollusk with a little frown creased into her brow, her lips pursed and rosy as a baby's.

I didn't want to wake her so early, but I needed to be outside. I needed the world firm and real beneath my feet, to breathe warm morning air until I could calibrate to this new normal.

Throwing a heather-gray cashmere wrap over my nightgowned shoulders, I eased the bedroom window open and dropped lightly onto the smooth stones of the courtyard. Čiča Jovan lived in a pied-à-terre in one of the renovated stone buildings near the North-ern River Gate, the Old Town's back entrance. It was right across from our favorite pizzeria, the Bastion, named after the fortifica-tions that led out of the Old Town along the clear, green water of the Škurda. The air was always cooler here, like spray to the face, and it already smelled like baking calzones: the insides a molten mass of cheese, prosciutto, and mushrooms spiced with oregano, and a rich dollop of sour cream on the top.

Whatever eagle eyes the police had posted to watch over our house had apparently called it a night long before dawn. I could see one drooping at his post, snoring in his chair in Jovan's wild little garden. Other than him and the bakers inside the pizzeria, the small square was deserted beneath the blazing pink and orange of a sky shot through with veins of molten gold.

There shouldn't have been anyone around watching me. But there was.

I could feel it, a tingle over the crown of my head that spread down the back of my neck like a flurry of pins and needles. People had stared at me plenty over the years, at me and Malina both, and I was intimately familiar with how the weight of eyes usually felt. But this was different, so intent I almost felt as if I was being touched, caressed by fingernails running lightly through my hair and down my nape.

It felt so weirdly delicious yet uncomfortable that I froze, scanning the square. Nothing stirred against the gray of the stone blocks, other than the whisper of lacy curtains behind open white shutters across the way, and a scattering of wildflowers nodding in

Jovan's garden. They pinwheeled into an unruly whorl as soon as my gaze landed on them, and I looked hastily away.

Then a flicker of movement drew my gaze up to the bastion itself, the rounded stone fortification with its crenelated edges. I'd never seen anyone up there before, but now a woman leaned on the edge right above the river gate, hair even blacker than my own spilling over like an inkfall.

I walked across the small square like a sleepwalker until I stood in front of the gate, my neck craned so I could look up at her with parted lips and squinted eyes. To her right the craggy mountains reared, patches of green against the sheer stone screes, and her silhouetted form was draped in dusky blue and silver, a loose Grecian dress pinned around her neck. From where I stood below her, the angle threw the architecture of her bones into stark relief, and I realized I *knew* her. I knew that powerful jaw, the full mouth and regal flare of the nostrils, the unyielding cheekbone sweep and thick black brows above pale eyes.

Then somehow her perfume reached me, as if it could seek me out despite the direction of the wind. With déjà vu rolling over me like a lurching tide, I didn't just know but I *remembered*.

FOUR YEARS AGO Lina and I had sat in the Arms Square on my threadbare blanket, hawking my glass flowers while Lina sang wanting songs at passing strangers. We'd already had a good day of it—three fractal poppies sold, scarlet with jet-black centers like singularities, and two lady's slipper orchids I'd sweated over for weeks—when they came.

Counting our coins and dinar bills, neither of us noticed until their shadows fell over us, and that sweet scent tightened around us like a grasping hand. It smelled like sandalwood and honey and bergamot, bright honeysuckle above and the tang of blood oranges below. It smelled so good it nearly hurt, and I could feel my lungs expanding painfully with the effort to draw it in, my bronchioles unfurling like cherry-blossom buds.

The black-haired woman had worn a gown then too, so extravagant it should have been silly in the milling crowd of T-shirted tourists, but it wasn't. Its full skirt was lined with stripes of shining peacock feathers alternating with raven black, as if she were heading to a masquerade. Her arms were swathed to the elbow with fingerless gloves, black leather and lace fine and dense as filigree. Deep copper shoulders glowed smooth above a satin hem.

But none of it compared to the sheer force of her face, a kind of bold that seemed almost wild: cheekbones flat and broad as steppes, a wide-bridged nose with a small bump between her eyes, a lush and perfect mouth. And those pale, pale eyes, black-rimmed and water gray. Exactly the color of my mother's, or Malina's, or my own.

And there was that hearthstone smell, like warmth and trust and mother-love. I wanted to be even closer to it, I realized. I wanted the black-haired woman to sit down with us, to somehow pull both me and Malina onto her lap as if we were still little girls who could fit.

"Look at them, Naisha," she whispered to the other in a rough-edged purr layered with more tones at once than I could count. It was a bit how Malina sounded when she sang, but I didn't think she could talk this way, and she wasn't anywhere near so multiple. "Look at how faint and little they are, that all these shamblers barely even see them. They should be so much *lovelier* by now."

"It's not their fault, Sorai," Naisha murmured back. She was lovely too, a blonde carved out of ivory, platinum, and silver. She had the same wolf-gray eyes, but her narrow features were both delicate and sharp, as if a sculptor had whittled her face using only a very pretty knife. She wore a man's white shirt unbuttoned to her breastbone and rolled up to her elbows, and in her worn-down, shapeless jeans she still looked like someone's queen. "She isn't teaching them, like I told you."

There was something familiar about her voice, sweet and stripped of the other's inhuman resonance, but the honeyed prison of perfume wouldn't let me think enough to place it.

"But they do look at us," I said, as if the blonde hadn't even spoken. My voice sounded strange and echoing, as if the three of us were underneath a dome, an upended goldfish bowl. It made the air feel like cotton stuffed in my ears. "They stare at us all the time."

"Of course they do, little one," the brunette—Sorai—said, and the slight smile she gave me warmed me to my core. Looking at her felt like staring at a darkened sun, watching an eclipse until it turned your eyes to cinders. "You were born to draw the gaze, to snare it like a butterfly in a net. But you are not nearly what you should be. Show them, Naisha. Show them what beauty should be like. Show them all they are missing."

Naisha's face stayed impassive, and I would never have noticed the struggle beneath if I hadn't seen Malina's eyes on her and heard my sister's dissonant little trill: *Don't tell me what to do.* It seemed strange, that childish note of defiance. Especially since they both looked around the same age to me, not much older or younger than Mama.

Moving so slowly, Naisha unbuttoned her shirt and let it fall, tossing her head so the gleaming corn-silk rope of her hair slid over one shoulder. Her bare torso shone long and lithe, small teardrop breasts tipped in pink. Every gesture was beyond deliberate, the bending of each wrist and crooking of her fingers like the precise steps of the most minute dance. I noticed she had an odd piercing, a tiny diamond embedded into her left wrist, sparking between the forking green threads of her veins. My heart pounded wildly in my chest; I'd seen women topless on the beach sometimes, but they'd never looked anything like this, a perfection vast and heartbreaking as a sunrise.

Beside me, I heard Malina catch a shuddering breath, but still no one else in the square even looked our way.

Patterns began to flicker across the pristine canvas of Naisha's skin, chasing one another. Tiger stripes of orange and black wound around her waist, then a silver spate of fish scales scattered across her ribs. Long, pale swan feathers fanned out over her chest, then bright-green and glossy black ones swept up her neck. Cheetah spots raced in trails down both her arms, and finally the skin around her eyes turned a stippled, tawny brown and beige, as if she had become part diamondback snake.

As she flicked through the patterns, her eyes and hair changed color to match, flowing from a brilliant, inhuman orange to a flaring peacock green, and even her features seemed to shift, sharpening or flattening out to mimic the animal she was showing for us. Yet it never went all the way; her face stayed beautiful in each incarnation, a gorgeous were-woman hybrid like a creature from one of my storybooks. A shape-shifter prettier than any succubus I'd ever read about.

I realized my jaw was hanging open, and closed it with a click as Naisha dipped to pluck her shirt from the ground, shaking her hair loose as she buttoned it briskly back up. Even that was gracefully done, nimble and quick like fingers flying over piano keys. My mouth had gone dry, and everything inside my head swam giddy. I should have been shocked to see something so dazzlingly strange, but the shock felt very far and faint, eclipsed by envy and wonder.

"Do you see?" Sorai said softly, reaching out to graze the crown of my head with her nails, Malina's with her other hand. A tingling current ran through me, and I nearly arched my back like a cat at her touch. "*This* is how you should be. So beautiful that you can wound with it. Your beauty is a force, you know, a power all its own. It can be both sword and shield for you, and win you anything you want."

"But I—I don't know how," I said hoarsely. Malina made an uncertain *hmm* beside me, as if *she* somehow almost knew what that meant, but I couldn't tear my eyes away from Sorai enough to question her. "Will you show us?" I yearned for them to stay so badly, to remind me how to gleam.

"Oh, you will learn again when you need to," she replied, still stroking my head. "It hasn't died inside you. I see it merely asleep, like a fox kit curled up in her den. And even what is deeply sleeping nearly always wakes again. But remember that it burns inside you, a fox fire in your chest. Even if it might be simpler, never let yourself forget."

"What about me," Malina asked thickly. "Why aren't you telling *me* not to forget?"

Sorai gave a bright, stirring laugh, a cluster of nested bells rung together. "Because you are my cuckoo, are you not, baby songbird? All that false meekness in your mother's nest."

"Are you going to . . ." Naisha hesitated, then cleared her throat. Sorai turned to her with a languid, too-slow swivel of her head, fine crow's-feet crinkling as her eyes narrowed. "Do you wish to take them, then?" she finished.

"No, let her keep them still. She'll serve as she needs to, when it's time. She will, and they will."

She turned back to me, dropping quick yet weightless to her knees, as if she were at once made of feathers and lead. The feathered gown pooled around her, and she tipped my chin up with a warm, curled finger—I could feel the sharp edge of her nail sink almost painfully into my skin—before leaning forward, her hair sliding like a curtain around both our faces. Her eyes were so bright I could barely stand to look at her, and my own slid closed as her lips covered mine in a smooth, chaste kiss, a long exhale of that dizzying perfume. It had deepened and darkened, too, turning closer to the earth; patchouli, frankincense, and even tobacco.

Everything seemed to slide away—the ground beneath me, the

grit of the stone block against my back, the warm brush of Lina's arm by mine—and I funneled into a thick and fragrant black.

AS I BLINKED against the darkened, frayed edge of the memory, I looked up to see the woman on the bastion gather her skirts in one hand and leap nimbly over the other side, beyond the Northern Gate—into the Škurda River. I raced headlong through the gate, but there was nothing, no one, just the lacy green-and-white churn of the water rippling around rocks beneath the bridge.

I stood for a moment with the back of my hand to my forehead, reeling; the way she moved had been so fluid it was nearly inhuman. And now that I remembered her—remembered them both—I couldn't believe that I had ever forgotten. I could recall the rest of that afternoon perfectly, almost too well, as if the excision of that memory had crystallized the remainder of the day. Lina and I had gone on as if nothing had happened, used some of the glasswork money to split a hazelnut and strawberry gelato before we headed to the beach with Luka and Niko. And there'd never been a single mention between us of a woman wrapped in feathers and scent, or another that could draw animal prints using nothing but her own skin.

It was the perfume that had done it: a perfume that made us feel things and then forget them, just like Mama had said our grandmother's gleam had done before she died.

And both of those women had our eyes.

Those women were family, somehow, they had to be. And if they were, then everything Mama had told us—*the three of us, all alone in the world*—was a lie. And from what Sorai had said, the gleam she saw inside us was something not to be tamped down, but to be coaxed into full flame just like I'd always wanted.

But who *were* they to us? Why had Sorai given me back a memory she had stolen from me years ago, just like she had considered stealing both me and Malina from our mother? Why had they even wanted to take us—and why had they left us with Mama anyway when they could have spirited us away so easily, luring us with that perfume like some scented pied piper?

The only thing I could latch onto was that one of these three women, Dunja, Sorai, or Naisha, had hurt our mother, then somehow suspended her just short of death. It was Dunja's name that Mama had spoken last, but then again, that "don't" . . . now I wondered if she was truly our only suspect. Everything felt like twist-tied nonsense, without end and beginning, like the world had spun itself into a Möbius strip. I yearned suddenly for Luka, who'd taught me about Möbius strips and then indulged me endlessly when I caught a fascination with them, wondering how they could be worked into my glass fractals. If he were here, what would he tell me to do? How would he cut to the root of this tangle?

The root. That was it. Mama was the root of this, and even if I couldn't go to her directly, I still had all her things.

TEN

I CROSSED THE BRIDGE OVER THE ŠKURDA, WHICH LED TO
the shop-lined street that backed ours. I was nearly home when it
struck me that I had no actual plan for confronting any potential
murderer lying in wait in our apartment, and that this was a thing
I might want to consider.

Glancing around the riverbank, I armed myself with a rock and
a sturdy branch snapped off from our oleander tree. Tucking the
stick under my arm, I tried the doorknob; it didn't budge under
my hand.

Squatting near the base of the oleander, I dug gingerly around
the roots, wary of beetles and things with stingers, until I found
the spare key nestled there. The apartment felt hushed and stale
as I let myself in, and my stomach contracted at the stubborn,

lingering tang of rakija. Still clutching my stick and rock, and feeling only slightly like an asshole but mostly like a subscriber to the "best have it and not need it" school, I poked through the kitchen, bathroom, tiny living room, and two bedrooms—the pile of Lina's shoes tipped precariously against one wall, like an abstract sculpture of stabby heels and glossy straps, seemed like it had multiplied exponentially, but that was always the case—until I was satisfied that no one was going to dart out at me from under a bed or behind a door.

Since there'd never been much of anything in our living room other than a TV with actual rabbit-ear antennas and more of Jovan's gorgeous driftwood furniture, I started my search in Mama's room. Other than two nights before, I couldn't remember the last time I'd been in there. She'd kept it locked during the day since she'd caught us playing dress-up with her clothes once, years ago—that once had been enough to keep Lina humming her danger song for weeks.

The space between bed and closet was so narrow I had to do a little sideways shuffle as I eased open one wing and then the other. The armoire exhaled lavender, sage, and lemon peel into my face; no mothballs for our mother. Wooden hangers clacked as I plunged my hands into an assembly line's worth of fitted dresses. Mama bought her clothes at the flea market stands and thrift shops just like we did, but she spent hours of her scarce free time painstakingly altering them until they somehow transformed into finery, as if she couldn't bear anything less than perfection against her skin. She took fastidious care of them, and threw them away so rarely that some of these were almost ten years old, ones she'd worn even before I lost her.

And they smelled so strongly of her.

I let the sobs come rolling out, the louder ones I'd held trapped in my rib cage the night before. Curling the fabrics between my fingers, I pressed her dresses against my flushed face. It felt as if I were turning myself inside out and my innards were spikier than expected, spiny like burrs.

Once I'd finally cried myself dry, I slid down to the floor, my back against the bed and my knees drawn up. If I hadn't been at that angle, I might not even have caught a glimpse of the folded chessboard at the bottom of the closet, wedged upright against the back so that most of it stood hidden behind longer dresses.

I dove into the closet face-first and dragged it out. It was a big board, and heavy, the squares black and white and the surrounding wood pale shisham, inlaid with silver diamonds and flower petals. I knew that Mama and Čiča Jovan loved playing chess together, so he must have made this for her; nothing strange about that. But when I gave it a shake no muffled rattle of queens and pawns sounded from the inside. I could hear only a papery slide as I tilted the board back and forth, along with a rumbly little roll. And the padlock that clasped to the hinge holding the two parts of the board together felt unusually sturdy.

Fortunately, I had a rock handy, and a right arm honed by years of stirring, rolling dough, and blowing glass. It had made me the arm-wrestling champion of the sixth grade, and now it let me deal a series of precise blows to the lock without damaging the board.

I had just eased the mangled lock out of the hinge and flipped the top back, revealing a plush, royal-blue lining, when a hand clamped down on my shoulder.

I leaped off the bed, scrambling for my rock.

"Riss! Jesus!" Malina backed away, hands held up. "Don't kill me, please, okay?"

I tossed the rock away and leaned on my thighs, panting. "Why would you sneak up on me like that, for fuck's sake? How did you even know I was here?"

"Well, the window was open, and the calzones baking at the Bastion woke me up." Of course they had. "You weren't there, and after that . . ." She shuddered, and a bright flush blotched down her neck. "That awful dream last night, I thought you'd come back here and look for, I don't know, clues or something. About what's happening to Mama. What's happening to us."

"That dream," I said, sinking back down onto the bed. "What *was* that? I *loved* her, Lina. I was all but looking around for the nearest cliff to jump from, just so I could show her how much I loved her. You know what I'm talking about."

"I know. I don't understand it either, how something could feel that way. Especially for us both. This is just—it's all too much." She took a deep breath and soldiered on. "Did you find something? What's in there?"

She sat beside me as I lifted a plain little apothecary vial from inside the chessboard. The thick brown liquid inside slid viscously back and forth as I tilted it.

"It looks like an absolute, I think?" Lina said. "They're always thicker than the essentials. Are you going to open it?"

"I was thinking we'd sit here and contemplate its visual properties for a while. See what we can see."

She frowned at me reproachfully, wrinkling the creamy expanse between her thick eyebrows. "Mean."

I worked the stopper out carefully, and Lina leaned in until we were almost touching foreheads. Then I brought the vial between our noses and took a wary sniff. The fragrance rushed up bitter, bright, and sweet all at once, vibrantly intense and underpinned by the faint hint of something darker.

Malina whistled softly, then bit her cherry-cleft lower lip. "Orange blossom absolute, wow. That's *wonderful*. I've never smelled one that dramatic. There's amber in there too, I think, and maybe myrrh? And lots of other things I can't recognize, I'm sorry. You know what's weird, though . . . ?"

"What?"

"Mama never used orange blossom absolute, even though it's stronger than neroli. That's the essential-oil version of bitter orange flower. Neroli she loved, but we never had any of the absolute around. I only know what it smells like because Niko bought me the Egyptian kind last year for us to play with."

"Why would she keep this locked up in here?" I wondered, working the stopper back in place. "It's gorgeous, but it's only perfume."

"Is there anything else in there?"

There was, a curling photograph tucked into the velvet-lined rim. I gently slid it loose. The photo was of a smiling girl who looked a little like our mother, but a much softer rendition, more along Malina's lines. She was maybe eighteen or nineteen, and her hair blazed a fiery copper, threaded through with ribbons just like ours. Her gray eyes were even bigger and clearer than our mother's as she smiled widely into the lens, lush wooded mountains and a pine-studded valley visible behind her. She wore an ivory dress, cap-sleeved with a black Peter Pan collar and a sheer lacy panel down the middle, exposing her fine clavicles and even the inner curves of her full breasts. It was both demure and aggressively sexy, and it seemed like a strange choice for a mountaintop in the middle of the day.

I turned the photo over; it simply said *Anais* in our mother's swooping, calligraphic handwriting.

"Anais," Malina breathed. "Ana."

I ran my fingers over the glossy contours of the woman's face. I'd never seen a photo of Mama's sister before. I hadn't even known any existed; Mama had always said she'd taken nothing with her when she ran, but I wondered now how we'd never thought to question that. How would she even have made it from a remote mountain village to Cattaro, without money or a car or any belongings? What would have happened to our grandfather, if he'd really killed our aunt and grandmother—and not just killed them, but flung them off a mountain?

We'd swallowed the story at the time, like a bitter tincture of truth, but now it seemed glaringly false. Gory as a Grimm fairy tale. A story meant to scare a child, to urge us never to dig deeper.

"But this doesn't make any sense," Malina murmured, echoing

my thoughts. "I thought Mama had to leave everything behind."

"Exactly. And it's not just that. I saw someone today, and remembered something that happened to us once. Do you remember two women coming to see us, about four years ago? A brunette and a blonde, Sorai and Naisha?"

She shook her head and frowned as I described the memory to her, chewing on her index finger. "I don't know, Riss . . . I want to say I almost remember, but I think it's just because you're telling it so well. Animal prints on a naked chick's skin, in the middle of Arms Square? I think I'd remember that. But I don't, I'm sorry."

Huffing with frustration, I set the chessboard aside. "Why don't you see if you can find anything else? Weird things like this, or something missing, like my sculpture from the café? I'll finish up in here."

Once I was done rummaging through Mama's closet, I riffled through her drawers too, and dipped my fingers beneath her mattress and under her pillows. But there was nothing.

It seemed wrong, somehow, to leave the room in such chaos, so I rehung the clothes and made her bed, then stacked up the velveteen pillows lining her window nook. Beside it lay the stained and crumpled dove-gray sheath she'd worn, and I picked that up too. A corner of it sagged in my grip. Frowning, I worked my hand into the hidden pockets. The left was empty, but the right held something cold and long, its end ridged beneath my fingertips.

A key, attached to a little magnetic fob.

I carefully worked it free as it snagged on the pocket's silken inner lining. It was heavy and ornate, the bow molded into the lion's head and fleur-de-lis I'd seen many times—the sigil of the Hotel Cattaro in the Arms Square of Old Town.

"Lina," I called out, twirling the blade of the key between my fingers, "I think I found something."

"Me too," she called back. "My violin, Riss. It's gone."

ELEVEN

"BUT WHY WOULD ANYONE EVEN WANT IT?" MALINA ASKED as she trotted next to me across the Škurda bridge. There'd been nothing else out of place at home, no new things or ones missing that should have been there. We'd called the detective to let him know about the stolen violin, but everything had careened so far from the mundane that I couldn't imagine what the police could possibly do for us now. What else would I have told him, anyway? *Look out for tiger-striped witches, Detective? Beware of perfumes that smell like commands?*

Any answers we wanted to find, we'd have to hunt down ourselves.

"It was just a Stagg, nothing special," she continued. "Not like anyone was going to mistake it for a vintage Stainer or Guarnerius or anything."

"Why would anyone want to take my glasswork from the café, either? Or, more to the point, karate-chop Mama to the heart?" Malina sucked in a breath, and I cursed myself silently. Just because being a callous shithead made it somehow less horrible to me, something I could begin to handle, didn't mean this was true for her. "I'm sorry, bunny. I didn't mean that. Let's just see what we find at the hotel."

The Hotel Cattaro had once been the Rector's Palace, built in the seventeenth century to shore up the western side of the Arms Square, back when the square had actually been used to make and store munitions for the city's defense. A gleaming suit of armor glowered in one corner of the reception area, plush wingback chairs were scattered around the lobby, and the polished wood of the reception desk stood wide and round like a ship's hull. Wearing gladiator sandals twined up to my knees and missing half of their studded spikes, and the black tunic with cutout shoulders I'd changed into back at home, I felt painfully out of place in this baroque haven of cream and gold.

The clerk behind the reception greeted us with an achingly sympathetic expression on his ruddy face, nodding to us each in turn as he smoothed back his sparse, combed-over dark hair. "Please accept my condolences. I was desperately sorry to hear about your mother. Wonderful woman, and that wonderful café—it's a terrible loss to us all. And most of all to you, of course."

So that was what the police were telling everyone else. That she was already dead.

If that was the tale they were spreading, of course everyone had already heard by now. The clerk's earnestness and his conviction that Mama was dead—that she was gone forever—made the truth all that much more terrible to bear. I bit the inside of my cheek hard, trying to gather myself. "Thank you. That's good of you. But there's something—we're hoping you could help us."

He spread his sunspotted hands over the reception desk's smooth surface. "Of course. Anything. What can I do for you?"

I steeled myself. "Do you know how our mother died?"

That took him aback. "I'd heard it was an accident, a terrible . . ." He trailed off, brow furrowed.

So the police were keeping the details contained. That was good; I needed the weight of shock on my side. "She was murdered. Someone *killed* her, sir. And the day before it happened, she had this in her pocket."

I held the key out to him, waiting until he took it from my palm with his dry, tobacco-stained fingers. The gesture sparked a glint of memory—the glimmering little thing that Dunja had held out to my mother before they parted—but I had to be sure. "Did you see her here? Do you know who she came to meet?"

The clerk had paled beneath his leathery tan. "Yes, Jasmina was here," he said finally. "I was here for that shift, and I saw her come in. She greeted me, but that was all. I let her pass. I should have stopped her—our procedure is to have all visitors check in, so we can call ahead—but I didn't. I thought . . ."

Malina came to the conclusion faster than I did. "That she was visiting someone she wanted to keep discreet."

Of course. A single mother, with no male companions anyone

ever knew of. A man of this generation would have assumed Mama was a lonely woman yearning for company, but intent on guarding her reputation. He'd have considered it a kindness, even chivalry, letting her preserve the privacy of the visit.

"Something like that, yes." His hands curled into fists on the counter, and I felt a stab of pity for him. This wasn't his fault, but now there'd always be the spidery niggle, the doubt that he could have done something differently. "I never thought that this might have anything to do with—with the death. If it does, I need to—"

"Yes." I cut him off. "The police should know, and they should hear it from you as soon as possible. But please, since we're here, could you tell us first? Is that what happened? Was she meeting a man here?" I let my voice tremble. "Probably it's nothing. But it would help so much to know."

He sucked in his lips, working them through his teeth. I could almost hear his thoughts; he'd already breached the protocol once, and look what had happened. Now there were tragic orphans, wanting things from him.

Sighing, he squinted at the serial number on the key fob, then pecked it into his computer system. "We have only seventeen rooms, and two apartment suites. This key is for one of those—suite eighteen."

Lina and I both leaned eagerly into the counter.

"No, it wasn't a man," he said finally, squinting at the screen. "A woman, I remember her. Sounded almost like one of us, but had a Russian name. Nina Ananiashvili. We get lots of Russians through here, but that's an unusual name even for them. I mentioned it to my wife, who nearly went crazy. Said this Nina was Georgian, once the prima ballerina of the Bolshoi Ballet, that she was in America now. But I told her it couldn't possibly be the same woman."

I felt light-headed from holding my breath. "Why not?"

"Because Nina Ananiashvili can't be more than forty or so, according to my wife. And the woman who stayed with us had completely white hair."

"And is she . . ." I had to swallow past the lump of risen dough in my throat. "Is she still here?"

"No, miss. She left yesterday, early in the morning."

"How early?"

He squinted at the log. "Around five thirty, it looks like."

Early enough that she could have been at the café that morning, in time to hurt Mama right before I got there.

I closed my eyes. *Please, please, please.* "And do you have any idea where she might have been going?"

"Well, she paid in cash, and there was no . . ." His eyes cleared. "Actually, yes, there *was* something. We have a shuttle that takes our guests to Perast every day, for the restaurants and the museum, and to see Our Lady of the Rocks, of course. I'm not sure if she took it or not, but she asked about it when she came looking for a room. Does that help at all?"

I NEARLY JOGGED to Luka's café, Lina by my side, my insides alive with adrenaline. Even if it hadn't been Dunja, maybe she knew who had done it—or even how Mama had been left stranded, like a traveler abandoned on the Styx's banks without the ferry fare. And whatever Dunja had told her had made her so afraid she'd wanted to be both drunk and numb, and even close to us. If there was the slightest chance that I might find her in Perast, that was where I had to go.

When I'd voiced all this to her, Malina had drawn me up short. "Why do you keep saying *I* like some lone-wolf vigilante, Riss?" she'd demanded.

"I thought it would be better if—"

"I know I'm not made of granite all the way through, like you, okay? But she's my mother, too. And if that woman really is at Our Lady of the Rocks, then we have to go. What do you think we should do about getting there?" We'd never been able to afford a car, or felt the lack of one. "Take the bus?"

I squared my shoulders. "Luka's going to lend us his car."

"What are you going to tell him?"

"Everything. And I'm going to need you."

The Roma Prince was tucked into one of the narrower alleyways in the Old Town's winding maze, gaslight lanterns swinging on either side of its ornate, bronze-clasped wooden door. Niko and Luka's mother, Koštana, had named it after her nickname for Luka—it was also very much in keeping with her tongue-in-cheek defiance toward those who still hadn't fully accepted a Romany woman in their midst, even one married to a Cattaro local whose family traced back generations. She'd decorated the café with Niko's help, and it looked like a sultan's harem flavored archly with Niko's own taste—clusters of embellished, black-and-silver darabukka goblet drums in place of tables, and luxuriant cushions instead of chairs, with gold-embroidered brocade curtains separating the little enclaves. The red walls were hung with strings of old threaded coins, frail bouquets of dried herbs, and Romany instruments in various stages of disassembly—an artfully broken cimbalom splayed out like some abstract sculpture, three pieces of a snapped pan flute, staved-in mandolins and tarnished tambourines everywhere.

Koštana had collected all of these. She apparently liked her pretty things on the broken side. Sometimes I'd wondered if that was why she'd loved having me and Lina underfoot so much over the years.

Some of the nargilehs squatting in corners as decoration, pipes coiled around them, were my own; I'd made their blown-glass bases using the flowers Luka gave me for inspiration, sometimes even capturing the original petals within the fractal folds. Years of scented tobacco haunted the air, and I could smell the ripe, wet cloy of fresh wads too.

It was too early yet for the throng of tourists and local teens who'd descend on the store later. Luka sat alone, reading, perched on the stool behind the counter with his back against the mirrored shelves of liquor and his feet propped on the bar. His eyes snapped up to mine as I stepped in, and a thrill flicked through me. He'd been gone for long enough that even after our reunion two days ago, he seemed more like a striking stranger with amber-bright hazel eyes than my best friend since I was nine. Beside me, I could feel Malina casting the room for Niko, but I didn't see her anywhere.

"Hi," I said tentatively as he eased out from behind the counter in his lithe, narrow-hipped way. "I don't know if you've—"

I abruptly found myself tucked beneath his chin, my nose nestled into the soapy hollow of his throat. It wasn't one of his bone-clenching hugs, either; he held me more than hugged me, letting me decide how close I wanted to be. The tenderness demolished me in a second, and I let out a strangled sob against him, my fingers curling into the blue linen of his shirt.

"I'm sorry," he whispered against the top of my head, rocking me a little. "Jesus, Missy, I'm so sorry. I can't believe it. Niko and I tried to come and see you yesterday, but the police wouldn't let anyone talk to you."

"They had to keep things quiet," I mumbled tearfully against his shirt. "It's bad, what happened. Worse than bad."

"That was the impression I got." His voice tightened. "Do they know what happened to Jasmina? Who killed her?"

So they'd heard she was dead, too. I shook my head beneath his chin, then pulled back, wiping haphazardly at my face with both hands. He let me go and held his arms out for Lina, murmuring, "Linka, heart, come here, accept my condolences," and she slipped into his arms in her graceful way, resting her cheek against his chest as he kissed the top of her head. I frowned at them, uneasy without any good reason. They'd never really been much for touching each other, easy as the four of us all were together—Niko was the cuddler, forever hugging all of us and dealing out kisses without provocation—but that hug had seemed so effortless. Like something they'd done many times before.

He caught my eyes above her head, brows lifted in question.

"She's not dead, Luka. Someone hurt her, enough that she should be dead, but isn't. They have no idea who did it. And they don't understand why she's even still alive, if you can call it that."

He hissed in a breath, then stepped away from Lina to lean back against the counter, arms crossed and eyes heavy-lidded. "Explain."

He listened as I frantically described Dunja, Mama's drunken night—Niko had already filled him in on that—what I'd seen at the café in the morning, and the moaning ruin of our mother in the hospital. His narrowed gaze stayed focused somewhere over my shoulder as I talked. Luka always did that, the sideways, thousand-yard stare when he was concentrating deeply, as if gesturing and facial expressions distracted him from absorbing the useful core of information he needed.

"So Jasmina should be dead," he murmured. "No vital signs, no functioning heart or lungs. But she has brain activity. She's alive, and not even just technically." He finally met my eyes, and I nearly buckled beneath their intensity, dropping my own in reflex. "Iris. How would that be possible?"

"I don't know," I nearly whispered, clasping my hands in front of me. I hated how easily he'd always done this to me in all the years we'd been friends. Lowering my volume, making me calm even when I didn't want to be. "But it is. Lina and I think there's some sort of . . . magic happening."

"Magic," he repeated quietly. "You think that's what's keeping Jasmina from dying. Or keeping her alive when she should be dead, rather."

"Yes," I said, bristling. "Like what Lina and I have."

"Magic, like what you and Lina have."

I flung up my hands. "What are you, a mountain valley now? Are you going to just echo everything back at me? *Yes*, magic. We've always called it a gleam. Mama has—had, I don't know—something like it, too."

"All right." He tilted his head. "Well, then. Show me yours."

I gritted my teeth. "The thing is, I can't. I used to be able to, but years ago Mama stopped teaching us, and—you know what, fine. I *knew* you'd be this way. Well, see about this, then." I turned to Lina, who was watching us nervously, eyes flicking back and forth between us like a fencing-match spectator. "Sing something for him. Whatever he's feeling. All the way through."

She cleared her throat, shifting from foot to foot and winding her hair around her wrist as Luka's implacable gaze settled on her like an alighting hawk. For all that he was so restrained, Luka could be unnerving as hell, his attention like a wide-winged shadow circling a grassy field.

With an encouraging nod from me, she sang a low, clear note, the fundamental. Then she layered it with overtones, first one and then the second, an unsettling melody of warm empathy twining around stark skepticism, bolstered by a harmony so simple, elegant, and soul-stirring it sounded like the beginning of a Russian balalaika love song.

I could see Luka's face wavering, and Lina's song fleshed out even further, taking on the dissonance of his shock. He staggered back, bracing himself against the bar behind him, his face paling and knuckles turning white where he gripped its lip. Abruptly I became aware of a percussive beat accompanying her song, and I looked over to one of the nooks; Niko had stolen in silently at some point, and now she held one of the darabukka drums tucked beneath her arm, her palm striking the center of the drum's head and then its edge. She nodded at me once, her eyes dark and intent with Lina's song.

She knew. There was no shock written on her anywhere, not even a footnote of surprise.

Lina had told her. I'd kept our secret all these years, locked inside me like a treasure trapped within a puzzle box, and Lina had *told* her.

As my fury rose like a juggernaut and my sister felt it, Lina's song shifted, churning into a tempest driven by the wild beat of Niko's answering drum. The surge of it was so powerful that my head fell back, and my gaze landed on the café's mad quilt of a ceiling—a series of overlapping Turkish carpets that Koštana had thought would be more fun there than on the floor.

The repeating designs of the rugs leaped out at me all at once, blocky, angular fauna and flora: a gridded fractal like the Minotaur's maze, cream and crimson, scarlet and royal blue, reaching down toward me as if to swallow me up. I wanted to tamp it down, but then also I didn't; it had been so many years since anything other than a flower bloomed for me, and this was *glorious*, so lush and complex—like the universe was giving me a Technicolor schematic of what these designs had looked like before they'd been born into physical being. My heart hammering against my ribs, I pulled even harder, made them multiply over and over as they echoed each other.

Abruptly, all that color began fading at the edges into black, and my insides boiled with nausea. I could hear myself make a miserable noise, a gag like a retching cat, along with the incongruously cheery tinkle of the bells strung above the café door behind me.

I staggered backward, sinking onto my knees on the scuffed parquet. My stomach heaved even as my head floated somewhere above me like a balloon with a snipped string. There was a warm, spicy smell—whiskey and chocolate, and just a hint of smoke—and a broad hand cupped the back of my head before it could strike the floor.

TWELVE

A FACE HOVERED ABOVE MINE, BLURRY AND OVERBRIGHT, as if I'd stared too long into sunlit water. I blinked a few times, waiting for it to resolve itself: a man, maybe twenty years old, with broad and bony Nordic features like a Viking's, white-blond hair swept back, and gas-flame-blue eyes lined with smudged black. His nose was long and ridged, and his mouth wide and soft, the lower lip much fuller than the top. Following the lines of his lips, I licked my own in reflex. His cleft chin was stubbled with blond, and through my haze he looked somehow foggily familiar.

Blinking, I reached up at him, trying to touch his face like a groping child.

"So handsy," he chided playfully, catching my hand. His long, blunt fingers wrapped around mine; they were very warm, with wide rings on almost every finger, the metal much colder than his skin. He flipped my hand over and brought it to his lips, brushing them over my knuckles. I felt the heat of the breath, and the shocking sear of something even warmer. From my very horizontal vantage point against his thigh, my belly bottomed out in the sweetest way. "Just like I remember. I told you next we met, I'd greet you properly, didn't I? Though you do seem very inclined to pass out on me. Wonder how I should take that."

"And where are you from, exactly, that a 'proper' greeting involves a girl lain out on her back?" Luka snapped from somewhere above us.

I focused on him, squinting, and Malina's and Niko's worried faces coalesced next to his. I abruptly remembered that there were other people here, and that I should start making an effort to move.

"Easy, now," the blond said to Luka. He had the mellowest voice, comfortable and somehow careless, on the brink of laughter. The heedlessness of it was the sexiest thing I'd ever heard. "I'm not the one who put her there, am I? I can't be blamed for catching a pretty apple already falling."

"*She* is not a *fruit*," Luka said, sounding so affronted it actually made me laugh out loud. The boy grinned down at me widely, his teeth very white and not quite straight.

"It's true, I'm not," I agreed, still giggling ridiculously. "I am, in fact, a female human. You—what is your name, anyway? Will you help me up?"

"It's Fjolar, swoony lady. And of course." He had a strange accent, clipped, upturned syllables, and an even stranger way of choosing words—like nothing I'd heard in Cattaro. Before I knew it, he'd wrapped his fingers around my upper arms and drawn me up easily against his broad chest, as if he were adjusting a piece of clothing rather than hauling up a person.

The inside of my head lurched back and forth as soon as I was upright. Everything sparkled for a moment—*how pretty, day-time shooting stars indoors!*—before I drew another breath of that tobacco, chocolate, and whiskey scent, and both my mind and stomach calmed. He was warm and very solid against my back, and I took a few more sips of air through parted lips, letting the smell rise up the back of my throat.

"Smell something you like, flower girl?" he murmured into my ear, too low for the others to hear.

I sat up away from him reluctantly, my cheeks flaming. "Why would you call me that? Only my . . ." *Only Mama ever called me that.*

"It is Iris, isn't it?" he said, leaning back on his haunches and running a hand over his hair. "That's what you told me at that party. That, and a few . . . other things."

I closed my eyes, mortified. If he was having this effect on me now, while I was still too woozy to stand, I could only imagine the things I'd wanted to say to him while my blood ran hot.

Luka offered me both hands, glowering so fiercely I nearly burst into fresh laughter despite the shame. I took them and he pulled me carefully to my feet, anchoring me with a warm, firm grip on my shoulders.

"You all right, Missy?" he said, peering into my face. "You gave us all a solid scare. I believe you about the—I believe it. I believe you and Malina both. No need to do that again, understood? The ceiling, or the falling."

"Yes, sir, got it, sir," I said, still stifling laughter. What was the matter with me, this ecstatic rush of hilarity? Malina was the giggler, out of the two of us. "No more falling down, and definitely no—wait. You *saw* the ceiling?"

"Hell yes, I saw it," he said grimly. "I don't think *he* did, though. He came in at the very end, once you'd already let go, and he was more focused on you than anything."

Still leaning on Luka, I turned to look at Fjolar again. He'd gotten up too, and he gave me a quirked smile as he dusted off the knees of his black trousers, as if to say, *look what you did, made me all dirty.* He wasn't nearly so tall as Luka, but he still stood a good bit taller than me, with a broad-shouldered, muscled frame, and veins prominent on the backs of his large, loose hands.

Now that I could actually see all of him, the modern Viking impression was even stronger. His pale hair would've brushed past shoulder-length had it not been scraped back into a careless bun, the undersides shaved. I usually hated that look, but all I could think of was how those shorn, soft sides would feel like felt against my palms. He had gauged metal earrings in each ear, spiraling like ibex horns, and a chunky silver bracelet around one thick wrist—a roped, open design with arrowheads on both ends. His silvery gray V-neck dipped over a smooth chest, the sleeves rolled up to his elbows.

And his forearms . . .

I nearly swayed, gaping at the designs inked into his skin. They were flowers of all kinds, but only in black and washes of gray, almost mathematical in their grid-like precision—as if someone had drawn up architectural plans of the way I saw flowers blooming with the gleam.

The gleam that had reared up in me so strongly just now, broken through like a swollen river tearing down a dam. Had it been him, somehow? But he hadn't even been in the café with us when it happened.

He tipped his head to the side, amused, raising his forearms for my inspection. "Like them? I did them myself. I told you that too, if you remember."

"I don't remember, actually," I said, my head clearing a little now that I wasn't near him any longer. "I only barely remember you at all. Why are you even here? How did you find me?"

"I've been looking for you since the party, to see if you still wanted to settle a bet you lost to me. Though I imagine you won't remember that, either. You mentioned this place a few times when we talked; it sounded like a favorite. Thought I might find you here."

"This isn't a good time," I said, after a moment.

He raised a pale eyebrow, tilting his head, and my insides heated again. "Is that so? And why not?"

"Because their mother's dead," Luka said when I hesitated, his jaw clenching when I turned to glare at him for the bluntness.

Fjolar's face sobered, and he looked to me. "I'm sorry to hear it." I nodded slowly. Better that he thought what everyone else did.

"My condolences to you." His bright eyes moved to Lina. "And to you. Malina, if I have it right. I'm sorry for your loss."

"Not all that much," Malina said quietly, but with such distaste I looked sharply at her. Her upturned nose was wrinkled, and her lips were pulled delicately away from her teeth, as if she smelled something only just gone putrid. "I wouldn't say you're that sorry about it at all."

"That isn't true," he said, sounding genuinely somber for the first time. "And I'm sorry to have barged in on all of you like this, when you were clearly . . . in the middle of something."

"We were," Niko said pointedly. "Want to see if Iris feels like settling her bets some other time, such as later? Or not now?"

That lazy half smile slid back into place at the unspoken "or never," eyes sparking like a flicked lighter flame. That sooty eyeliner against the impossible blue of his irises and his blond lashes was such an unsettling combination, but instead of dissuading my gaze it just made me want to stare openly at him. "Understood. If you're up to finding me later, Iris, when you're feeling more"—his eyes slid over Luka, Malina, and Niko, then back to me—"unchaperoned, I'd be very happy to hear from you."

"But"—I licked my lips again—"how would I do that? I don't have your number."

He was already halfway out the door, but he paused to smile over his shoulder. "Oh, you do. Just check, whenever you have the time. I won't have gone anywhere."

THIRTEEN

"I'M GOING!"

"You absolutely are not."

Lina and I watched in bemused fascination as Luka and Niko faced each other down across the bar top like opposing generals. They'd launched into it as soon as Fjolar had left, after I'd had the chance to sum up what Lina and I had learned at the hotel. Hazel eyes glaring into brown, her profile like a cameo version of his with their stubborn chins, fine lips, and classical noses, they reminded me of that optical illusion, the vase that melted into two faces when you looked at it differently.

"Yes I *am*, you miserable wildebeest!" Niko gave Luka a robust shove against his chest, growling in frustration when he barely budged a half step. "Ugh, why are you so *big*, God."

He growled back at her, about ten octaves lower. "Do you understand that this is dangerous, Nikoleta? We have no idea what's happening here, or what we're going to find in Perast. The police are supposed to be doing the investigating, and if *this* one didn't make mazes come alive out of ceilings, and *that* one didn't sound like a Guillermo del Toro angel, I wouldn't be letting any of this happen. But no police is going to do anything good with this, especially not ours, who handle nothing more dangerous than Mihajlo the Widower bellowing at lampposts and palm trees on the weekends. And if I don't take them myself, *these* two will go off to Perast alone, and I. Cannot. Have that."

These two? Malina mouthed at me. I looked away from her. I hadn't forgotten how furious I was with her, even if now wasn't the time to air that out.

"What even happened to you, Riss?" she said cautiously. "That *ceiling*. You haven't done something like that in so long. I didn't think you . . ."

"No," I agreed coolly. "I didn't think I could either, and I didn't mean to do it. It happened on its own, and it was so strong. What about you? Why were you looking at him that way? That boy, Fjolar, I mean. I don't think I've ever seen you talk to anyone like that."

Her nose wrinkled again, as if she couldn't help it. "He just sounded so . . . one-note? He really didn't mean it, that he was sorry about Mama. Or maybe he did, a little, but there wasn't much room for that. I've never heard anyone sound so single-minded before."

"And what was it? The one note?"

She shuddered, shoulders twitching. "I don't want to think about it."

"Well, do it anyway. Sing it, I don't care. If it bothered you so much, I need to know."

She made a disgruntled sound, then hummed a perfunctory snatch of song, but it was enough. I caught the sense of voracious hunger-lust, conjuring images of me with tousled hair and dewy lips, straddling Fjolar with his arms flung over his head in abandon, his eyes latched to mine.

I let out my breath in a long rush, rubbing at my arms.

"Yes," Lina said emphatically. "It was just like that. Pure wanting. Hungry. Like he really meant it when he called you a fruit, something to eat. It was disgusting."

I didn't think it was at all. It should have bothered me, coming from a stranger, but instead the idea of it made my insides feel like they'd been melted into molasses and twirled around a spoon. I dipped into my tunic pocket for my phone when Lina looked away, and found an entry for *Fjolar Winnnerr of bet: owe two warm sticky kiss to!!*

I hastily tucked my phone away.

"You're not Tata, *Luka*," Niko was saying as I forced my attention back to them, my cheeks burning. "You don't get to 'let' anything happen. No one made you Grand Deciding Vizier of Significant Decision Things just because Mama died. I'm saying that I'm going, so I'm going. You literally cannot stop me unless you punch me in the face hard enough to knock me out, and you always say—super annoyingly, I might add—that that causes permanent brain damage when it happens in movies. Are you prepared to brain damage me, brother? Are you, truly? Go on, peer deep into that patriarchal soul."

Luka put a hand over his face.

"Why, Heavenly Father?" he moaned into his own palm. "Why saddle me with this brat, when everything was so fine without her for three glorious years? Why give her the will of a thousand mules in this incredibly tiny gnat body?"

"Oh, stop it, beast, you're not even religious," Niko said, bouncing up and down on her toes as she smelled victory, the bell around her ankle tinkling merrily. "Besides, brats are your favorite. Look how you like Iris."

"Hey!" I protested. "My brattiness, which is not even a thing, is beside the point here. If we don't go now, we'll miss the last ferry from Perast to Our Lady today; there won't be any after five. We don't have *time* for this."

"Luka," Niko began again, taking a softer tack this time. "I know how you feel. Probably better than anyone. And that's why I have to come. I can't not be there. You understand me, right?"

They stared at each other for a long moment, and Luka finally slapped his palm on the counter in defeat. "*Fine,*" he said through clenched teeth. "Fine, Nikoleta. But only because—"

"Yes, yes, *thank you,*" she broke in, grabbing his hand and giving it a sound kiss. I watched the two of them uncertainly, not sure what had shifted the tide, but I put the thought aside as anticipation surged through me. We were going. We were doing *something.*

HALF AN HOUR later, all four of us had somehow jammed our-selves into Luka's ancient cherry-red Mazda. As we set off north along the Adriatic Highway I still felt a little giddy, a helium sort of high that buoyed me up even though I knew it would leave me dizzy and deflated once it faded. Luka glanced at me a few times, as if he wanted to say something, but each time he bit back whatever it was.

Outside, the narrow highway wound along the contours of the bay, overhung with the cliffs above us. The surface of the water had swallowed both the mountains and sky, reflecting slick, blurred replicas of blinding blue, gray stone, and even the whites of the clouds that had settled midway down the cliffs like curls of exhaled breath. Beside us, neat ranks and files of buoys bobbed in the water, hosting acres of mussel plantations.

Barely twenty minutes later, the highway dipped west and the first stone houses of Perast came into view. The little fishermen's town nestled at the gently sloping base of Mount Saint Elias, shel-tered from the northern winds during winter, and angled toward the cool breezes that funneled through the Verige Strait in high summer.

"Look," Luka said, and I followed his gaze. Across from Per-ast, stranded in the middle of the bay and dwarfed by the granite loom of the mountains all around, two islets stood guard like tiny, twinned versions of lost Avalon. "You can see them from here. Saint George, and Our Lady of the Rocks."

Malina stirred in the backseat, propping herself up in the space between us. "Saint George is abandoned, right? Just the old Benedictine abbey."

Luka shook his head. "The abbey's from the twelfth century, but the Saint George church is from the seventeenth. There's a cemetery there, too, for old nobles from Perast."

"How do you know?"

"Mama wanted to be buried there," he said simply. "When nothing was working anymore, she wanted us to take her on a tour of the monasteries and churches, the nicest ones. Remember, Niko? We thought it was a last-resort thing, hedging her bets with all the saints. But really, she just thought they were beautiful. She wanted to say good-bye, and find the right one."

I snuck a look at Luka, my throat clenching. I hadn't known that about his mother. Koštana had died three years ago from leukemia, and Luka had been wrecked for years after. It was part of the reason I'd never fully believed he'd go to college in Belgrade until he was gone; I couldn't imagine him leaving his father and Niko after she died. But he had. Life went on.

"I'm sorry," I said softly, catching Niko's glistening dark eyes in the rearview mirror. "I didn't know."

She pressed her lips into a wavering half smile. "It's okay. They don't bury anyone out there anymore, anyway. She's back in Cattaro. But she'd have liked that we stopped by here, don't you think, Luka? And that it made us think of her."

I glanced back out at the islet, the ancient, blocky silhouettes of the church and the abandoned abbey, overgrown with dense vegetation and slender cypress trees. There was a deep and sacred sort of beauty to it, as if it stood still even as the currents of time parted and flowed neatly around it, leaving it untouched. It looked like the kind of place that could keep a soul safe.

"Why aren't there any trees on Our Lady of the Rocks?" I asked, tracing the outlines of the other islet on the window. The church of the Blessed Mary was stone, too, but more elaborate, with a domed apse, a round bell tower, and what looked like a guardian's house attached. The rest of the isle was flat and bare, empty of anything green.

"Because it's man-made, not like Saint George." He cast me a skeptical look. "Have you really never heard any of this?"

I shrugged. "Mama was never much for churches."

He craned his neck as he eased us into a parking spot, next to a restaurant tucked behind a grapevine trellis. "I'll tell you all about it on the ferry. It's an unusual story, not the kind of thing you forget."

There were two ferries tagging each other back and forth to the island, and we caught one, ducking our heads beneath the canopy that protected the simple boat on rainy days.

Once settled on the wooden bench that ran down the center, slick with waterproof white paint, Luka continued. "Our Lady isn't just a Roman Catholic church—it's a sailors' votive shrine. They say that in 1452, the Mortesić brothers, who were recovering from some seafarers' disease—scurvy, probably— found an icon on a rock in the middle of the bay, a painting of the Madonna and the baby Jesus. Right afterward they made a miraculous recovery. Due to the painting, of course, or possibly the sudden availability of oranges and sauerkraut."

I nudged him with an elbow to the ribs. "Spoken like a true believer, Damjanac."

"Just laying out the facts. Anyway, the townspeople took this as a sign that this spot was marked as holy, and began sinking boats heaped with stones around that original rock. They layered a foundation so that the main altar of the shrine would perch on the reef where the painting was found."

The hull scraped along the islet's wooden dock, and Luka swung off first once the captain had secured the ropes. Malina and then Niko caught his outstretched hand and hopped off the makeshift steps that had been propped along the boat's side, heading toward the bronze door of the church's main portal. I laid my hand on Luka's palm and lingered on the boat for a moment longer, feeling the lurching bob beneath my feet. The roots of my hair prickled oddly, and I felt suddenly hesitant to step onto the dock.

Luke gave me a little tug and I hopped off, trailing after him reluctantly. *"Hail the Queen / Of the Boka sea."* He read the inscription off the bronze door as we walked across the threshold. *"You are the red dawn / The shield of our faith."*

"What is that?" I whispered to him. There was none of that cold density in here that some churches exerted, a silent demand for continued silence. But somehow even this cool, sweeter hush felt cloying to me, itchy on my skin.

"A hymn for Our Lady, looks like."

He wandered off toward the altar, but I stayed in the nave, turning in a little circle over the blue and gray diamond-tiled floor.

The ceiling was painted elaborately with celestial motifs, each scene cordoned off by braided gilt. The walls were lavished with framed paintings, the bottom row above the choir benches featuring images I recognized from the Old Testament, of both male and female prophets. The topmost row held four massive paintings, two on each side of the nave, a gleaming silver frieze in between them.

The entire inside of the church was rife with repeating patterns, and again I could feel the beginnings of the gleam swelling in my sight. I wanted to wallow in it, to be delighted in this sudden resurgence—I'd missed it so badly, for so many years—but this felt almost hostile in a way I didn't remember from before. As if it wanted to multiply this church's insides into endless fractals and then shatter them, like a mallet brought down on a block of ice.

"Missy?" Luka said, hand on the small of my back. "You okay?"

I took a deep breath. "I'm fine. I just need a minute."

Trying to narrow my focus, I drew closer to one of the silver plates, an exquisite rendering of a storm-wracked ship with one splintered mast, a cloud-borne Madonna hovering above it in blessing. The metalwork was so finely done that the waves beneath the ship's prow churned in a fine, almost lacy froth.

"They're votive plates," a tentative voice said over my shoulder. "Perast has always been home to sailors. Whenever they survived some tragedy at sea, they would make a solemn oath."

I turned from the plate. A gangly, green-eyed boy about my age stood behind me, his freckled cheeks flushing adorably when I met his gaze. I smiled at him. "What kind of oath?"

"The sailor would pledge that, if he survived and returned

to port, he'd leave some mark on something lasting like silver—usually a picture of whatever kind of ship he'd sailed on, and an inscription naming the vessel and its captain. Local goldsmiths made these plates, here in Perast and in Cattaro."

"What about these?" I asked, pointing to a silver heart, nestled into the crook of a miniature arm. "What are they for?"

"Same thing. Sometimes the sailors thought they were sure to lose an arm or a leg, falling overboard or getting tangled in the rigging, and that it would have happened if Our Lady's love hadn't protected them. This isn't nearly as many as we once had. Our Lady was looted twice." His eyes dimmed. "People always want to take what isn't theirs. Even today."

He tried a fretful smile. "I'm Ivan—I'm sorry, I should have said. I'm the curator's son. Let me show you and your friends the altar. The museum is closed today, so that's all you'll be able to see."

I followed him between two smaller marble altars on either side of the nave, censers dangling above us, to the enclosure of the main altar. Its walls were painted a deep maroon, like the inside of a heart; Malina, Niko, and Luka were already there, on the narrow benches on either side. Three curved tiers rose up from the altar, each wider than the previous one, the last holding a tabernacle supported by mottled green marble pillars. Above them stood the painting of the Madonna and child, surrounded by cherubs and seraphim, a chiseled marble curtain shielding it from above.

"This is a replica of the painting found by the Mortešić brothers, painted over plaster," he said. "The original icon is in a museum. Safer than it would be here," he added, again with that trace of outrage.

Looking up, I saw a delicate confection of glass, its loops so finely wrought it made me long for the blowpipe at my lips, the molten give of the bubble, or the *gather*, at the end of the pipe. From below, some of the shapes even looked like the bulbs and buds of flowers. They practically quivered in my sight, wanting to burst into fractals like some hostile hybrid of glass and weedy plant, and my breathing went shallow. I screwed my eyes shut and snapped the band around my wrist, trying to rein myself in.

"And see all these dried wreaths and bouquets hanging from the lintels?" I heard Ivan saying, but I didn't dare look at actual flowers, even dead ones. "Those are votive gifts from brides who get married here. They give their bouquets and ribbons and jewels as offerings to Our Lady, to safeguard their marriages and their husbands when they go off to sea."

Why would Dunja have wanted to come here? I wondered. Despite my reaction, my still-buzzing scalp and the milling unease like centipedes down my spine, I could feel that this place was meant to be a sanctuary, if not one for me. What could she have been looking for in this homespun little church?

I turned my attention back to our reluctant guide, who was biting his chapped lower lip. "There's one more thing," he said. "We don't usually show this to the larger groups in case of damage or accidents, but since it's just the four of you . . . do you want to touch the first stone, behind the altar? The one that held the painting when the brothers found it on the sea?"

Luka's face brightened like a little boy's, despite all the skepticism. "We'd love to," he said. "Thank you."

Ivan squeezed behind the altar, his voice growing muffled. "It's tight back here, but you'll come through just fine."

I startled as his hand wrapped around mine, and he gently tugged me forward, placing my palm against the altar's cool, dusty back. I edged in sideways, trying not to breathe too shallowly. The dark, tight space smelled as clean as the rest of the chapel, nothing but the fresh saltwater breeze from outside and the ghostly undertone of faded incense. Still, my flesh crawled as Ivan guided my hand around the dry rim of an opening carved into the altar's back, as if there might be creatures in there, a snake or swarming beetles, a scorpion with its barbed tail held poised to strike.

But when I finally slipped my hand into the smooth, rounded opening and ran my fingers over stone polished by countless palms, I felt a deep wash of disappointment, as if I *had* thought there might be something here. A clue, maybe, something we could use to begin picking at this thorny tangle with Mama—and the two of us—at its center.

But nothing was ever so easy.

After all four of us wriggled out the other side, Ivan gestured toward the doorway to the left of the altar. "The museum is through there. It's a shame that I can't show it to you, but after yesterday, my father thought it'd be best to be a little careful, even if we can't close down the church itself."

Malina stiffened beside me. "What . . ." My voice came out

raspy. I could practically taste my heart in my throat. "What happened yesterday?"

"Someone stole our most precious votive offering. It was a tapestry of the Madonna and child, embroidered by Jacinta Kunić-Mijović, from Perast. She worked on it for twenty-five years while her husband was away at sea, until she lost her eyesight. She used gold and silver fibers, and seed pearls, but by the end, when she ran out of money and could barely see, she used her own hair. You can see how it pales from dark to white where she wove it in."

He turned away from us, as if to straighten a little display of candles, but I could hear the fury in his voice. "Can you imagine how much love went into something like that? Her wealth, her sight, her own hair—just in the hope that her husband would come home. And now it's gone forever. It was given to Our Lady, and someone *stole* it. Our Lady wouldn't ever be vengeful, but I don't think it's blasphemy to say that I hope that woman pays for it."

"Were you here when it happened?"

"I was," he said bitterly. "I showed her *everything*, even the first stone. And I let her stay upstairs alone so I could tour a French group that had come in. She seemed so . . . She didn't seem like the kind of person who'd do something like that. But what do I know. I can't even be remembering her right."

"Why not?"

"I thought she was old, to begin with. Her hair was white. But when she took her sunglasses off inside, I could have sworn she wasn't any older than me."

FOURTEEN

"WHAT IS SHE DOING?" I DEMANDED. WE SAT AT THE outermost table of the trellis-shrouded restaurant's terrace, overlooking the water as the sun dipped behind the mountains across from us. I'd wanted to head straight back to Cattaro, as if simple movement could make up for how stagnant and lost I felt, but apparently I'd still looked pale when we got off the ferry. Luka had insisted we get something to eat. "What could she possibly want with a tapestry? And if she burgled a church, it seems likely that she's the one who took our things, too."

Malina dipped her chin, her cascade of curls rushing over her cheeks. "But what for? It's not just why a tapestry—it's why *that* one."

"Maybe if we understood the context better," Luka mused.

He was sitting next to me, across from Malina and Niko, one arm slung across the back of my chair. "This gleam, these things you both can do, and Jasmina too." He leveled a gaze at his sister. "That *you* knew about, apparently."

"Yes," I said flatly, looking at Malina, who met my eyes with a guilty dart of a gaze. "About that."

Niko shrugged, one brown shoulder slipping free of her black-and-gold top, slim as a sparrow wing. "Well, I obviously wasn't going to *tell* you, Luka. I didn't think it was such a terribly big deal anyway. Mama did things for us sometimes, cantrips and blessings, little songs for health and wealth. No need to look so shocked about it—you were the one who never wanted to hear about her old family, her compania in Bosnia, before she married Tata. Anyway, this seemed like that, just scaled up. And it was Lina's secret, which she didn't exactly mean to tell me in the first place. We were singing together, and then—"

"Yeah," Lina broke in. "Niko was teaching me one of Koštana's songs, the Romany rounds. We were singing on top of each other, and it just happened. I showed too much. It was three or four years ago. I was still doing it by accident a lot more than I do now."

I looked between the two of them. They were staring away from each other, Lina's eyes near silver in the dimming light, as if her irises were limned with mercury, Niko's dark and gleaming like a doe's, blackened with liner. There was something glinting right beneath the surface there, a goldfish flicker in a pond, but I lost it just as quickly. Niko's eyeliner reminded me of Fjolar, and I wondered if he might be free when we got back tonight. If he might want to see me.

Thinking of him put me in mind of my flaring gleam, like a candle flame caught in a cross breeze. "Lina, do you feel like you've been getting stronger at all? Or more unpredictable, anyway? It kept happening to me at Our Lady, like in the café. Also, I'm not sure if that's all it was, but I almost hated being in there."

"Yes!" Lina burst out. "Not about the strength—I'm not feeling much different, though maybe it's been a little easier to sing things out—but there was something about that place. This feeling, you know, like when you're visiting with someone and you can tell they're just itching for you to leave?"

"Hmm, a bit like that," I said. "Though it was more . . . visceral for me. More mutual, maybe. It wanted me out. And I wanted to hurt it."

"So, what else?" Luka said, drumming his fingers on the table. "This is an equation, like everything else. A really damned weird one, but still. The more variables we can fill in, the better we'll understand it."

"Mathematics to the rescue!" Niko cheered under her breath, giving a sarcastic fist pump. "Calculus will find a way!"

"Oh, shush, brat. It's just a way to consider it. Think of it as a criminal case, if that works better for your gnatty brain. The more clues we have, the closer we are to understanding how the whole is supposed to look. Right now we have Jasmina, our Schrödinger's cat. Alive and not alive."

"Luka!" Niko hissed. "She's their *mother*. You can't just turn her into a physics paradox."

"I'm just trying to help, and this is the only place I know to start," Luka said equably, squeezing the back of my neck. "Why don't you two walk us through what else you know?"

Lina and I took turns respooling the past few days. Niko's brow had wrinkled while Lina and I described the nightmare of Mara, and she broke in before I could even finish telling them about Sorai and Naisha.

"The woman that you saw, in the winter valley. You said one of her names was Marzanna?"

"Yes." I closed my eyes and tilted my head back, a chill running down my spine like a trickle of water as I recited the rest. "Also Mara, Maržena, Marmora. There were others, too, I think. Why?"

"It sounds familiar, is all. I can't quite remember it—it might have been a song Mama sang us, or maybe one of her stories, Luka, remember the ones?"

He pulled a face. "How could I forget? We probably had a few nightmares of our own about them, not that that ever stopped Mama."

"She just wanted us to remember, is all," Niko countered. "That's what we come from; it's not something to be scared of, or ashamed. I wrote a lot of them down in the last months, along with her tinctures and recipes, when she"—her slim throat worked—"when it got worse than bad. I'll look through them for you when we get home."

We all fell silent, watching the sun set. Layers of mountains reared above the bay, each receding tier like a paler charcoal rendering of the first. The pinks of the sky turned the rippling water a silvered mauve, with the early moon rising fat above the mountain peaks. Despite everything, I could feel my heart swell with the majesty. Sitting here, you understood why so many monasteries and churches clustered in Montenegro, perched on every other cliff top and wedged into folds of mountain stone. It was beautiful on top of beautiful with beautiful tucked inside, like one of my fractals, and watching it you could almost sense the slipstream of eternity, the holy, breathing soul of the universe.

The waiter returned then, carrying a tray loaded with the gleaming catch of the day. A massive two-pound bass served as a centerpiece, with fleshy sea bream fanned out around it, along with an ugly, gawping monkfish. As we waited for the fish to grill, we tore into dense, chewy rolls spread with *kajmak*—the buttery cream cheese made from ripened curd—washing our bites down with tart, tannin-laced sips of the dark Vranac merlot Luka had ordered.

I was wondering if I'd even have room for the fish when Malina let her fork clatter to her plate, her eyes brimming. "The *kajmak* is perfect. The balance is exactly right. Mama would have loved it."

The roll turned to ash in my mouth, and I struggled to swallow. Luka draped his arm over my shoulder and pulled me against his side, sliding my chair along with me. "Hey, now. It's not a sad thing. Flavor was everything to Jasmina, even I knew that. Even before I knew it meant anything more." He gestured toward the dusky water. "And she would have liked that, wouldn't she? Maybe . . . maybe she'd have made it into one of those little cake squares. What are those things called?"

"Petits fours," Malina whispered. "It would be really pale pink ones, with mille-feuille and strawberry filling, and a sprinkle of sea salt for the surprise. And silver foil for the decoration."

I took another swig of the wine, feeling the kick of warmth in my stomach displace the hurt. Maybe that's why they had named it after a *vranac*, a rearing black horse, I thought muzzily. Because it bucked so nicely in your belly. If I had another glass, I would be fully tipsy.

Our fish arrived, and the waiter prepared it for us, separating the steaming, flaky white meat from the tiny needles of the skeleton in one smooth slice with the fish knife. He slid portions of the bass and the sea bream onto our plates, complete with the salty crisp of skin beneath, along with potatoes boiled with spinach. I ladled dollops of the slick marinade onto the meat—olive oil, parsley, and minced garlic—letting each tender bite saturate my mouth.

After we finished, we sat with our feet propped up against the restaurant's ivy-twined railing, sipping the last of the wine and watching the night sky. The day's heat had broken into a rainless thunderstorm, and the dense bank of clouds had gathered low above the inlet, flickering and bursting with bright bolts of jagged lightning, like a Polaroid negative of a daytime sky. I thought of Peter Pan, of celestial pirate ships dueling between clouds. The salty, ozone-laden wind blew into our faces, carrying with it that soapy scent of pine sap that was always strongest in summer.

Despite the storm, the restaurant was doing a lively business. A live band had struck up, covering classic, older hits from bands like

Bijelo Dugme, Merlin, Hari Mata Hari. Luka eventually stood and held out a hand to Malina, bowing extravagantly in front of her. Giggling, she stood a little shakily and stepped into his arms. He led her through a loose, improvised waltz, his steps sure and hips swaying just slightly.

"Where did he learn how to dance like that?" I asked Niko, who was smiling a bit as she watched them, one corner of her mouth turned up.

"Mama and Tata used to take dance classes together. They were amazing—they could do anything from this silly tango to a ballroom waltz. They'd dance sometimes when the bands played at the cafés on the *riva*. Luka and I loved watching them. Tata so fair and tall, Mama gorgeous and dark and little."

"Like you," I said.

She smiled again, faintly, acknowledging the compliment. "She taught me all of them, and her Romany dances too. Sometimes—near the end—I used to dance with her, just a little, very slowly. It reminded her of her compania. They wouldn't acknowledge her anymore, after she married a *gadje*. But she was happy with us. She was."

"You must miss her so much," I said. "She was so wonderful, so warm. We used to talk about it, Lina and I, sometimes. What it would have been like to have her as a mother, instead of ours."

"And me as a sister?" she teased. "Not ideal."

"What do you mean?"

"Oh, you know." She waved her hand vaguely. "You've seen me and Luka tear into each other, and you and I butt heads plenty even without being blood. There you are," she said to Lina as Luka led her back to our table, her cheeks still flushed. I felt a surprising needle-stab of jealousy slide between my ribs. "I was just telling Iris how Mama and I used to dance, while you played us a *sevdalinka* on the guitar and sang for her."

"I didn't know you sang, Luka," I said. I loved *sevdalinke*, too. They were my favorite kind of folk music, love songs that tasted like Turkish delights, slowly and sweetly strummed in a minor key that seemed to resonate in your own heart's valves. "I thought you only played."

"Of course I sing, Riss," he said as Niko stood and twirled Lina back onto the dance floor, Lina laughing as she tucked a damp curl behind her ear. "You know what they say about Roma."

The band drifted into "Emina," a haunting Hari Mata Hari song about the forbidden love between a Bosnian Christian and his Muslim beauty. Luka spread his arms open for me. I stood unsteadily, moving toward him as if through molasses.

"Actually, I don't think I do," I said into his shoulder as he took my hand and began gently guiding me back and forth. Dimly, I realized that I'd never really been close to him like this before, my breasts against his chest, his hand like an ember at the small of my back."

I could feel him smile. "When you take a Roma's wife, they say, he laughs. And when you take his horse, he cries." He shifted against me, dropping his head so we were cheek to cheek, his hand sliding gently up my back as he whispered into my ear. "But when you take a Roma's song, he dies."

An electric warmth swept through me, like I'd swallowed one of the lightning bolts that still flickered above the water. This was Luka, I reminded myself sternly. My best friend, and likely owner of an entire harem of Belgrade girls with high heels, full lips, and shining hair.

"Lina's the song," I whispered. "Not me. So I don't know about this metaphor."

He snorted quietly. "That's not what I meant, and you know it."

I tried to slide my hand free of his. He wouldn't let me go.

"Why didn't you tell me?" he murmured, swaying me back and forth. A few feet away from us, Niko was turning in a slow, sensual circle, her hips flicking beneath the tight band of her beaded skirt with each step. Lina was clapping the beat for her, cheeks flushed, one foot tapping in time. All the eyes in the restaurant were on them.

"Tell you what?"

"About the gleam. Lina told Niko. Why wouldn't you tell me?"

His closeness was making my head swim. "Because I . . . because . . ."

"It wouldn't have changed anything. I would still have—"

I stepped abruptly out of his arms. "I think we should head for home, if you're all right to drive. I'm feeling a little dizzy again."

Luka watched my face for another moment, the fine narrowing of his jaw below his winging cheekbones illuminated by the light from inside the restaurant. "Why don't you head for the car, then.

I'll stay out here for just a little while longer, for a smoke. I'll be right there."

Before he turned away, I could see the flaring cherry of a lit cigarette as he settled down into one of the chairs, followed by a smoky exhale that sounded like a sigh.

FIFTEEN

LUKA DROVE US HOME IN SILENCE SO LEADEN THAT IT tamped down even Niko's usual helium-light chatter. It was so quiet I could hear each of Lina's unsteady breaths as she sensed the contained maelstrom of everything the rest of us were feeling. I couldn't hear Luka like she could, but I knew how I felt: like the apex of a collapsed triangle, having failed him all these years by not telling him something so big, while Lina failed me terribly in turn by telling Niko.

They dropped us off by the bridge that led to the Old Town's Southern Gate, Niko murmuring a subdued good night to both of us while Luka death-gripped the wheel and stared mutely ahead. I stormed up the bridge, taking deep lungfuls of the sweet night-and-river air while Malina scrambled to keep up with her shorter stride.

Now that we were finally alone, the full breadth of my anger and betrayal had expanded and slid into full view, like a hidden planet inside me with its own mass and orbital plane. Even with that, I thought to glance at the crenelated fortification of the bastion up ahead, wondering if I would see Sorai there again.

But there was no one. Just the two of us, me and my wretched liar of a sister.

Beside me, Lina heaved a ragged sigh as she struggled not to cry. For once it made me viciously glad that I could hurt her with nothing more than feeling, that she could sense every iota of my pain.

"How could you do it?" I finally said through gritted teeth, letting us into Čiča Jovan's garden. The gate wheezed rustily shut behind us. "How could you tell her? Don't you think I wanted to tell Luka myself, a thousand times? But I didn't, did I? Because Mama said not to, to keep us all safe. And all that bullshit you gave me how it was all right, it was *better* that I barely had any gleam left. It was what all of us needed. While you were singing for Niko, spilling out all our secrets to her."

"It wasn't *like* that," she said, her voice shaking. "I swear it wasn't. I just . . ."

"'Pie,'" I broke in, rounding on her. "Is that why she calls you that? Pie, like cherry pie? Did you tell her Mama's story about you and me, the fruit and the flower? Even that?"

"Yes." Almost under her breath. "I'm sorry."

"You are *not*," I whispered furiously, my stomach hollowing. "You say that all the time, just throwing it around, like it means nothing. Sweet Lina who'll do whatever she likes, but not to worry, she'll be so sorry for it later."

"Unlike you," she mumbled, sullen and tearful. "Who never apologizes for anything, no matter what."

"Apparently I don't need to," I snapped, slapping my hand on the wrought-iron table beside us, so hard my palm stung. "Compared to this, apparently I've never done anything to you worse than maybe a three, possibly a four, on the 'accidentally flat-tiring someone' to 'breaking the most sacred of vows' scale. Does that sound about right?"

"I just don't . . ." She trailed off, running her hands over her face and into the thick, shining mass of hair backlit by the lantern light from the Bastion, her curls both brighter and darker than the clouded night above us. She looked so much like a tragic damsel in deep, melodramatic distress, as if *she* were the injured party, that the sight of her pissed me off that much more. Fuming, I turned away, fumbling with the door.

Inside, the lights were blazing and the doors to all the rooms flung open. I cringed inwardly at the thought of Čiča Jovan waiting for us for hours as the sun peaked and then sank, pacing up and down the gauntlet of the apartment and puffing at his cherrywood pipe. In the whirlwind of the day, we'd forgotten to worry what he might think had happened to us.

"Jovan?" I called out, heading for the studio. If he'd managed to settle anywhere, it would be there.

"Riss, wait," Lina said, and the strained pitch of her voice stranded me in place. "There's a note for us. It says he's at the hospital. It says we need to go as soon as we get back."

THE CAB RIDE to the hospital was the closest thing I could imagine to being trapped in purgatory. Lina kept reaching out for me, then remembering we were fighting and dropping her hand to twine it frantically in her skirt.

"Do you think she died? All the way?" she finally whispered hoarsely.

My insides contracted around my pounding heart. I was so queasy with twinned dread and anticipation that every bump and pothole made my stomach come climbing up my throat. "I don't know."

"Or do you think she—"

"Lina, I don't *know*!"

We lapsed into quiet after that, both of us laboring just to breathe.

Čiča Jovan met us in the hospital's dismal entryway, his haggard face flicking from relief to devastation and finally to fury, like a flurry of projector slides. "Where have you been?" he demanded, gripping me by the shoulders and giving me a shake. This was the angriest I'd ever seen him, his thick white hair rumpled from raking his hand through it, his eyes blazing beneath bushy white brows. "How could you go and not tell me, with who knows what maniacs out there waiting for you? And you too, Malina. I would have thought at least *you* might have more sense than this. One of you could have picked up your phone, or checked your messages. Given me a single moment's thought."

I bit the inside of my cheek, steeling myself for yet another lie.

"We just . . . Luka offered to drive us to Perast to our Lady of the Rocks, so we could leave an offering for Mama. A prayer and a love token, if it makes any difference to her now. Jovan, why are we here? What's happened to her?"

Čiča Jovan closed his eyes for a long moment. When he finally opened them, they were bleak as quarry water. "It's not a quarantine any longer. It's a different secret they're keeping now."

"Why?" Malina whispered, the question like a wince. "What's happening?"

"They don't know, my girls. She's gone. Someone stole her away from them. Apparently the hospital's too godforsaken to afford security cameras, so they have no trace of what happened to her. The nurse maintaining quarantine swore up and down that no one slipped by her, that she saw nothing." He hitched his shoulder at an attendant hovering several feet behind, hands clasped tight in front of her bleached-out scrubs. I recognized her from the last time: the same sallow-faced woman who had let Mirko pass with us in tow. "She's the one I spoke to."

"And nothing? She can't remember seeing anything at all?"

His jaw worked beneath the muscle of his cheek. "That's what she says, though I can't fathom it. They had our Jasmina here, and now she's gone. *Someone* must have taken her, by God. She certainly didn't walk out of here on her own! So I've railed at all of them, my girl, all the way up to the hospital director; Mirko was here earlier, too, to interrogate them in turn. None of them have a thing to say for themselves."

I could feel myself swaying from the inside, like some rickety stilt hut in high winds. *Could* Mama have somehow left by herself, in the state she was in? A shudder tore through me at the thought of her dragging herself out of the bed, eyes half lidded and twitching blindly, tubes trailing from her slack limbs, her chest concave beneath the papery hospital gown. But how could the nurse have possibly missed it? Lina and I exchanged frantic looks, and I could see her come to the same conclusion.

Someone would have needed to have been there with the nurse, to lure away her memories.

Someone like Sorai.

I squeezed Jovan's shoulder. "Let me talk to her, Jovan. Before we leave."

He nodded once, and held an arm out to Malina. "Why don't you stay with me, sweetheart. I need someone to lean on for a spell."

The woman's narrow face folded in on itself as I approached her. Her gray-threaded dark ponytail was loose and scraggly, and her fingers flitted up to pluck nervously at it as she struggled to meet my eyes. I glanced at her name tag. "Jelena—it's okay if you don't know what happened. Really. I don't think this was your fault. None of us do."

She snorted a little, weakly. "Thank you for saying so, though it's not true—they're going to be rid of me for sure now. Someone has to take the blame for this. I was the one outside that door, how could I not have seen anything? It's—it's impossible. There's only one way in and out of that room, and I was *there*, I swear I hadn't left for a moment. I'd checked in on her just an hour before, and the next time I went in—gone. Vanished like a ghost."

I pressed my lips together, pulled them through my teeth. "This might sound strange, but do you remember anything else at all? Something like a smell, maybe? Perfume, even?"

Her brown eyes flashed up to mine. "That's—yes! I smelled peaches, strong, very sweet. Almost like there was a fresh-cut plate of them tucked somewhere close that I couldn't see. I even looked around for it first, and then I was nervous that maybe I'd had a small stroke or the like. Phantom smells can happen after that. But I could see just fine, and move my hands properly. And there was another smell, something like flowers, then it faded completely too. I thought maybe . . . the vents here can be strange. There wasn't any other explanation."

Except for Sorai. She'd taken this woman's memory, just like she'd taken ours years ago, siphoned out with the power of her scent.

And now she had stolen our mother whole.

BACK AT ČIČA Jovan's, the three of us collapsed in the living room, Jovan in his massive, hand-carved rocking chair, Lina and me on the couch. "I don't understand what's happening here, my girls, I swear on my heart," he said heavily, massaging his temples. "It's beyond me. How could they have *lost* her, and why are they lying? Because it must be lies. Human beings don't simply disappear into thin air."

Malina shifted uneasily beside me. On the way out of the hospital, I'd quietly shared with her what the attendant had told me, and we'd both agreed there was no need to tangle Jovan in whatever spiderweb Sorai, or whoever else, was weaving around us. Involving

Luka and Niko was already dangerous enough, given how little we knew of anything.

"In any case, we're all worn out," Jovan said. "If you've eaten already, it might do us all good to make an early night of it. Could be we'll hear something in the morning."

"I'm going to sit in the studio for a while, I think," I said. "I'm not ready to sleep yet." Or to be alone with Malina, especially now. I didn't have any spare comfort to lend her, or the inclination.

In the studio, I sat on the little wooden bench across from the furnace, my back against the stone wall, breathing in the familiar, lingering tang of molten glass and wood shavings. It brought me back to the first time I'd slept over at Jovan's. Mama had made me cry that night, two years ago. By then I almost never let myself cry in front of her, but I'd been so furious that it couldn't be helped. Lina had been playing for us before it happened, and for once our living room was almost peaceful with the warm contentment of her song, a sleepy-sweet melody like a heavy-eyed pup curled by a fireplace.

And then one of her strings had snapped with a twang.

It wasn't her fault. The violin was cheap and already old, but Mama had flown into one of her senseless rages over it, rolling in that storm front of fury Lina and I both knew so well. Why couldn't Lina take better care of her things, why couldn't she have a lighter touch with the rosin, why couldn't she be more graceful? Even if the words weren't aimed at me—and even if they were utterly false, given how much grace Lina had even then—I felt each one drop heavy into my stomach like a swallowed bullet, until I finally moved to shield my sister.

"Jasmina, just *stop*," I said. "She didn't mean—"

"Not 'Jasmina,'" she hissed back. "I'm your *mother*."

"Not really," I retorted, chin quivering. "You're not."

She slapped me across the face. And without thinking, I hit her back, hard.

The shock on her face—the sheer hurt beneath it, the unfamiliar etch of betrayal—frightened me so much I burst into tears. She reached for me as I darted past her and out the door, into the humid, salt-laden August night. I sprinted all the way to Čiča Jovan's house on bare feet, my sides throbbing with stitches and sobs. I pounded on his door like a lunatic, and when he finally let me in and gathered me into his arms, I could barely speak.

"She . . . she . . ." I sobbed into the silk-lined vest he wore even in high summer, that smelled of pipe tobacco, resin, and hot glass. My cheek still flamed with the imprint of her hand. "*Why?*"

He sighed deeply, his lungs creaking. "Oh, sweetheart. I couldn't tell you why. Your mother is a fine, fine woman, but hard. Heavy as the earth, like they say sometimes. I think it may all be a bit much for her, that's all."

I pulled away from him. "And what about us? It's not too much for *us*? You know what, I don't care why. I just wish she'd die and leave us alone."

His craggy face crumpled, eyes dimming beneath the overhang of his brow. "Don't say that, my girl. Come, let's go sit in the studio. Let's make something together. Anything you want."

I watched as he fired up the furnace, the crucible in which we heated the glass all the way to 2,400 degrees, a white sun-heat that looked like it might match the level of my fury. Then we cooled the piece down to around 2,000 degrees, still a bright, fiery orange but cooler enough to "fine out" or release the bubbles from within. By myself, I spooled the gather of glass from the furnace onto my blowpipe, like honey twirled around a stick, and transferred it to the marver—his was the traditional marble slab, not the steel most people used these days for their working surface.

And when the cool skin formed along the blob's glowing surface, the glass was mine to mold: to blow with short, sharp bursts of breath, tweeze and shape with straight and diamond shears. I slowly exhaled my fury as I turned the glass into my bougainvillea through cane and murrine, rolling the sticky, molten scraps in colored powders for their hues.

"Slow and careful with your hands," Čiča Jovan murmured as I worked. "And careful with your breath. We can reheat each piece unless it cracks, but we can't reskin your fingers."

I worked with him for hours, building fractal offshoots from the leaves and petals of that primary flower, reheating glass when I needed to in the glory hole. I hadn't known what that secondary furnace was called before, and it made me laugh when he told me. By the time we transferred the piece to the annealer, where it would cool slowly over the next day to keep from cracking or shattering, my rage and hatred had smoothed over and cooled as well.

Now, the studio's heavy door scraped open, startling me out of the memory. Čiča Jovan shuffled in, offering me a mug purling with minty steam. I wrapped my hands around it and he lowered himself onto the bench next to me, grunting a little as his knees cracked.

"You're bearing up so well, my girl," he said, shaking his head. "Like a proper hero. It's unbelievable how strong you're being, both for you and your sister. Even when the world's turned impossible on you."

I leaned against his side, breathing out a laugh through my nose. "Hardly. It's just that I don't know what to do, and I don't understand any of this. How could she be just *gone*, Jovan? Who is she, really? Or who was she, I suppose. I don't even know how to say it."

He gave a labored sigh. "I always wondered when you'd finally ask me that. Surprised you never did before, with that auger of a mind of yours. And I wish I had something to give you."

"But you don't?"

"She never did tell me where she came from," he said, hiking up his sharp-creased trousers as he leaned back against the wall. One of his socks had a hole in the ankle, above his fur-lined slipper; it snagged at my heart. "I found her outside the gallery one night, high summer. July, near eighteen years ago. She was sitting on the ground, slumped against the glass like a beggar, but she was wearing the finest dress, white and black. I remember it shimmered in the dark, and all that wild hair of hers was down."

I could hear the echo of old longing in his voice. If he thought of Mama as his daughter now, he hadn't always. And all those gifts he'd made for her over the years looked different to me now, too. Tokens of another kind of love.

"Even run ragged as she was," he went on, "she looked like art herself."

I held my breath; I'd never heard any of this before. "And you just took her in? A complete stranger?"

"She told me she thought my work in the window was beautiful, the loveliest things she'd seen in the town. That they reminded her of home. And she said she had no money for a hotel or food, no baggage other than a little silk satchel. She looked so sad, so worn out, my girl. I couldn't turn her away in such a shape. I offered her a place to stay, and I truly believed it would be just for the one night, but then . . . you know how she is, Iris. She's changed over the years—loosened a little, maybe, though I know it won't have seemed that way to you—but she was the most elegant woman I had ever known. Everything she did or said was such a wonder to behold, and sometimes it felt . . ."

He cleared his throat uncomfortably, a deep tobacco-roughened rumble.

Such delicacy, such deliberation. It was a marvelous thing to witness. That's how your mother was when she was young. Every movement done in degrees, to please the eye. And I used to think to myself, no one is simply born this way. Someone taught her this."

Spider-leg chills skittered down my spine. *This is how you should be*, Sorai's voice echoed in my mind. *So beautiful that you can wound with it. Your beauty is a force, you know, a power all its own. It can be both sword and shield for you, and win you anything you want.*

Had our mother grown up with those women? Had they taught her to be beautiful as they were? I remembered the way she always seemed poised on the edge of flirtation, on the brink of kept-back laughter, with everyone but us. How men and even women nearly tripped over themselves around her. And that was almost a decade later, after she'd fled whoever it was that taught her how to do it. Something about the thought struck me as so sinister, the notion of purpose behind beauty. That my mother had been *for* something.

That maybe Malina and I were, too.

"And you never made her tell you?"

He snorted. "When has anyone ever made Jasmina do anything? I know you think the two of you couldn't be more different, but where do you think you came by all that steel?"

I felt a twinge of pleasure at that, pale and raw, like a spring shoot nosing through winter soil. It had been such a long time since I took any comparison with Jasmina as a compliment. "Still. You let her stay with you. It seems like the least she could have done was tell you the truth."

"She said that a terrible thing had happened to her. That she had lost her sister, and her mother. And that if I wanted her to stay with me—and by then, I couldn't imagine her gone—I would never ask again. You and Malina came soon after, and she refused to burden me with your care, as if I wouldn't have loved raising you like a father. All she would take from me was the money to start the café."

Again, I thought of all his gifts to her over the years, all the furniture and ornaments. He'd been trying to make her life lovely, in the only way she would accept.

"I would never have told you this before, my girl," he said. "It was against your mother's wishes, and I'm only telling you now because keeping it from you might do more harm than good. But Jasmina was a haunted woman, even a fool could see it. That's why I shouted at you tonight. I can't bear the thought of it, of something happening to you or your sister. It's too much for this old heart to take."

SIXTEEN

TUCKED UP IN THE GUEST-ROOM BED, I LAY AS FAR AWAY FROM
Malina as I could get, my back turned to her. I knew I should tell her
what Jovan had told me, wrap myself around her and split the weight
of Mama's new absence between us, but I couldn't bring myself to
pierce the surface of the silence between us yet. Everything was still
too raw. Finally, my thrashing became too much to take. Sleep was
so far away that it felt like some distant horizon I would never reach.
I needed to be elsewhere, and I needed not to think.

I tossed the covers back and flung my feet to the floor. Malina
pulled herself up in bed as I dragged my tunic back over my head
and laced up my sandals, her knees drawn up to her chest and her
face curtained by the darkness of her curls on either side. "Riss,
where are you going?"

"Out."

I'D ONLY BEEN to the beach at night a few times by myself. Usually it was with Filip and Nev and a Pepsi-vodka flask, a few times with Luka. Lina had never been much for sneaking out of the house for midnight swims.

At least not with me, I thought bitterly. Maybe she'd been here with Niko hundreds of times, for all that I knew.

Either way, it wasn't always so solemnly wonderful as this. The moonlight was bright as lanterns, and houses twinkled on the bay's opposite shore, sparking halfway up the looming black mountains like scattered bonfires. Every breath of balmy air was thick with salt. The water lapped at the moonlight, silvered tips above the oily black, and the pebbles beneath my bare feet were still warm from all the sun they'd drunk during the day.

I could hear them crunching as Fjolar picked his way toward me.

"Flower girl," he said, bracing himself on one hand as he eased down beside me, bringing a waft of whiskey and chocolate. "I didn't think I'd hear from you quite this much sooner rather than later."

"But you thought it would be soon, regardless," I tossed back. "A little presumptuous, no?"

"Well, you do owe me," he pointed out. "And you don't seem like a girl given to welshing on her bets."

"Right," I muttered, my cheeks lightening. The moonlight was so bright I wondered if he could see my skin flushing with color; I could feel his eyes on me even as I looked straight ahead. "And what was this bet I lost, exactly? Maybe we should start with that."

"Fair enough," he agreed. "If you're going to be parting with my two kisses, seems reasonable to tell you why."

The certainty behind the words—the sureness that those kisses were his—caught fire like a sparkler lit in my stomach, a hissing mix of excitement and indignation.

"Well, we'll see about that," I said, trying to keep my voice steady. "The honorable don't usually finagle drunk girls into bets. I'm still deciding if this one even stands."

"One, I never claimed any honor to my name," he replied, ticking the points off on his fingers. "Two, I thought it might be in my favor that we had so much in common, what with fractal magic between us. Not a quality you find in a beautiful witch every day. And three, I won fair and square. You told me you couldn't make the ceiling bloom for me—I told you that you could. And so you did."

My face went numb, but even as my mind blanked with shock, a small part of me spun in giddy circles at having been called beautiful. "Fractal magic?" I stammered. "Witch?"

"You are one, aren't you? You and your sister, both. I heard her singing at that café before I came in, and you made me the prettiest Christmas-light nebula at that party. You just needed a little nudge, was all. I can't do it myself, exactly, but I can help. Make it easier for you to bloom."

"How?" I breathed. "Who *are* you?"

A match flared, illuminating his broad-boned face, eyes glinting and mouth soft amid faint stubble. I heard him suck in a long breath, a pungent waft of tobacco from a hand-rolled cigarette.

"I'm like you," he said through the smoke. "My mother was a

witch, and among other things, she could summon fractals. I can see them—and draw them, hence the tattoos, that's actually what I do for work—but I can't pluck them from thin air like you can, make others see the fabric of the world." He chuckled softly. "It's spectacular, what you do. Wild, stunning. I've never seen another one like you."

I sifted through everything he'd said, still reeling. "*Was* a witch?" I said carefully.

"Yes. She's gone, has been for a few years. It's just me and my younger brother now, in Reykjavík, she and our father split very long ago. She was from here before she moved to Iceland, taught us both the tongue. I thought this might be the right summer to see it for myself, her Montenegro."

That explained the accent, the unusual, rocking rhythms of his speech. I stole another glance at his sharp profile, watched him blink slowly like a sleepy lion. "Maybe this is where the magic comes from," he added, "and she simply brought it with her."

"I just never . . . I had no idea there were others. My mother always told us we were all alone in the world." And somehow, even after remembering Sorai and Naisha, I hadn't thought past it enough to glimpse the notion that there might be other families in the world like mine. "But I'm starting to think she might have told us a lot of things that aren't true. And I'm sorry. I'm sorry that you lost your mother."

"She wasn't an exceedingly nice woman," he said dryly. "Pleasantness was not so much her forte. But even still. It's always hard to let a mother go."

I pressed my lips together, scraping my teeth over their tender insides. "It is. I—I wouldn't have thought that I'd miss mine."

"Why not?"

"She wasn't 'exceedingly nice' either," I replied, mimicking his tone. "Especially not to me. Have you ever heard of those people who have overactive immune systems, and they're allergic to ridiculous things, like to their own spit or skin? It was like that with us. I'm half of her, but the way she tore into me you'd think I was made from all her castoffs, all her warts and wrinkles and crooked joints. All the things she ever hated about herself, things she wished she could cut out. Or would have, if she hadn't been so fucking perfect."

"Maybe it's the opposite," he mused quietly. "Maybe there was too much of everything shared between you, and not merely the bad. Two magnets face-to-face, repelling."

I closed my eyes against the searing swell of tears. Silently he passed me the cigarette, and as I pinched it between my fingers, his hand landed lightly on my thigh. I nearly flinched at the sudden contact and the warmth of his skin, but the first potent lungful chased the doubts away. My mind opened up like it always did, unfurling and unfolding. Heat dripped through me like some sweet sap, and I tipped my head back as he just barely stroked my thigh, trailing caresses on the very surface of my skin.

"What kind of magic did your mother have? Was it like yours?"

"No," I murmured, eyes still closed. Each word felt discrete and sticky, like a melting bonbon on my tongue. It was work stringing them together, but sweet. "She baked things, made flavors. You'd taste them and see something like a memory, but of a place you'd never even been. A moment in time that she'd seen or imagined, and translated into taste."

"Taste is very powerful that way. Together with smell, they're like the strongest time machine. Take you anywhere you like, and even where you don't."

"I don't know," I said, my insides still rising and falling, aloft on a warm tide. "I don't know why I'm telling you any of this. You don't know me. You didn't know her."

"I'd wager you can feel how similar we are," he suggested. His eyes were so intent on mine that even in the dark it made me squirm, scrabbling for someplace safe, a shell to drag over my most tender parts. These were the insides I kept sealed away, from air and from everybody else. "You look at me and simply know me, the way I looked at you and knew you. Even our names. Iris, Fjolar. My name means 'violet flower,' a bit like yours. And it means 'warrior' as well."

"No more wagers, please," I said with mock haste, trying to lighten the weight between us. "If we keep going this way, I might wind up in your debt forever."

He huffed out a low, growly laugh. "I imagine you'd make the time pass very quickly."

"Maybe once I could," I said, thinking of my whirlpools and spirals. "Not as much anymore. It's mostly just flowers now, and before you, I couldn't even make anyone see them."

"So you say, and yet, ceilings keep turning so interesting around you." He gestured at the water with his free hand, the other still curled warm and heavy around my thigh. I could feel the width of his palm and the pressure of each fingertip so acutely I wondered if I could draw his fingerprints just by feel. "Have you ever tried to bloom that?"

"Yes," I said. My voice came out raspier than I expected, and I cleared my throat. "Though only in daytime, with the sun on it. And just for myself, of course. It was one of my favorite things. Like a bonfire made of sun and water."

"How about from beneath?"

"What do you mean?"

"Come. I'll show you."

He stubbed out the cigarette and heaved himself up in one smooth movement, then turned to stand in front of me, holding out his hands. I took them and he pulled me up, so hard I stumbled into him with a surprised squeak, palms flat against his chest. We stood there for a moment, his eyes on mine, his mouth so close my lips parted in response to the tickle of his breath.

"My, my," he murmured, running his hands down my bare arms, over my shoulders, and down my back. "That was a very adorable little mouse sound. Not what I would expect from you. Tell me, do you make any others?"

I felt that giddy rush again, like a globe filled with sparkling water being tilted back and forth. "That's just—do you *always* say things like that to girls you barely know?"

"Sometimes, yes," he whispered in my ear, brushing his stubbled cheek against mine. "But definitely never always."

"Why do I feel so sparkly around you?"

He swirled one hand into a courtier's bow. "Turning girls' blood into glitter happens to be my specialty."

I burst into giggles against his chest. Being around him was so much better than drinks, better than the smoke that still wisped through my blood. It was making me forget entirely how angry I was at Malina, how adrift I had felt when we returned from Perast with near nothing to show for it.

It nearly made me forget my missing mother.

"You, sir, are ridiculous."

"And you, miss, are the same." He took one of my hands and lifted it to his mouth, turning it over to press an openmouthed kiss into my wrist, and this time I was sure I felt the hot flick of his tongue against it. "So . . . wild. Iris suits you, you know. Irises grow everywhere, in cold and heat and desert, set down roots even in rocks. A warrior of a flower, no kind of lady."

"It's true," I murmured back. "I've never been strong in the ladyship department."

"And a very good thing that you're so lacking. Because ladies don't take off their tunics and leap into dark waters with strangers, do they?"

"Wait, what—" He flashed me a lazy half smile and abruptly let me go, pivoting on a bare foot to set off down one of the short concrete piers that jutted off into the water, stairs cut into their sides. He stripped down as he walked, tugging his V-neck over his head. The muscles in his wide back corded in the moonlight, shifting black and gray shadows. His torso tapered sharply at the waist, and as he stepped out of his jeans, I caught my breath at how dense his thighs and calves were, how solid all of him was, like he had been carved out of a single slab.

I swallowed hard. He glanced at me over his shoulder, his cheek creasing from his smile.

"Are you coming or not, then, flower? I'm not going to stand here for your inspection all night." He let his hair down from its bun; it just brushed his shoulders as it fell loose. "Unless that happens to be your thing."

It could be made to be my thing, I thought as I followed him. If he was willing to continue looking that way.

I pulled my tunic over my head, so aware of the fabric's whisper against my skin. Everything felt high-pitched and sensuous, my mind and body vibrating at the same high frequency as I stepped next to him in my bra and panties, trying not to shiver as he took my hand. His thumb stroked over my knuckles, and his eyes went heavy-lidded as he ran a slow gaze over my body.

"What is it like," he said, low and rough, "to be made so perfect as you are?"

"I'm not perfect," I stammered, ducking my head. "My sister is the perfect one. Curves from here to everywhere. In all the right places."

He stroked three fingers down my throat, tracing out its hollow. "And where exactly do you think yours are? Not in any wrong places I can see." He tipped his head toward the water. "Lead the way. If you're game to go, that is."

Everything inside me roused at once. "Of course I'm game." I dropped his hand and broke into a run to the edge of the concrete pier, calling, "Don't forget to take the biggest breath!" over my shoulder.

Then warm air parted around me as I jumped, a wobbly, delicious plummet in my stomach as I dropped toward the water and broke its surface with pointed toes. I nearly exhaled the long breath I'd taken as the silken warmth rushed around me, sealing over my skin. A fizz of bubbles like popped champagne tickled against my face; Fjolar had landed almost exactly beside me, both of us kicking to stay underwater.

The salt stung like fury when I opened my eyes and water surged into them, but I could stand it and I could see, enough to make out the bright wavering coin of the moon's reflection on the surface, and the rippling silver facets where its light broke on the waves all around it. Fjolar took my hand and squeezed it hard, my bones grinding together until I nearly gasped. And just like in the café the gleam went roaring through me. The facets multiplied over each other, and so did the central orb of the moon, spiraling into concentric rings around itself. I pulled at the gleam until I'd made the underside of the water into some strange, brilliant night sky, the glittering overlay of the moonlight like perfect constellations—as if someone had graphed out all the stars and forced them into order.

My lungs burned and my head went light from lack of air, but I didn't stop pulling until the constellations came alive, blooming into silver fireworks that arced down toward us. I had never wondered how far I could take the gleam, what would happen if the fractal bloom actually touched me, but I wondered now as it came surging down.

I ran out of air before I could find out. Two kicks launched me back above the surface, gasping and laughing through salty water as I rubbed at my stinging eyes.

"What a glory," Fjolar was saying breathlessly, laughing low in his throat. "What a work of wonder you are."

"Thank you," I replied, running a hand over my head to slick the hair back, licking the salt off my lips. "I—just, thank you."

We stopped laughing at the same moment, rising and dipping as we faced each other, kicking to stay afloat with little fin-flicks of my feet. There was nothing but silence, the quiet splishing of the water right around us. His hair had slicked back too, and he was shining with sluicing water, his cheekbones curved and thick as ribs, his lips and lashes glistening as he watched me. My insides went tight with hunger.

I swam toward him in one quick burst, pushing his back against the pier. He gasped a little, and I wondered if the barnacles that clung to the concrete had cut him. I didn't care. His nearness and that bright jolt of uncut tobacco, the quality of the night, had made me bold.

I cupped his face in my hands, feeling reckless and wild in the way I'd always pretended to be but never fully felt. I swept my thumbs over his cheekbones as his hands ringed my waist.

"Iris . . . ," he said, an exhale of my name.

"Quiet," I said, then kissed him. His lips parted beneath mine and the kiss went deep, tongue against tongue all silky wet. Beneath the lacing of smoke, he tasted fresh and sweet, and I kissed him like I was parched, like drinking a glass of cold water down in long and greedy gulps.

He groaned low into my mouth, and my hips writhed against his in response. He drew me closer and turned us around twice, until we were on the pier's other side, him sitting on the steps and me straddling his lap. I pulled back just enough to look into his face, still breathing into his mouth.

"Is this what you were thinking about, this morning?" I barely recognized my own voice, so low and rough. "Is this what you wanted? Malina heard you wanting me. So you can't lie."

"Why would I ever lie about that?" he said. "Of course it's what I wanted. Just like I want you now, any way you like."

A thrill pierced through me, like a red-hot needle pulling fiery thread. All that permission. All of it mine. I wound my fingers through his hair and pulled, licking the salty water from where his neck met the thick muscle of his shoulder, sucking on his skin until he hissed between his teeth. I even used my own teeth, biting down until I felt him tense beneath me, hoping that I'd leave a mark. He let me kiss him wherever I wanted, my hands tight in his hair in a way I knew must hurt. But his own touch stayed infuriatingly light.

There'd been two boys before this, tourists who'd come through the café and stayed for a week or two. One of them I'd slept with when I turned sixteen, but nothing with either of them had come even close to this driving need. I wanted him so badly I was afraid of how fast my heart was beating.

"Why won't you touch me harder?" I demanded, nearly panting against him.

"You're the one on top from where I'm looking, flower," he said, brushing his thumb over my collarbone. "If that's what you want,

179

then tell me so. Though it seems like you could use a little softness."

"That's true," I whispered, suddenly near tears. It was the oddest combination, wanting him so much while also wanting to nest my face into his shoulder and cry into it. "I don't get very much of that."

He traced his fingers over my profile, over my forehead and down the straight line of my nose, dipping above and below the crests of my lips. He even fanned his fingertip through my spiky lashes. "I think you might need some now."

I kissed him again, slower this time, lingering and long. His lips felt so soft against the stubble that surrounded them. "It's not fair," I whispered. "I've already given you more than the allotted two."

"I *have* been known to be a very wily son of a bitch," he teased. "Maybe all this tenderness is entirely to my benefit."

"Maybe. But thank you anyway. It's been . . . I don't know how to feel anymore. With everything that's happened with my mother. And then my sister upset me tonight, made me so angry at her." I paused. "I could tell you what happened, if you want."

"Doesn't matter what it was. It brought you to me. And if this is what comes of such upset, could be I'll write her a thank-you note."

"I don't think she'd appreciate any kind of note from you," I admitted. "She doesn't seem to like you very much."

"She doesn't need to," he said simply. "I happen to like you lots more than her. She seems nothing like you at all."

That shouldn't have made me so happy—she was still my sister, and usually a very good one—but I'd never had this, someone who would so clearly rather have me. Someone who looked at me as if I blazed against the night, like a trailing comet. Like I was blinding.

"And what do I seem like?"

"Like wildfire. Like beauty that dies as soon as it's curbed."

"I guess we know what you'll need to do with me, then."

He ran his fingers down the ridges of my spine. "And what's that?"

I rested my temple against his. "Don't curb me, and you can watch as long as you want."

SEVENTEEN

LINA WAS STILL AWAKE WHEN I CREPT BACK THROUGH THE window—I was really getting to be an expert at avoiding doors—my tunic clinging to my damp bra and panties. She'd turned a lamp on, one of Čiča Jovan's whimsies, its base a bottle with a schooner trapped inside it and the shade in the shape of a mast and sails.

In its faint light, her cheek was striped with dried tears, and with her lips still trembling she looked like a lost and desperate little girl. I found that I just couldn't be angry with her anymore, as if it had become physically impossible to summon that much spleen. Fjolar had bled it out of me with tenderness. Instead I felt a smooth, vast sense of peace, like a windless desert at twilight—anything unruly had burrowed deep underground, an expanse unruffled by living things.

Her eyes narrowed as I sat down on her side of the bed, her thick lashes nearly meshing. "I think you're not mad at me anymore," she said, each word blunt and careful, like a child picking out marbles.

"No," I agreed. "I'm done with that, for now."

Her brow wrinkled. "Why?"

"Does it matter why? We could just agree to be okay."

"But you never just stop this way, Riss. Not without hashing things out, not without a fight. It's not like you."

The digging should have irritated me, but I couldn't find any residual embers to fan, nothing that even threatened to grow into a flame. "I'm just feeling peaceful, is all. Can you let me have that, after everything we've been through for the past few days? It's not that I've forgotten about you and Niko. I just don't have it in me to care at this very moment."

"That's what I mean." She scraped at her lower lip with her teeth. "I wanted to tell you that you were right, before. I shouldn't have told her—especially not without asking you first. She's my best friend. But you're my sister. I should have been protecting you. I'm selfish like that sometimes, you're right. Being sorry doesn't always fix everything, and I know that I—that sometimes I use it like a patch."

I stood and peeled the tunic and underwear off, shivering a little as the air hit my still-damp skin. "So, we're good then."

She was still frowning as I slipped back into bed, the heavier cotton of my borrowed nightgown wicking the last of the wet from my skin. "I just . . ." Her voice sharpened. "Did you go see that boy,

Riss? Is that where you went?"

She wouldn't like it, but I couldn't be bothered with a lie. "Yes," I said simply. "I smoked with him out on the beach. Then I made the water bloom for him, and then I kissed him on the pier stairs, and then I slept with him. See that? That's honesty, right there. You could take notes."

"But you only just met him!"

"So what? I wanted to. And we were safe."

"Fine, okay, you always do what you want. Everybody knows that. But you made the *water* bloom, and he could see it? You don't think that's something to talk about?"

"Not at this moment, no."

Her mouth went slack with incredulity. "He shows up out of nowhere right before Mama's attacked, right before she goes *missing*, and you don't even think twice about him? How do you know he doesn't have something to do with this?"

"Why would he have anything to do with Mama? He's just visiting from Iceland. His mother was from here. It's the start of the season, there's probably hundreds of tourists who showed up in the last few days."

"Not ones who can't get enough of you all of a sudden, who think about you like you're made for dessert."

I felt a distant bolt of fury, like a glimpse of lightning two mountain ranges over. "Because that's such a crazy thing to consider, that a boy I met might want me?"

She dug both hands into her hair. "That's not what I meant! I'm just saying—"

I reached over her to flick off the lamp, feeling her flinch as my wrung-out hair dripped salt water onto her face. "I want to go to bed. We'll talk more tomorrow."

I WOKE BLEARILY, squinting against the glare of late-morning sunlight. My muscles felt dull and sluggish, a hungover ache more intense than I would have expected from the wine and single cigarette I'd had the night before. All the stress and exhaustion of the past few days finally crashing over me, most likely.

Lina was already up and about, for a wonder, wearing a peach maxi dress with a tiered skirt, patterned with tiny wild strawberries, ferns, and sleeping mice with curled forepaws. A corded bracelet of braided leather and silver thread had been wound around one wrist, and I could see the peep of her silver espadrilles beneath the dress's hem. Čiča Jovan must have brought over some of our things yesterday, while we were still out.

She turned to me cautiously, hands stilling on the shirt she'd been folding to put in the dresser. Her hair was in a loose braid, its curling ends and ribbons trailing over her chest, and with it drawn back she looked even more like a watercolor version of our mother.

I could see the moment she felt my stab of pain; her face softened with sympathy. "*There* you are," she said. "How are you feeling?"

I dug a knuckle into one crusty eye. "Pretty far from phenomenal, actually. Not sure what's wrong with me. I never sleep this late."

Malina had always been the one able to plunge into sleep like an Olympic diver, willing herself into oblivion whenever the world around her grew too intense. But this morning I still felt half asleep even with my eyes open, the waking world around me tilting swimmy and unreal.

I stretched my arms gingerly over my head, wincing. "And I feel like I spent last night in a mosh pit instead of . . ." Gleaming for Fjolar, I didn't say. Just thinking of him revived a surge of lust, and I dug my nails into my palm, trying to quell it before Lina caught its sound. I didn't want to disrupt this fragile peace between us.

It was futile as usual, and I could see Lina's nostrils flare in response before she chose to let it go. "Well, if you're feeling up to it, Niko said she'd meet us at the Prince. She's bringing her mother's book with her. Do you want to come with me? You don't have to, I could go alone while you keep resting—"

"No, I want to come. If you don't mind. If she's found anything, I'd like to see it for myself."

"Sure. I put up your clothes, too—I hope that's okay? They're all in these two drawers, next to mine."

I dredged up a smile for her. "Thank you for that. You didn't have to do that."

She flicked one shoulder in a tentative shrug. "I was up anyway. I think Jovan's made breakfast for us, if you want to eat together?"

"I do. Let me just take a quick shower first."

I dragged myself to the bathroom, feeling like a prizefighter who'd lost a particularly vicious bout. Despite all the sleep, my eyes were heavy with plummy bags, and my temples felt tender. In the shower, I let near-scalding water pound over me until my skin turned red. By the time I'd wriggled into shorts with radioactive symbols stamped onto the pockets and a black tank with a mesh racerback, my head had cleared a little.

Outside, Čiča Jovan had laid out a breakfast banquet for us, as if we were actually starving orphans. He'd been cooking lavishly for himself for years, since his wife, Anita, had died so young, and even when I worked with him in the studio he was forever interrupting to spoon-feed me bites of whatever he had simmering. We ate with him at the wrought-iron table in his garden, between patches of neatly tended vegetables and wildflowers trailing tendrils everywhere. He watched us like an anxious mother hen, offering us feta cheese omelets, spooning extra sour-cherry preserves onto our plates. Lina had loaded her plate with a chocolate Eurokrem crepe, and was carefully dotting mayonnaise onto her toast, which she'd smeared with Carnex vegetable pâté.

"What?" she said through a mouthful, catching my look. "Why are you looking at me like I'm eating roadkill or something?"

"I think Carnex pâté might be worse than that. Roadkill is too close to organic."

She shrugged. "Well, it's delicious. Better than your crepe of the Spartans there, for sure."

"I know not of what you speak. Cocoa and sugar is a classic."

Čiča Jovan frowned at me over a steaming sip of black coffee. "You're barely pecking at that, Iris. Have some of the omelet, my girl, you're beginning to look like a whalebone corset. Or I can cut you some *gibanica* from yesterday if you want."

My insides turned over at the thought of the cheese pie leaking grease. "No, thank you. I'll eat more at the Prince, I promise." I looked up at him, gauging his reaction. "Lina and I were thinking of spending the day there. It helps to be around Niko and Luka, and they're both working today."

It was painfully easy to lie to him, when he was so clearly unmoored when it came to us—how to keep us both safe and happy, now that we were in his care. "I would rather you stayed with me today, at least until we hear something from the police or the hospital. I know you want to be with your friends—"

"Jovan, please?" Malina broke in softly, reaching across the table for his knobby-knuckled hand. "We'll be with Niko and Luka, and their father will be there too. It's such a public place, who'd come after us there? It might even be safer for us there, maybe?"

His eyebrows drew together at the thought that he might not be able to protect us on his own. He'd always been a fiercely proud man, and even though I'd only ever known him old, I'd seen how it frustrated him that age had stolen so much of his skill and strength—his once-steady fingers trembling and a stoop hunching his tall frame. But he'd never let the prickling of his pride get in the way of keeping us safe.

"All right, then," he said stoutly. "But I'll walk you there, and take my battle cane. Let someone try to cross either of my girls' paths with me standing in their way."

THE PRINCE WAS a little busier than usual, for so early in the day, but it was Friday; the flood of tourists would be swelling over the summer weekends, regular as the tide. There was already a group of giggly Dutch girls in one of the nooks, nibbling on biscuits and coffee as they puffed on a peach-mint nargileh.

Otherwise it was just us, Luka tending the bar and serving while Niko knelt on the tasseled cushions with us, striking in a scarlet wrap dress and a choker of tambourine zils strung on black cord; it had the look of Koštana's handiwork, and I wondered if she had made it for Niko, if Niko was wearing it in her mother's memory.

Niko's collection of her mother's writings sat on the floor between us. I had been expecting something more mystical, somehow, maybe a leather-bound grimoire with tarnished clasps. But I'd forgotten that Niko had been barely thirteen when she made it, out of a simple black binder that she'd plastered with a collage of Koštana's photos. Koštana was smiling in all of them, so widely you could see her one gold molar glinting—Luka had once told me how much it mortified him that she adamantly refused to swap it out for a regular white cap—and her children's faces pressed next to hers like a gradient of color. Luka's tan skin, Niko's olive, and their mother's even deeper brown. Her right ear was cuffed with piercings, from the shell down to the lobe, just like Niko's was.

There were even gummy bits of glue where a younger Niko had bejeweled the binder with little plastic gems that had dried and fallen off, though a few clung to the edges. At the very top, she'd written in sparkly, looping cursive, "My Mother Koštana's Book of Everything." And beneath it, the saying, "*Jedna je majka.*"

There is only one mother.

It broke my heart to look at it, to know what she must have been feeling, both now and when Koštana died. Niko's face was painstakingly placid as she flipped it open, but Lina's eyes swam with held-back tears.

"Thank you for showing this to us," she said. "Really. I know how precious this is to you."

Niko leaned her temple against Lina's shoulder. "It doesn't do anyone any good moldering in the dark, does it? She would have wanted it to be useful. Especially to you two."

"Even still," I said. "Thank you. Lina said you'd already looked through it, that you found something?"

"I was right—it *was* in one of her songs." Niko flicked deftly through the pages with her slim fingers. "That name you mentioned, of the woman in your dream. Marzanna. The song is Romany, but I translated it for you this morning, set it to rhyme as best I could. She only sang it for me once; I remember because I was asking her about magic, the little things she sometimes did for the changing of the seasons. I asked her why, what it was for. And she sang me this."

She ran her finger down each line. "It's called 'Kill Her in Winter, So She Can Birth Spring.'"

My stomach felt like a nest of baby snakes had hatched in it all at once. I clutched a fist against it, and looked over to Lina, whose face had gone bloodless.

Niko began:

Her bones are of nightmares, her face cut from dreams,
Her eyes are twinned ice chips, cold glimmering things,
Her hair is the scent that will drive you to death,

Her lips are the kiss that will steal your last breath.
Kill her in winter, so she can birth spring.

Strip her arms bare of glitter or silver,
Choke her and flay her, force her to deliver,
Drown her in lakebeds, or quick-running streams,
Dunk her in pond scum to smother her screams,
Kill her in winter, so she can birth spring.

To chase out the winter, build her to burn her,
Make her a body, the better to spurn her,
Build her of twigs, and of scraps, and of sticks,
Then build up the fire, and sing loud as it licks,
Kill her in winter, so she can birth spring.

Niko stopped, laying her hand flat on the page as if she could blot out the words. Lina's eyes were so wide I could see the whites all around them, and I wondered if I looked like that too, like a cornered animal.

It sounded exactly like her, like the woman in the clearing. And like Sorai, too.

"Is that it?" I whispered. "Is there anything else?"

"Mama told me a story to go with it," Niko said. "Because it scared me so much, and also made me sorry for Marzanna. It's a mishmash of things, a patchwork tale. A lot of these legends crossed the country borders, carried by the Romany. Mama said she was a Polish witch-goddess who ruled over winter, nightmares, and love. They say even Death was so fascinated by her that she never died."

"So, Mara and Death, biffles, understood," I said. "But what about all those other names?"

Malina looked up from her phone. "They're all the same person. Deity, whatever. I just checked. They're what they call her in different places. Polish, Lithuanian, Czech, Slovak. Everyone has a name for her, all the Slavs and Baltic people."

"But Mara," I said softly. "Mara is her first name. Is there anything else, Lina?"

"It says that in Poland, they kill her every spring equinox. First they make an effigy of rags and clothing, and they decorate her with ribbons and baubles before they burn her. And then whatever's left, they dunk into every body of water along the way of the parade, drowning her in every lake, pond, and puddle. They sing witch-burning songs the entire time. The one Niko has must be a Romany version of those. Oh, and . . . wow."

"What?"

Lina chewed thoughtfully on her lower lip. "It even mentions Our Lady of the Rocks. Apparently there's a side story—sort of like an urban legend, I guess, but religious—that the Mortesić brothers who found that icon actually found something much older there, an ancient figurine of Marzanna. And that they intended to dedicate the island to her name, but were too afraid of being labeled heretic pagans. So they pretended they'd found the Virgin Mary icon instead."

"But why?" I whispered, tugging at the ribbons in my own

hair. "Why is she so terrible that she needs to be both burned and drowned?"

"That was the part Mama told me," Niko said. "To make her sound less like she might eat me in the night. I wrote it down along with the song. The story goes that she was a human woman long ago, back when migrants crossed all the way from India, before they settled here and split into the Indo-European tribes who became us. And even though she's been deathless since she befriended Death, she isn't evil."

"Yeah," Lina added. "That's what this says, too. That there has to be a sacrifice to keep things orderly. For winter to end, Mara has to die and birth Jarilo, god of spring—though really, he's just another form of her, because she never truly dies." She shuddered. "I don't know. It still sounds awful to me. Maybe you just have a higher tolerance for the hideous. You did make me watch *Paranormal Activity* three times."

"Only twice, the third time was the sequel. The good one."

Lina rolled her eyes. "It's always the fine print with you."

I thought of the woman in the frozen, snowy clearing, her intensity and wildness, the bloody powders pounded from murdered things smeared all over her face. The fractaled sigils and dried flowers around her, the sharpened stones for cutting, and that glittering pile gathered up in front of her. Whoever that woman was—whatever she was, witch or god or both—the things she had done had been intentional. There was no mistaking the willfulness that blazed in her. Whatever she had done, maybe she'd earned herself this endless burning and drowning.

"But what does this have to do with us, or Mama?" Lina was saying. "Why are we dreaming about her?"

"And why do we have ribbons in our hair?" I mused. "That seems related, if it's important enough that even a story about her would mention them."

We all fell silent, frowning at our hands, until the tinkle of the bell above the door and Nev's brassy voice broke our quiet.

"Riss! Lina!" She rushed at us in her gangly way, dropping a massive plastic bag beside her as she knelt and flung her arms around me. "Oh, dollface, I'm so fucking glad to see you. And you, Lina, my condolences, sweetheart. I'm so, so sorry about Jasmina. I still—I just still can't believe it's true. I can't imagine how this is for you."

She smelled so wonderfully familiar, the vanilla extract that reminded me of all the hours I'd spent working beside her in the café as she baked with Mama. I fought back tears even as I pulled away from the hug like a kitten squirming out of fond arms; it was too much to feel her sympathy. It made the strangeness of the truth feel worse somehow, a confinement Lina and I could share only with Luka and Niko.

She let me go, with a wordless look of understanding at my discomfort. "I baked some baklava for you," she said tearfully. "I didn't know what else to do. I thought Luka or Niko could bring it over for you, but this is much better." She cupped my cheek for just a moment before pulling back, and I thought for the thousandth time how nice it would have been to have her as an older sister.

She dove headlong into the bag and lifted out pan after pan of the sticky, glossy dessert, liberally sprinkled with nuts, enough for a battalion. Even Niko began looking a little fazed as stacked pans teetered on top of each other on the table between us.

"Go on, have a little," Nev said, flapping a hand in the general direction of the baklava. Her ivory sailor dress was smudged with syrup on the bodice; I wondered how long she had been toiling away at this, if this was the shape of her grief. "I made it with hazelnuts instead of walnuts, I know you both like those better."

At her urging, we all dug into the pan with our fingers, cupping our palms beneath the sweet, flaky squares to catch falling crumbs. I'd always loved baklava, the crisp layers of phyllo as they melted in your mouth, the almost cloying sweetness of the honey, syrup, and chopped nuts cut by the acid nip of lemon. We'd made variations of it at the café so often that it tasted exactly like home to me. It made me hungry in a way I hadn't really been in days.

"When is . . ." Nev cleared her throat. "When is the funeral? I hadn't heard anything, and I didn't want to be a bother by asking, but I was so afraid I'd miss it."

"We don't know yet," I said when Malina hesitated, shooting me a beseeching look. "Because it's a—because it's a murder, the police protocol is stricter. They might need to keep her for longer before they give her back to us."

Nev looked so stricken I wanted to slap myself for the lie, but there was nothing better to tell her. "I'm so sorry to hear that. What utter bullshit. I mean, I'm sure it's necessary and all that, but it probably doesn't help that they're morons and probably running all amok what with everything else that happened yesterday." She clapped a hand over her mouth. "Shit, I'm sorry. You don't need to hear that, either, what is the *matter* with me."

The nape of my neck began to prickle. "What do you mean? Nev, what's happened?"

"Oh, it's nothing, really, I shouldn't have even brought it up, it's just that Tata hasn't been able to shut up about it and—"

Nev's father, Uroš Stefanović, the councilman. My pulse sped up, and I grabbed her arm, squeezing so hard her eyes widened. "Nev, what *happened*?"

"It looks like someone's stealing relics from our churches, and it's—Iris, that fucking hurts, let go!" She rubbed her arm, eyes wide. "First it was Our Lady of the Rocks, but that was just a votive gift. Then it was the monastery of Ostrog, and Tata's being very tight-lipped, but it sounds like someone's tampered with Saint Basil's remains. Everyone's clutching their prayer beads over it, pun totally intended."

"Do they know who it was?" Malina broke in.

"No, but apparently it was a woman. Which is driving everyone nuts, all hail the misogyny, as if women can't be good at stealing and sacrilege—"

"But we have to go," I interrupted. "We have to go to Ostrog."

Nev stared at me as if I'd lost my mind. "Why in the shit would you need to go there? And you can't anyway, the monastery is on lockdown to visitors. They're not letting anyone in."

"Can you ask your father? Please? It's—" I geared up for another heinous lie. "We promised Mama we would go, when we found her. It was the last thing she said to us before she passed. Malina, tell her."

"Right," Malina said, warming to the story. "She could barely talk, you know? But she managed that. It's something she always wanted, and you know she wasn't even very religious, Nev. But it was like—like her deathbed wish that we go there in her place. And since we don't even know when we can bury her properly . . . please, could you just ask for us?"

Nev looked narrowly between the two of us, as if she sniffed something off, but the desperation must have been scrawled over our faces. "Jesus, what a thing. All right, then. I'll see what I can do for you."

EIGHTEEN

NEV REFUSED TO TELL US THE BRIBERY AND STRING-pulling that had been necessary to grant us permission for an Ostrog pilgrimage; I got the sense that whatever sacrifice she'd made had been big enough that even if it was for Jasmina's sake, she still resented us a little for it. But three hours later we had it—two of us would be allowed to go, but only two.

Luka wouldn't hear of Lina and me striking out on our own; protecting us trumped everything, like it always did with him.

"Missy, Ostrog is a cliff monastery, and those roads are hell even for seasoned drivers. I'm not trying to be some 'girls can't drive' asshole, don't give me that look, Niko. I'm just saying they haven't had much of a chance to practice. And if this woman is still out there, and is the one who attacked Jasmina, she could be waiting for you in those mountains. If only two can go, it should be me and one of you."

"Iris," Niko jumped in. "Take Iris."

"Hey!" Lina bridled. "I don't even get a say in this?"

"You couldn't even climb that runt tree in the schoolyard without wanting to pass out, pie," Niko pointed out. "You couldn't handle the *jungle gym*. Do you really want to be trapped in a moving metal prison thousands of feet up, nothing between you and the plummet, just all that empty air and—"

"Okay, would you please stop?" The skin beneath Lina's eyes had turned green, translucent like dragonfly wings. "You're right. That doesn't sound . . . ideal for me."

"Exactly." Niko crossed her slim arms over her chest, satisfied. "You can stay with me, and we'll see if there's anything else helpful in Mama's book. There's so much in there, and I haven't had a chance to fully delve into it. Maybe we'll find something more."

Lina nodded, chewing on her lip, her eyes clouded with uncertainty. She reached for me, and I pulled her into a quick, fierce hug. "Don't worry, bunny," I whispered into her ear. "Let me handle this one. Luka will keep me safe, promise. And about last night, I'm . . ."

"It's okay," she murmured back. "You don't have to say it, I know you are. Just come back to me soon, please?"

"GODDAMN IT, LUKA, how do I get this off?" I demanded, twisting around in the front seat as the seat belt threatened to throttle me.

He shrugged, eyes on the road. "You don't. Not safe to ride with your feet all tucked up under you like that. Very fetching, but not safe."

Huffing with frustration, I levered my chair back and jack-knifed my knees up to my chest in protest, resting my heels on the dashboard with my soles pressed against the glass.

"Wow, princess," Luka commented with a sidelong glance. "By all means, smear my windshield with your improbably tiny feet. I wouldn't want you to feel like you're not traveling first class."

"My feet are not tiny."

"They are so, look at them. I don't understand how you walk around with those. Probably you could be in a circus, they're so small. It's very cute."

"What about if I take one and put it in your face?" I suggested. "How cute would that be?"

"If you're looking to drive us into a ravine, you should try it out."

We'd only been driving for forty-five minutes, but aside from the coast, most of Montenegro was at least three thousand feet above sea level—a whole kingdom of untamed mountains with gentler, fertile plateaus and valleys dipping between them. I thought of Čiča Jovan as the road wound us up the mountainside, through the fir, spruce, and towering black pines that had given Montenegro its name, their gangly trunks bare of branch and needle until they burst into life high above the rest of the trees. When I'd told Jovan once that I'd like to see skyscraper buildings in person, he'd laughed his hoarse smoker's laugh and said, "Trust me, sweetheart, people in cities have no idea what truly scrapes the sky."

I could see now what he meant. Even as we gained altitude, the mountains loomed above us like monoliths, so thickly forested in places that they rolled with greenery as if furred with moss, in others stark and scraped down to the limestone beneath. Some of the exposed stone was creamy as a layered dessert, swirled with butterscotch and russet—I couldn't look at those too long without the striations beginning to waver, trembling in my vision as the gleam threatened to seize and multiply them into whorling fractals.

Lina would have hated it. Even with my general indifference to heights, I still couldn't glance past the low guardrail without my stomach pinching a little at the drop.

"How do you think the *hajduci* ever lived in these mountains?" I asked Luka. The *hajduci* had been outlaws in the seventeenth century, fighting the Ottoman Empire as guerrilla warriors. "Look at how steep it is out there."

"Ah, those were rugged highland folk," he drawled, lengthening our already slow vowels until I smiled despite myself, watching his knuckles shift beneath tanned skin as he rearranged his grip on the wheel. "Montenegrin manhood at its finest. Finer, even, than your chauffeur, if you can conceive of a thing like that."

"Forsooth, I cannot."

"I know, the mind boggles. Plus, they were busy hiding from the Ottomans and also chopping them up whenever the opportunity presented itself. So I assume that was pretty motivational. Lots of adrenaline."

As we wound up and up, I could see a linked series of glacier lakes in the distance, gleaming beneath the morning sun like pools of sky and gold. The more distant sets of mountains looked like they were rising from an ancient sea, bucking out of the water like the coils of some leviathan.

"It's magnificent, isn't it?" Luka said softly, taking his eyes off the road to glance at the lakes through my window. "Almost primordial."

"It does make all this a little easier to accept somehow, doesn't it? A world that looks like this, I mean. Speaking of which, how are you taking all this so well?" I'd told him about what Niko had found for us as he drove, Marzanna's story and its echo in our dreams. "Being friends with a pair of witches, whose mother happens to be not only undead but also kidnapped. Magic suddenly real. A white-haired woman running all over creation, stealing from us and from churches. I'd have thought the epic shifting of your paradigm would be triggering countrywide earthquakes."

"I don't really know, Riss. This does all seem too surreal, way too out of hand, but . . ." He trailed off. "I don't know exactly how to formulate this, and could you try to not be offended?"

"Oh, definitely I won't, since you started it that way."

He hissed out a sigh. "What I mean to say is, as completely bizarre as this all is—as far out of any normal, real-world depths that I can navigate—it doesn't feel nearly as strange as it should. And that's because of the three of you, I think."

I stiffened until my back felt like a staff against the pleather seat. "What do you mean by that?"

"Have you ever heard of the uncanny valley hypothesis?"

"Do you *think* I've heard of the uncanny valley hypothesis, Luka?"

"Nobody likes your attitude."

He licked the corner of his mouth with the tip of his tongue, the way he always did when he was focusing. Or nervous. Despite everything, the glisten of his tongue sent my belly into a shower of sparks, and for the first time, I felt faintly disgusted with myself. If I wouldn't even let Luka close enough to me for a proper dance, I could imagine how he would feel knowing what I'd been doing the night before with someone I'd known for all of four days. Not even the sex so much as the talking. And the telling and the showing, all the things behind the curtain that I never drew back for him.

"It's a hypothesis in human aesthetics," he went on. "A Japanese robotics professor, Masahiro Mori, coined it in 1970. It applies to things like robots and computer animation, and it means that when something looks and moves almost, but not quite, like an actual human being, it can make people uncomfortable. Disgusted, even. The closer you get to human without the thing actually being human, the more people find it revolting."

A prickling pressure built behind my eyes. "I think I know where you're going with this, Luka. And I don't think I'm going to like where you end up."

"Just bear with me. If you want to, you can slap me when I'm done. Or kick me in the face with your baby foot, whatever you need. But I think you should hear this."

"Fine," I said through clenched teeth. "Go for it, then."

"You and Malina, and your mother. None of you have ever had many friends, right? Just me and Niko, mostly, and Nev. Jasmina was close to Jovan, and spent a little time with my mother, but that's it, as far as I know. And I think . . ."

"Go on." My lips felt numb. "Tell me what you think. Too late to spare me now."

He drew a deep breath. He didn't want to tell me this, and that made it all the worse. "I think it's because the three of you look the way you do. You're so beautiful, Iris. All three of you so stunning that it's *stupid*, it makes people uncomfortable because it doesn't feel real, somehow. You give people chills." He stole an earnest glance at me. "But it's just an illusion. As soon as you talk—as soon as anyone gets to know you—the feeling shatters."

"But it's there. It's there to begin with, you're saying."

"Yes." His voice dipped much deeper than normal, like it always did when he was uncomfortable. "It is."

I huddled against the door as if I could somehow teleport through it and out into the ravine below. Because I knew exactly what he was talking about. It reminded me uncomfortably of what Čiča Jovan had said last night about our mother, the uncanny quality of her beauty and poise. Maybe she hadn't merely been trained to be beautiful. Maybe she'd somehow been born to be trained.

And if Lina and I were of her blood, maybe we were somehow the same.

"So, what, it's like *Blade Runner*? You think we're androids. Something that just wears human skin."

"Damn it, Iris, I think you're *gorgeous*." His voice was low and vehement. "I used to look at you every day, and even though I could practically graph a model of your face, I always want to look at it more because it's never exactly like I remember. It's always better. It's—"

I looked into the rearview mirror, at the sliver of my features visible in the glass. Sunlight slanted over me through the window, playing on the creamy skin I shared with Lina and our mother, smooth as a nectarine, poreless like a baby's. "I know you're only trying to help. But I don't really need to hear your compliments, or whatever you think they are, at this very moment."

"I wouldn't have told you if I didn't think it mattered." He reached over and slipped his hand behind the back of my neck. There was nowhere to go, so I tolerated it. "Please believe me, Iris. I think it has something to do with this Dunja, with Marzanna, with all this. And I'd rather tell you everything I know if it might help. Even if it hurts at first."

I dropped my chin into my chest, and we were both quiet for a while. He kept his arm draped over my seat, his hand buried in my hair.

"I'm still going to wallow for at least thirty-seven minutes," I finally said, tipping my head back so his palm cupped my nape. "Possibly thirty-eight."

I could see him smile from the corner of my eye. "I can live with that."

I TRIED TO nap after that, huddled uneasily against the door. I had no idea what might be waiting for us at Ostrog, but I had the queasy, churning sense that it was going to be worse than anything I could dream up. The feeling I'd had at Our Lady of the Rocks, the low-level revulsion, was beginning to seep into my skin again, as if I'd been coated with something itchy and loathsome, like mustard seed and lard. I hadn't even noticed it when we set out, but by the time we'd descended into the Zeta River Valley, the plain that cupped Podgorica, Montenegro's capital, and Nikšić, the next biggest town, I was about ready to shred off my own skin.

The sky had darkened, clotting with gray clouds; I hoped it wouldn't rain too hard for us to reach the mountain monastery. Luka drove us around Nikšić's rustic outskirts, through dirt roads that wound around brick houses with trellises, little orchards, and plots of cabbages, their heads round and ruffled like flower buds.

"How far are we?" I asked him, scratching at my tingling scalp.

"It's right up there," Luka said, pointing through the windshield. "See? We'll have to pass underneath the pipeline that carries gravel from the mountaintops down to the plain. And then go even farther up."

"Holy shit," I whispered, following his gaze. "That is—that is *very* high up. How did people used to get up there? It's practically vertical."

"There you go again, underestimating our forebears. They got up there the old-school way, with horses and donkeys and on foot, on paths carved into the side. There's still a series of steps cut into the cliff through the car road, for pilgrims who want to climb."

My stomach bottomed out as soon as we began to ascend onto the road that led up to Ostroška Greda, the sheer slab of rock into which the monastery had been carved. As we rose higher, the road's serpentine curves coiled back on each other ever tighter. Without speaking, Luka took my clammy hand and placed it over the gearshift. It shuddered beneath my palm, and he curled his hand around mine. We shifted from gear to gear, cutting the switchbacks together, and this small scrap of control calmed me until a measure of awe crept in. The lush valley seemed impossibly far below us, a deep, rich green like algae, scale models of forests bisected by farm fields, villages, and vineyards between them.

"We're almost there," he said. "This is the tightest portion of the road, but Saint Basil is the patron saint of travelers. They say no one's ever had an accident on the way here."

"Well, they would say that, wouldn't they," I said through gritted teeth. "I doubt any plummeting peasants ever made it onto his permanent record."

We finally reached the little cliffside plateau that held the monastery's two tiers, and Luka eased us into the empty parking lot outside the monastery gates. I nearly tripped over myself in my urge to scramble, weak-kneed, out of the car. "I think I need something to eat," I said tightly. That queasy, skin-crawling feeling kept sweeping over me, and I thought I might throw up if I didn't line my stomach with something.

"There's a shop that sells relics and food over in the Lower Church, on the first tier of the monastery," Luka said. "We can get something there before we go into the monastery proper."

The Lower Church's facade reminded me of a film set, as if the stone archways, cream-colored balcony, and three inlaid mosaic icons had simply been rested against the stone of the cliff behind it. Inside the shop, the shelves groaned with golden jars of honey, herbal creams and tonics blessed by the monastery, and rows of wine from the vineyards in the villages below.

I picked one of the busier honey jars, dense with dates, almonds, and apple slices, and we carried it up the steps that led to the monastery proper and its terrace. The prune-faced, kerchiefed woman at the shop had given us some plastic spoons, and Luka and I dipped into the honeyed fruit.

"It looks like something your mother would have made, doesn't it?" Luka said, swirling his spoon through the sticky mass. My heart went raw at the thought of her, and of Lina back in Cattaro, without me. "Although messier. A little lacking in presentation."

"I think it's perfect," I said. I propped my elbows on the stone wall and gazed over the lowland plain below, emerald beneath the leaden sky, a cool, piney breeze stirring my hair. Looking down over the valley seemed to settle me a little, soothe the feeling that my skin had flipped inside out, nerves dangling raw on the outside. "It tastes just like this valley looks."

"That's what they say about honey," Luka agreed. "Every kind is different depending on where and when it was harvested. Even a batch from the same hive can taste completely different two weeks later. People who really know honey can tell exactly where each batch is from, and when."

We looked up as a priest approached us, his black robes brushing the dusty stone. He was in his thirties, almost as tall as Luka and the peregrine kind of handsome so many Montenegrin men were, hawk-nosed and full-lipped beneath a neat beard. He was eyeing us sourly, and I could see his gaze flick to me and then purposely away, his Adam's apple bobbing beneath stubble. It reminded me of what Luka had said, and I wondered if I'd spent my entire life misinterpreting the way people looked at me.

"The reliquary is closed," he said finally, sighing. "No one should be allowed in there until we've properly resanctified it, but I hear the powers that be have decreed otherwise for you. Even still, I'm hesitant to let you pass. It isn't right, adding insult to injury that way."

"I'm not sure what you were told, Father," I tried, tugging at the hem of my shorts, wishing I'd worn something longer. The buzzing on my skin was growing so thick and uncomfortable I felt like I was covered in a swarming blanket of flies. "But our—my mother died, not three days ago. She was murdered, and the police don't know why or by whom. I'm just looking for some peace on her behalf, Father. Please."

He wavered for a moment longer. "All right, child," he finally conceded, his eyes sliding away from mine again. "For the sake of your mother's soul, then. I'll come in with you and administer the saint's blessing, but you may not approach the remains as we'd normally allow. You will stand in the doorway, both of you."

He turned and swept ahead of us, robes swishing.

The rock-hewn monastery was smaller and blockier than the Lower Church, square and snowy against the sheer cliff it had been carved into, its whitewashed surface scored with tiny slits for windows. It looked as though it had been partially swallowed by the rusty, yellow-streaked rock around it, as if the mountain had once been a ravenous stone Titan before it settled.

The priest led us past the main entrance, toward a terraced area that ended in a tiny black metal door emblazoned with a cross. "This is the cave-church of the Holy Cross," he said, fishing a heavy, bronze key out of his robe pocket. "Normally there would be many gathered here to receive blessing, but we've been turning pilgrims away since yesterday."

"What happened?" I asked. "If you can say."

"The remains were desecrated, child. Some devil-ridden blasphemer stole one of our saint's finger bones, if you can imagine something so grotesque."

My gorge rose, and I abruptly wished I hadn't had so much honey. Whatever was happening here wasn't just beyond the pale. It was sin, mealy and soiled.

My stomach still churned as I followed Luka into the cave-church, ducking my head under the door's low threshold. The father stood in the farthest corner of the little grotto, next to a massive cross of wood and gold. Biblical frescoes, richly pigmented like cave-paintings, covered the rocky walls and low ceiling, from which hung gilded censers. The reliquary that held the saint's bones was swaddled in burgundy velvet with a golden fringe of tassels, like some morbid bassinet.

As soon as I set foot inside the cave and took a breath of ancient stone and incense, the nausea and roaring wrongness swelled until I choked back a dry heave. My scalp tingled, my ears buzzing as though we'd stepped into an apiary. Instead of fear, a strange, blind rage began howling inside me—*like a gale of winter, like the roaring song of storms*—and I barged ahead, pushing past Luka until

I stood with my fingers wrapped around the wooden edge of the shrine. The priest's shrill voice echoed faintly, as though from somewhere far away, because he couldn't touch me here. This had nothing to do with him. This was between me and *it*, the aura that surrounded these dry and shrouded bones.

And it hated me. Just like I hated it.

How dare you hate me, a whisper curled inside of me like smoke. *How dare the remnants of you pitiful man, who groveled for a mewling child-god only to be reduced to withered tendon and dusty bone, lay judgment upon the likes of me? The ancient gods attend to me, you skeletal, marrowless heap. WHO ARE YOU TO SPURN ME AFTER EVERYTHING I'VE DONE?*

The grotto had fallen away from me entirely, and all I could see was Mara's face as it had been in the dream—her black hair whipping in the snowy wind, her teeth white as winter flurries in her smeared face as she shrieked through my own mouth. And I adored her just like I had before, waves of toxic love pounding over me, glistening like rainbows in puddles of black oil. This pile of human kindling in its cradle had no right to hate her. Feeling anything toward her was a privilege, and even hatred was too good for him.

By the time I came to myself, I realized I was standing with my fists clenched and my teeth bared so widely I could feel the ache up to my temples—I had said all of that aloud, snarled it at the reliquary in a lock-jawed hiss. I was still making a growling noise in the back of my throat, and the fug that surrounded the remains was so dense it felt like a malarial pool, like this place would seep into my blood and sicken me if I let it. The roots of my hair itched furiously, and I could nearly feel every separate length of ribbon that twined through the strands, as if the ribbons had come alive.

The next thing I knew, the priest had seized me by the shoulder, his fingers digging painfully into my bone, and hauled me out of the cave. I stumbled and nearly fell as he flung me out onto the terrace, his blue eyes ringed with white, his face pale with fury.

"*How dare you*," he spat. "How dare you use such words in the presence of our saint, you daughter of hell? What *are* you?"

Luka stepped between us, breaking the priest's hold. "Father, please, calm down," he urged. "Something's wrong with her, can't you see that? She's—she's having a spell of some kind."

"A witch's spell, maybe! Did you see her, son? Did you see her *hissing* at our holiness like a devil's cat? That girl is evil, son. Or there's something inside of her that is."

Luka glanced over his shoulder at me, and I could see the shock and fear on his own face before he turned back to the priest to appease him. "It's just the grief, Father. She's lost her mother, she's not in her right mind—"

I was crying by then, deep racking sobs that were more terror than grief. My arms wrapped around my chest, I stumbled against Luka's side. "I'm so sorry," I wept. "I don't know what that was, but I swear, I didn't mean to . . ."

"Keep away from me, demon!" The priest backed away from me, his face contorted, frantically crossing himself. "*Keep away from me!*"

I went blind with tears, the world blurring around me as Luka half dragged me away. But even through the haze, I could see the wrath warring with disgust on the priest's face as he stormed back into the monastery.

Like I was some foul thing, unnatural, everything Luka had said to me before along with everything I'd always felt inside.

NINETEEN

EVEN WITH THE RAIN THAT LASHED AT THE WINDOWS, I knew it was hot inside the Stari Mlini, but not even the shawl wrapped around my shoulders could keep me warm. Usually I loved it here, the exposed wooden beams, rough-hewn furniture, and bronze candelabras on every table, the water wheel spinning in the stream outside as the night rain sheeted down on it. And it smelled of warm things, curling cigarette smoke, beeswax, and grilling fish. But I couldn't stop trembling. My insides felt like slush, sliding around a skeleton of ice instead of bone.

Someone had set a bowl of bean stew in front of me at some point, recently enough that it still steamed. Plump sausages bobbed between the kidney beans, and I caught a savory waft of spices, enough to make my stomach growl. So I was hungry, then. That was good to know.

Malina sat across from me, her hands wrapped around her own bowl. I could see her fingers shaking, the torn edges of her cuticles. Niko was next to her, an arm slung around her shoulders. By my side, Luka gripped my own arm, massaging me briskly as if I actually needed a boost in circulation.

"It wasn't you, Riss," he said. I had the dim sense that he'd been saying this for a while. "That was *not* you. Those things you said . . . they didn't come from your mind. Not the mind I know."

"It was me. It was her, speaking through me, but it was me, too." That also sounded like something I'd said before. From the moment I'd stepped up to that reliquary, time had taken on an elastic quality that reminded me of how I'd felt after finding Mama broken. Every moment felt as long as an opium dream, but at the same time I barely remembered the ride back to Cattaro after Luka wrapped me up in the shawl and tucked me into the backseat. He'd kept me on his lap for a long time, his long body folded awkwardly in the small space so he could hold me, rocking me and crooning in my ear as I shook with tears against him. He'd asked Malina and Niko to meet us here on our way home, so neither his father nor Čiča Jovan would see me like this.

"How can this be happening?" I said through numb lips. "Who is she to us? Is she—is she even real? Because this is more than just dreams. This is some kind of open connection, a conduit. She was *in* me, I could *feel* her, and I wanted . . ." Aftershocks rippled through me, and I took a shuddering breath. "I wanted to rip apart that reliquary. Crush all those bones. Because they hate her, and she hates them for hating her, and even then I loved her so much I wanted to keep her safe."

Malina reached across the table and grasped my hand. "I felt it too. A shadow of it, at least, nothing as strong as you. Maybe it's because I wasn't there, but I'm still plugged in somehow, like you are. Do you think it's these?" She reached tentatively for her hair, stopping short before her fingers grazed the ribbons, as if they might singe her. "I don't think they have anything to do with Mama, anymore. I think someone else put these in for us. Maybe we should take them out, Riss? I hate it, I hate it so much thinking that something at the other end can *feel* us through them."

A violent shudder ripped through me at the thought of a stranger creeping over our windowsill, bending over us as we slept the way I'd imagined Mama had. "We can't do that," I murmured. "What if we do, and they don't work anymore? We need to know what they do, and what they have to do with the thefts. Maybe they can bring us to wherever Mama is."

"I was thinking about that," Niko said. Her dark eyes had taken on that hawk focus she shared with Luka. "It could be that these are two separate things—a bifurcation of what was once a single process or event. Ribbons aside, think of all the objects this Dunja has been taking. So far, it's your belongings, a votive gift, and a saint's bone."

"That we know of," Malina added.

"Right. Looking through Mama's recipes and cantrips today reminded me of why it was bothering me. For spellwork—at least the small kind Mama did, sympathetic magic—you need symbolic ingredients that have specific connections with whatever you're trying to achieve. Like parts to represent the whole. I have no idea what that would be in this case, obviously, but that's what this reminded me of. Someone gathering ingredients for a spell."

I met Niko's eyes with an effort. I was saggingly tired, exhausted to my marrow, but it wasn't time to stop yet. "But without talking to her, to Dunja, we have no idea what she's trying to do, or what it has to do with Mama and us. And we don't know how to find her. So that's a dead end. Did you find anything else while you were looking?"

"Just one thing," Niko replied. "It's one of Mama's original tincture recipes—it looks like Jasmina asked Mama to craft a scent for her."

"Why couldn't Jasmina have done that for herself?" I asked. "She used fragrances and essentials all the time in her cooking."

"But she didn't blend tinctures on her own, and Mama and I did," Niko said, sounding a little miffed. "It's not like it's a witch-exclusive skill, last I heard. The rest of us can muddle through making nice things, too."

"Fair enough, peace," I said wearily, holding up a hand. "What's in the one Koštana made for Jasmina?"

"Orange blossom absolute, lots of it," Niko said. Lina's eyes flicked to mine, and I knew she was thinking of the vial we'd found in Mama's treasure chessboard. "Also amber, myrrh, a touch of honey, and three different kinds of musk—pink, skin, and Egyptian."

Something about that list niggled at me, but I couldn't put my finger on it. "And that was it? Just the recipe?"

"There was the name of the perfume, too. Mama called it 'the Scent of Home.' And below it said, 'for Jasmina.' But that was it."

I huffed out a frustrated breath. "So it would have reminded Mama of home, somehow, but what are we supposed to do with that? Go to Egypt? The Middle East, maybe? And I don't even know where orange blossom absolute usually comes from."

Luka drummed his fingers on the tabletop. "We have a big enough data set here. Maybe we're just not looking at it from the right angle."

I dragged my spoon despondently through the beans, tracing swirls in the cooling, gluey mess. "Or maybe the problem is that our data set contains things like 'dreams' and 'possession' and 'memories stolen from Iris and Malina.' Not exactly the stuff deductions are made of."

"Maybe that's our missing variable," Luka said, hazel eyes sharpening. "That one memory. It's the only thing you have that none of the rest of us can see, Iris. And you said it seemed deliberate. Like that woman *let* you have it back. Why? Maybe there's something important in it, something you're not seeing."

"But I've already retold it four times," I groused. "What else could possibly be in there?"

"Just one more time, Missy," Luka coaxed. "The last days have been such a whirlwind for you. None of us are thinking clearly. Maybe play it out again, methodically, step by step. Remember the smell of the perfume, if you can. It'll trigger the memories like nothing else."

I let out a whoosh of air, working my jaw back and forth. My fingers worried at the band around my wrist. "I'm just so tired. But I'll try."

I closed my eyes and took a deep breath, trying to resurrect the layers of the perfume—and not just the blood orange, honeysuckle, and bergamot, but the smell of the Arms Square as it had been that day. I spoke it as I went; the dry warmth of sun on stone, suntan lotion from the tourists who swarmed blindly around us like schools of fish, foamy cappuccino from one of the cafés in the square. With every added layer, the memory expanded in scope and breadth, fleshing out as I spoke it aloud like a city being built in fast-forward. I focused especially on Naisha's exhibition, the animals chasing across her skin like a shadow play and the careful movements of her hands, the swishing of her hair, the briefly blinding glint as the sun caught the diamond piercing in her wrist—

"Riss!" Malina broke in breathlessly. "You didn't tell me about that!"

I squinted one eye open. "What, the piercing? It didn't seem that important, what with all the shape-shifting and such going on around it. And regular people have body piercings, sometimes."

"But Mama had one like that too!"

"What?" I frowned. "No, she didn't."

"She didn't *before*." Malina wrung her hands together. "But that morning when I found you both in the café, I saw it. It was just a sparkle under all the blood—I saw it because I felt something there when I went to take her pulse—and I forgot about it after. I only remember it at all because I'd only ever seen something like that on one other person."

My hands flattened on the rough wood of the table, fingertips sinking in. "Who?"

"Natalija. My violin teacher."

The room seemed to shift around me. "That's *it*. I couldn't place it, and she looked so different, but that's what it was. That's who Naisha sounded like. Natalija."

"SHE ISN'T ANSWERING."

"Try again."

"I've already called her six times, and texted," Malina said, leaning against the stone wall beside Natalija's music shop, the light from the lantern above spilling through her curls. "She's not going to answer. Either it's too late, or she doesn't want to talk to me."

The storefront was in one of the Old Town's narrowest alleys, hemmed in by apartments. Lines of laundry strung between buildings fluttered over our heads like spirits in the dark, bringing faint, clean whiffs of detergent. We were far enough away from the three main squares that we could barely hear the nighttime hubbub of tourists partying in the cafés and clubs, just distant, wispy snatches of music and laughter, like sounds drifting distorted across a pond.

"I bet she doesn't," I muttered, jiggling the doorknob. Locked. "If she's been here this whole time, it must have been to watch us. Like a spy. Like a sleeper agent."

"But she didn't look anything like that woman," Lina protested. "Like what you said. Natalija's a brunette, and at least forty. You've seen her yourself. Even if she'd dyed her hair, she wasn't exactly a beauty queen."

I thought of Natalija's plain, warm face; I hadn't seen her very often, and she never came to the café, but we'd run into each other enough times that I recognized her bright, crystalline voice, ice cubes clinking in sweet water. The voice was unmistakably Naisha's, and now that I thought about it, even those unremarkable features—wide-set, small brown eyes, squinted and muddy, and a lumpy nose—held a slight but compelling echo of the icy beauty I had seen. As if she'd purposely constructed the opposite of her own face, a photograph negative of herself.

"If she could mimic animals, change her own coloring and features, why couldn't she make herself look like someone else?" I asked. "We have no idea how this works. If she's related to us at all, if that's what this is, maybe her version of the gleam is still completely different from ours. Either way, we need to get in here, see what we can find."

Niko stepped between us. "I could help with that, if I may." She held a hand out to Lina, palm up. "Pie, can I have two of your pins?"

Lina worked her fingers through her curls, plucking out the hairpins that swept the front section away from her face. She handed them to Niko, who pried one open and bent it into an L.

"*Nikoleta!*" Luka hissed beside me. "Are you trying to get us all arrested? More to the point, do you think they're going to let you into law school with a record?"

Dropping to her knees, Niko slid the shorter end into the lock, fumbling it around. "There's no one around at this hour, and I'll be quick about it. Relax, brother. You just say that because you hate yourself and spit in the eye of our culture."

"Our *culture* does not have to include breaking and entering, that's some very convenient cherry-picking you're doing for a future lawyer. We could just wait until morning and—"

"Oh, be quiet, you self-loather. You're distracting me from my creative process." She squinched her eyes shut, tipping her head forward as she pressed her cheek against the door. "*Yes*," she crowed a moment later. "It's just a pin-and-tumbler lock. Give me the other one, Lina. I have to keep holding this one to apply torque to the cylinder."

Luka snorted through his nose. "Torque to the cylinder, dear God. I still can't believe Mama thought it would somehow be a good thing to teach you this."

Niko flipped her hair over one shoulder and tilted her face up to give him a stark look. Her dark eyes glittered in the dim light. "It's a good thing at this moment, isn't it? And she'd have taught you too, if you hadn't been exactly like this with her. Nothing but judgment, all the time."

Luka went quiet, hurt flitting across his face. Niko turned back to the lock, mumbling, "Sorry, beast. I didn't need to say that. This isn't the time."

Just then, the lock gave way with a neat click. Niko released a victorious hiss, all of us crowding behind her as she cracked the door open. We spilled together into the dark, quiet store. Racks of violins and guitars took up the lengthwise center of the room, and the walls were lined with shining woodwinds. In the dark, and with the lantern light washing in from the street, the instruments cast shadows like some grotesquely enchanted wood, everything too bulbous, elongated, or sprouting strings like curled, spiky ferns. Lina must have caught my unease—or maybe all four of us felt it—and the melody she began to hum wound around the room like the encroaching creep of vines, as if the instruments could crawl toward us on twisted roots. Stalk us until they drove us out.

Niko growled low in irritation, her bow mouth pursed. "Does anyone else feel like the cellos are plotting murder?"

"Oh, good," I said under my breath, stepping closer to Luka. My arm brushed against his, and I could feel the raised pattern of goose bumps on his skin. "Not just me, then."

"Definitely not just you," Niko confirmed through clenched teeth. "Pie, can you stop that? It's a little too on point for in here."

"Sorry," Lina said, cutting herself off. "I didn't mean to do that. It's the smell in here. It's slight, but definitely there. I think it's meant to disturb? It's never smelled like this during the day here, ever."

Now that she had mentioned it, I could catch it too: a low-level, pungent reek, metallic and astringent, that smelled nothing like Lina's rosin or the materials of the instruments themselves. It smelled vividly like death still too fresh for rotting, as if a slit-throated body might be sprawled behind the counter, eyes gelled and staring into nothing. My skin crawled at the idea, but now that it had come to me I couldn't shake it.

"Maybe it's like a protective spell," I mused. "An olfactory Do Not Enter. Better than a burglar alarm."

"If it is, it's effective as hell," Luka observed. "I can't wait to get out of here."

Niko snorted loudly.

"What?"

"Nothing, brother. You're just so manly, is all. I'm overwhelmed with awe."

"Don't make me smack you, brat. I'm not trying to die to prove my manhood to you."

Their banter dispelled the ominous miasma a little, but we all continued to cluster together, huddling for comfort. "So," I said, "if someone thought it was necessary to protect this place, we must be on the right track. Obviously, next step, we split up and explore."

Niko burst into her raspy, two-pack-a-day laughter. "Oh, good one. Or the alternative—we hold hands at all times and go everywhere together."

We poked around the store in a pack, touching one another like a kindergarten class clinging to a shared rope. The strobe of our phone flashlights revealed nothing other than the instruments and music tools on display. A jaw-clenching foray behind the counter turned up only the cash register, guitar picks and strings and pens, and drawers full of paper scraps: the same daily detritus of running a small business I'd seen at Mama's café and Jovan's small gallery.

"We could try Natalija's apartment?" Lina offered. "It's right above here. That's where I took my lessons with her."

"Yes," I said. "And if she's there, even better. She can't hide from us knocking on her door. Lina, do we have to go back outside, or can we get up there from here?"

"I've gone up from in here, I know the way."

Lina led us to the back door, which opened onto a low-ceilinged, winding stone stairway leading directly into Natalija's penthouse apartment. The door at the top was unlocked—she really didn't expect unwelcome visitors coming through her shop, and no wonder, if it smelled like a haunted horror show every night—and when Luka's series of sharp raps faded into silence, he eased the door open and led the way through.

Natalija's living room was as black and deserted as the shop below, dappled with yellow light from the street. It was spare and utilitarian, a few pieces of simple, modern furniture of wood and glass on bare parquet, but it smelled marvelous—a rich, complex fruit scent like an orchard that had caught a frost out of season, crisp apples and soft peaches with glittering, frozen skin, their leaves chips of fresh emerald suspended above them.

Behind me, I could hear Lina breathing deeply. "I forgot how nice it always smelled in here," she said. "She smelled just like this, too, even when I met her downstairs."

Luka flicked on the lights, and we all stood squinting blearily at each other for a moment.

"Why don't Lina and I take the kitchen," Niko suggested. "And you two can have the *bedroom*."

Lina smothered a giggle at that, biting her lip when Luka glared at her.

"Oh, that's hysterical, coming from you, Nikoleta," he muttered, turning on his heel and stalking toward the bedroom. "Riss, let's go take a look while the children play."

I trailed after him, nearly gasping as we stepped across the threshold. The bedroom was as opulent as the rest of the apartment had been sparse. A massive four-poster bed beckoned, with a sweeping canopy, looping sheets of white silk embroidered with fat golden roses that echoed the heavy duvet. A glass chessboard with figures hewn from crystal sat on one bedside table, and the vanity was white and gold, carved with a scene from the Garden of Eden—except that both Adam and Eve were biting the apple, entwined together beneath a tree like a weeping willow, drooping fronds of branches sheltering them. A trio of massive, intricately flowered courtesan's fans splayed over one of the walls. Paintings hung all over, too, night skies and glittering cityscapes, and blossoms drifting in shining pools of water. Little curiosities dangled everywhere from the ceiling, a suspended constellation made from sea glass here, a set of wooden oddments there that resolved into the skeleton of a rocking horse when you looked at it from just the right angle.

Luka whistled low. "I would never have guessed it, from all the times I've bought guitar strings and picks from her, that Natalija would live in a place like this. How much would all this have cost?"

"I don't think 'Natalija' would," I said, picking up an ivory-backed brush with blond hair wound around the bristles like silk thread on a spindle. "But another woman pretending to be her might."

"Riss." His tone had changed. "Come look at this."

I laid the brush down and joined him, sitting on the edge of the bed. He'd tugged open one of the bedside table drawers, and even from where I was sitting I could smell the rolling waves of that icy orchard scent, as if distilled to its essence. It didn't smell just like

226

frozen fruits, I realized as I breathed it in; the smell of it brought Naisha's face to vivid life in my mind, the foxy finesse of her small, sharp features. As if the perfume projected her like a picture onto the strung canvas of my mind.

Leaning over Luka's shoulder, I saw a spool of fine ribbons in the drawer, like the ones Malina and I had in our hair. Luka plunged his hand into them and offered them to me—I flinched back as soon as my fingers closed around them, feeling a jolt like a static shock as a flash of Mara's face imprinted in front of my eyes.

Hands shaking, I dropped the ribbons on the bed. Lina and Niko had crept in, kneeling at the bedside in front of us, and as the full force of the scent broke over her, I could see Lina's eyes turn so glassy they looked almost metallic. "They smell like Natalija," she said, brow furrowing. "But they somehow . . . look like someone else?"

"I know. I see it, too. Don't touch them!" I rushed as she reached for the ribbons. "They're very . . . aggressive."

Before I could stop her, Niko gathered them up, bringing them to her nose. I caught my breath and watched her closely, but there wasn't even a flicker of shock. She hadn't caught that glimpse of Mara that I had. "How strange," she said, eyes narrowing as she breathed them in, nose twitching like a bunny's. "They do smell like a woman. Not a lady-smell, I mean, but they actually make me think of a woman I don't think I've ever seen. A blonde, is that right? With eyes like the two of you?"

I nodded. "That's Naisha. The woman from the memory."

Luka was shaking his head with disbelief. "How could that be possible? Changing your appearance so completely. No, I know, I've seen what you two can do, but that seems . . ." He trailed off, spreading his hands in defeat, as if it was all too much for him to hold in two palms.

"I can't believe it," Lina said, her voice tremulous. "She was someone else, all this time. I talked to her while she taught me, Riss. I told her so much, about you and Mama and . . . about how hard it was, sometimes. It felt so good, being around her. Like doing the right thing. Who knows what all she learned from me?"

I squeezed her hand. "It's not your fault. How could you have known? And if she was family, somehow, maybe it *was* the right thing. Luka, is there anything else in there?"

He twisted, rummaging in the drawer. I could see his spine stiffen and he turned back to us, holding something that looked like a scroll. He offered it to me and I accepted it gingerly, breathing out a sigh of pleasure as the fabric slid like water over my palm. If it was vellum, it was softer than I had ever thought that would feel, like felt or deerskin as I carefully unrolled it, its fabric whispering over the embroidered duvet without a snag.

Unscrolled to its full length, it spanned across the bed. I could feel Lina's and Niko's breath fanning over my neck as I ran my finger up its length. Like an illuminated manuscript, the edges were filled with beautiful women in black and gray, rendered in the bare minimum of strokes it took to hold them. One had hair that cascaded to the floor, butterflies suspended in its length; another hung upside down, one ankle and one wrist wrapped in the hint of trailing bolts of silk. A third had leopard spots patterned on her skin, and a fourth sat cross-legged in the suggestion of a winter storm, some of the snowflakes as large around as her limbs.

They surrounded what looked like a family tree, but with first names only, and no years marked. And instead of spidering branches, the names ran down a single column, two in every generation. In each, one was crossed out with a glittering silver strike-through, and the other provided the snaking line leading down to the next two names. I saw Naisha's name about eight lines up; it sprang alive from the parchment, more embellished than any of the others. Maybe it meant ownership, a mark that this scroll belonged to her.

"Look," Malina whispered, her voice catching. "It's *us*."

It was—we were at the bottom, both of our names in black calligraphy that reminded me of Mama's fine handwriting, though this was even more stylized and sharply graceful, as if each name had been rendered in a single perfect stroke like a lovely fencing stab. The two names above us were *Faisali* and *Anais*. Anais was struck out with silver, and Faisali connected to the two of us. The last third of the scroll was blank.

"But that's not Jasmina's name," I said.

"And Natalija's face wasn't her face," Lina reminded me. "Maybe this used to be Mama's name?"

"Wait," Niko said. Her hoarse voice sounded scratchier than usual, almost warbling. "*Look*."

Lina and I followed her finger up the strange, laddered tree. At the very top was a single name, rendered with none of the flair. Because it needed none. Just its four stark letters were enough.

MARA, the scroll proclaimed at its apex. Hundreds of lines separated us from her, but the connection was direct—Iris and Malina at the bottom, Mara at the top. The blood flowed from her straight down to us, connecting us to her through ribbons of ink.

She was the first mother.

She was what we'd come from.

TWENTY

ČIČA JOVAN HAD ALREADY GONE TO BED BY THE TIME WE staggered in, Niko and Luka having walked us home. He'd be surprised in the morning to find us there, after having been told that we would be spending the night at the Damjanac house, but we'd wanted to be alone, together. And even talking to him in the light of day was difficult to imagine. Lina and I had stepped off the edge of the earth in the night, and the coming morning felt like a different world, some undiscovered continent. A modern age full of mundane things, like McDonald's, talk shows, and machines, that would either never come or had already passed us by.

As if we were the sole survivors of an apocalypse, even with the rest of the world spinning around us fast asleep.

We'd tucked the scroll into the farthest back of one of the knobbly drawers. It was too much for either of us to look at any longer. Then we'd talked in circles for an hour, facing each other with hands tangled.

"If she's alive—if Mara's alive," I began. "And we're related to her . . ."

"But how could she be, whoever—whatever—she is? Did you see all those names, Riss? If that's a family tree, that would make her, what, *thousands* of years old? That's impossible. There are no . . . no *witch-goddesses* that are just too interesting to die. No matter what the legend says."

"Well, there's clearly witches," I pointed out. "There's us, and Mama—who didn't die when she should have. There's Sorai and Naisha, possibly Dunja. And how do you even know the two of us are categorically mortal? We've never been sick, not in any real way. We haven't tried to die so far, so we can't know what would happen if we did."

"Let's not make an experiment out of it yet, maybe?"

"Agree. Early yet."

"It's just—" She pinched the bridge of her nose. "It's *crazy* to think it."

"You've felt her, too, though," I argued. "We both saw her in the dream, and we've been feeling her through the ribbons somehow. She's alive. Or at least a piece of her is. Otherwise, what's happening to us?"

"So let's say she *is* alive. How are we going to find her?"

And if we do, neither of us said, *does she have our mother? And could she give her back to us?*

We stalled out there every time, islanded in a sea of questions.

If Mara existed, how, and where to find her? Maybe Natalija—Naisha—knew, but she had disappeared—why? And Sorai too might know, but why hadn't she come back for us after that single glimpse of herself she'd let me have? Why had she given me back that stolen memory, like a note pressed into my palm, and then melted back into nowhere instead of approaching us?

Finally I flung the light covers off me, my limbs so heavy with fatigue that they almost felt light, like a magician's trick.

"Lina, I have to go," I said, pacing the length of the room. "I have to walk. There's something, I almost have it, it's that perfume Koštana made for Mama. My mind keeps snagging on it, and I don't know why. I'll think better if I'm walking."

She rubbed her knuckles into her eyes, like a little girl. "Then I'll come with you."

"You're tired. And you don't think better on your feet like I do."

"You're tired, too. And I don't want to be alone. Please?" She peered up at me, fists still balled against her cheekbones. "Let me come? Or stay with me?"

"I can't." She closed her eyes so slowly, like shutters lowering, and I steeled myself against the pain of abandoning her like this, of how selfish I was being. "I'll be back soon, I promise. Just try to sleep."

"I know why you're really going, Riss. I can *feel* it." She shifted, covers and mattress rustling like husks beneath her, until her back was turned to me. I nearly winced at the venom in her voice, so unusual from her. "I wish you'd at least try not to lie to me, you know?"

I stood in the darkness for a moment, shifting from foot to foot, listening to her ragged breathing and trying to think of a single thing to say that wouldn't be a lie. When I couldn't, I climbed out the window before I could say anything worse.

Outside, I leaned against the side of the house, stones still warm from the day breathing their heat into my back. My phone screen glowed overbright, like an artifact from the future that had no place in my hands.

Are you awake? I typed, my fingers trembling. I'd seen him just the night before, and I couldn't understand why I felt this way, so desperate and fretful. Like I would sooner collapse from his absence than beneath the weight of everything I'd learned tonight.

The response chimed in seconds, only three snaps of my wristband in. *Of course.*

I snorted a laugh, a wave of relief washing over me. He was there. I would see him soon. *Why? It's so late.*

Waiting for a rare specimen of the Night-Blooming Iris. I'm told the color and the scent are second to none.

My cheeks rushed with blood. *That was cheesier than expected. Not saying I don't like it, exactly. Just an observation.*

I'd like to see you say that to my face, flower girl.

What's my prize if I do?

Anything you like. More of a promise than a prize, really.

I leaned my head back against the stones and took a long, open-mouthed breath. *The beach again, then. I'll see you soon.*

HE'D BROUGHT ME flowers and fairy lights. The flowers were clipped, stemless and strewn all across a fluffy red blanket, with battery-powered LED strings spooled around and through them. There were candles, too, along a broader perimeter, little tea lights that marked out the edges of our territory. An oasis on the dark beach.

I smiled at him as I eased myself cross-legged onto an edge of the blanket, the petals spotlighted in the glimmering, holiday light between us. I rubbed one between my fingers, silk on the topside, fuzzy velvet underneath. He smiled back, so wide and white, his face breathtaking with its Valhalla angles lit up from beneath. He was shirtless already, an amber pendant dangling from a leather cord around his neck, a tiny fossil suspended in it. I couldn't quite tell what it was. A centipede caught midwriggle, maybe, something sectioned with too many legs.

"Did I miss something?" I said. "Is it our two-day anniversary, and me without a gift for you?"

"That's five-day counting from when we met, and not to worry, we aren't official," he assured me, running his hand through his hair. It was already down, the spiraling silver earrings glinting from amid the blond, and I wanted to reach over and bury my hands in it with an almost feral desire, as if touch had become a need like breathing. "Though I did bring you something special to mark this nonoccasion."

He twisted behind him—the muscles in his abdomen leaped at the swivel in the most interesting way—and turned back to me with his hand held out, a cupcake glistening with dark berries sitting incongruously small and dainty on his large palm.

"It's a skyr cake, with blueberries," he said at my bemused look, and for the first time he looked a shade uncertain. "A very small one, obviously. Usually they're full-size, proper cakes. I thought you might like it; it doesn't taste like anything you have here. We were speaking of flavors the other night, and your mother's desserts . . . my mother always prepared this for my birthday. It tastes like home to me, more than anything else. The happiest of my home. So I thought I would make some for you, whisk you there with me for a moment."

"I . . ." I swiped my hand across my eyes. At least it was too late to make a mess of any lingering eyeliner. The slim silver lining of these long days. "Thank you."

The cake was little even in my hand; I peeled back the wrapper and took half of it in one bite. The blueberries burst across my tongue first, a bright dominance of flavor, crushed tart and sweet between my teeth. The cake's base was crumbled butter biscuits and the frosting cold and densely creamy, something like cheesecake but much lighter, more air and less tang, with a startling, earthy hint of resin. Fjolar was watching me so intently he must have seen the moment I tasted it, that surprising, ghostly scrape of bark against my palate.

"*Birkir*," he said. "Birch liquor. Unusual flavor, isn't it? And the skyr is like your yogurt, but without quite so much zest."

I took the second bite and chewed it slowly, rolling the cream across my tongue, savoring the grit and butter of the crust. As soon as I swallowed the last of it, I set the paper aside and nearly vaulted myself across the blanket, settling onto his lap with my legs wound around his hips. "Thank you," I said again, against his mouth.

"That was so kind. No one's ever—"

Liar liar liar, a small, outraged part of me sneered. *You know someone has. Think of all the flowers he gave you, for no reason at all. Think of all the quiet and strength, all those years of holding your hand and expecting nothing back.*

"—done something so thoughtful for me," I finished, nose to nose with Fjolar.

He exhaled once into my mouth, then buried his hands in my hair and kissed me, hard and deep. As soon as his tongue swept wet against mine I could feel everything inside me clench and rise up toward him, wanting deeper, wanting more. But he pulled back as soon as I leaned into him, brushing his lips lightly over my cheek and the lobe of my ear.

"Will you show me?" he whispered, his breath setting every minute hair inside my ear to tingling, like tiny lightning rods. "I'd like to see these flowers bloom, Iris. To see them burn as wild and beautiful as you."

My heart beat frantically against his chest. I wanted to do it so badly, to call the flowers' fractals for him, but I was so *tired.* Even abuzz as my body was, electrified from all his nearness, I didn't think my muscles had it in me to power that bright surge.

"Fjolar . . . ," I said hesitantly. "I'm not sure I can. . . . It's been such a long day, I haven't even told you all of it. . . ."

"Would you like to try? I'll be here to help you, make you stronger."

I considered it. Why not? Why not make something gorgeous out of this hideous day, show him what beauty I could muster?

I nodded, and he lifted me like I weighed nothing, like my bones were a hollow bird's and not my own, then shifted me around so that I sat in his lap with my back against his chest. With one hand he swept all my hair over my right shoulder and sank his open mouth onto the tender space at the base of my neck. I arched against him like a strung bow, feeling all surging quicksilver on the inside, his lips and tongue the sweetest, tickling pleasure against my skin.

"Will you bloom them for me?" he whispered.

I could barely breathe, and I so desperately didn't want him to stop. "Yes," I said faintly. "Just let me . . . I just need a minute."

I focused on the cluster closest to me, a pile of black-eyed Susans and pale crocuses, their colors both muted and strange in the LED light. My eyes nearly crossed with the effort as the flowers multiplied, murky yellow petals and muddy blues racing around each other, like spirals of falling dominoes tipping each other over. Fjolar chuckled into my ear, nipping at the lobe.

"Very nice, flower girl, so nice. Could we see a true spectacle, do you think? All of them together, rising toward the infinite."

He gripped my upper arms until I gasped, and it would have been almost painful if he hadn't run his lips down the line of my neck. I could feel the heat spread between my legs and flare into a pulsing throb, and even with my vision blurred I pulled at the flowers as hard as I could.

I would do it. For him, I would do it.

They burst into the spectacle he'd wanted, a fractal of component fractals like a massive, turning clockwork flower. It rotated like some steampunk dream, as if my glass sculptures had been used to build a gorgeous and infernal machine powered by petals. Gears of gum cistus, white with crimson-and-orange insides, notched into spears of violet larkspur, while silk vine and rose bay roped between and through them. Leaves, stems, and ferny frills spiderwebbed throughout in precise patterns, like an overlay of a stained-glass mosaic. And the fairy lights shed a luminous corona around it all—halo within halo of strung beads of light, shaping the fractal into a glowing orb.

I dimly wondered if somewhere nearby, a thoroughly mind-blown individual thought they were seeing a UFO hovering over the beach.

"Oh," Fjolar breathed into my ear. "Oh, *Iris.*"

I sagged against him, my heart beating sluggishly, as if it were pumping bog water instead of blood. I was so tired my muscles fired twitches at random, and *still* I wanted him, the contours of his chest in sharp relief against my back. He feathered his fingers down my arms and gently flipped us so that I lay on my back, my hair fanned out as he hovered above me, propped up on his forearms. The ends of his hair tickled on my face, got in my mouth, made me want to sneeze. But I didn't dare move for fear he would.

Exhausted as I was, I felt so lit by the way he looked at me, lips parted in awe, eyes heavy-lidded with desire. The flowers and loops of lights beneath me dug painfully into my spine, but they also reflected in his irises. Almost by instinct, I tugged at that too.

I'd never fractaled eyes before, had never thought to. Even as my own eyelids grew swollen-heavy, dragging toward sleep, his irises filled the space between us like a single compound eye. Silver and gray striations flickered above electric-blue orbs, like captive lightning bolts, and even his pale eyelashes were fringed throughout like transparent lace, around white sclera threaded faintly through with red.

It was stunning. It was also improbably grotesque, the ugliest thing I'd ever made.

"Look at that!" he whispered, delighted as a child. "*My* eyes! Look what you made for me, you wondrous thing."

"Thank you, I . . ." My mouth was so dry. It was hard to talk. "I'm glad you like it."

"I don't like it," he said, low, eyes narrowing. "I fucking love it, flower girl."

He began kissing me then, like hot summer rain, a shower down my neck and chest.

I tried to raise my head, only to find my neck wouldn't hold it before it thumped back down. "Fjolar, I think I need—I need to sleep."

He hummed a disapproving sound against my skin. "But it's still early. Play a little more, hmm?"

Biting my lip, I stared up at the sky, which was already bleeding into dawn. His mouth was searing on my stomach; I could hear and feel his quickened breath, and I strained up toward it despite myself as he traced his lips around each hip bone. The faintest *stop stop stop* echoed in my mind before I gave up, and I fell asleep with him still kissing me lightly, that hollow echo plaintive, like a stranded girl calling from a distant mountaintop.

⚜

I DREAMED OF honey.

There was a meadow first, alive with rippling waves of grass, a green sea bobbing with a regatta of wildflowers. Bees flitted between them, too fat, gold, and friendly for waking life; I could see the tiny dangle of their legs spotted with bright yellow pollen. Pines circled the clearing like guardian soldiers, tall and so densely needled they were nearly black, and behind them in the distance there were craggy mountains everywhere, sere and snowcapped and rolling with these same proud pines.

It felt like a place I knew. And it smelled like the place I was born. Sunlit air and a cool breeze that still held a breath of the mountaintop snow it had swept over, the invisible ice crystals it had stolen in its wake. Sharp grass and wildflowers, too, and piercing evergreen.

Somehow I watched it all from the Ostrog monastery ledge with Luka, a spoonful of honeyed apples sticky in my mouth.

Even a batch from the same hive can taste completely different two weeks later. People who really know honey can tell exactly where each batch is from, and when.

And then instead of honey, the skyr cake was back on my tongue, milk cultures and crushed biscuits melting.

It tastes like home to me, more than anything else. The happiest of my home.

Taste and smell together, like a time machine.

I burst awake like a surfacing diver, gasping. Lina's face was directly above mine, gorgeous with pallor in the unearthly bright early-morning light, her eyes nearly silver above plum shadows. Her cold hands were wrapped around my face.

"Are you okay?" she whispered fiercely. "I knew you'd have come back here to see him. Did he do something to you? I'll *kill* him if he did, I'll—"

"No," I mumbled, trying to pry my tongue loose from the roof of my mouth. I was thirsty and starving and nauseous, all at once. I ran my shaking hands over my body, searching, a far-off panic beating inside me like a distant drum. But everything was where it should be, my shorts and tank top snugly on, bra straps digging comfortingly into my skin. In the simplest physical sense, my body felt undisturbed. "I don't think so. I'm fine."

But even if he hadn't touched me after I passed out, I was nowhere near fine. I'd seen Mama debone a whole duck once, and that was how I felt. Like a limp sack of muscles, a tangle of flaccid veins and tendons with no chassis to support them. Sitting up made me groan with pain, even with Lina's arm behind my back.

"Where're Luka and Niko?" I forced out.

"You were still gone when I woke up, and I didn't want to wait for them." Her nostrils flared with fury, exactly like Mama's in high temper. "What's wrong, Riss? What did that bastard do to you?"

"He didn't do anything, really, it wasn't his fault. . . ."

But he'd known I was tired; I'd told him over and over. And even then he'd wanted me to show him, to bloom fractals for him until I drained myself into exhaustion.

I felt on the cusp of a very great rage, but I was still too tired to take the step. And there was something else we had to do, besides.

I met Lina's furious eyes, so grateful for her. She could do it for me while I rallied. She could cup my fury in her hands and blow on the embers when they guttered. "No, you're right. He *did* do something to me. But that's not the important thing right now, not the most important, anyway. I know what it *means*, Lina. I know why Mama's perfume was called the Scent of Home. There was honey in it; we have to find out exactly where it came from."

TWENTY-ONE

THE BUS JUDDERED BENEATH US, STRAINING ALONG THE narrow mountain roads. I sat next to the window so Lina wouldn't have to look at the plunging depths beyond the mountainside, but both of us were too exhausted to care much either way. She held my hand in her lap, cradled in both of hers; my head was tucked into her neck. The pilled seats were so saggy I kept feeling like I was going to collapse right through mine, like falling down a rabbit hole, and the air was stale and warm from the feeble AC.

Even worse, that quivery, unstable feeling of emptiness refused to recede, as if Fjolar had sucked the marrow from my bones. I'd gone limp as a jellyfish washed out onto a beach. Even deadened with fatigue, it scared me badly how empty I felt.

Still, I passed out almost as soon as we'd boarded and settled in, right after wolfing down two smoked-ham and cheese sandwiches that Lina pressed on me, washed down with a liter bottle of orange Fanta. I dreamed about him in jolts and flashes as I drowsed on Lina's shoulder. Every time I woke up enough to be aware of her, I could hear her grinding her teeth in silent fury, jaw clicking.

"You were right about him," I whispered up to her, and even defenseless as I was, the words stuck like burrs in my mouth. "I shouldn't have—"

"It's not your fault, Riss."

"But you warned me—"

"It doesn't matter. I can hear you hurting and tired, and still I can't even tell what happened. So whatever it is, you couldn't have been ready for it, okay? Whatever it is, it was *his* fault."

I grasped her hand tight, hoping she could hear my unspoken thanks.

As I slipped in and out of sleep, my temple tilted against the window after Lina curled up away from me, my mind batted vaguely at the happenings of the morning. Niko had checked her mother's book for us and confirmed that the honey in Mama's perfume had been very specific—a batch harvested in Žabljak, in early spring. Žabljak was the highest-altitude town in all the Balkans, perched on the imposing Durmitor range; Lina and I had both known that much from school.

It was far from the kind of cliffside-clinging village I'd always imagined from Mama's story. But it felt, at least, like another version of the truth. As if everything she'd ever told us had been like a matryoshka nesting doll, and we had to crack open shell after shell to find the kernel of pure truth at the heart.

Luka and Niko had raged in every way they could think of, but Lina and I had found our way back to each other and clasped tight. No amount of their battering against our seamless united front would budge us. We'd left Niko in raging tears, pounding her tiny clenched fist against the Prince's bar top.

"Why won't you let us come?" Luka had asked me after she turned away from us to pour herself a shot of tequila, slamming both glass and bottle with abandon, refusing to talk or to accept a good-bye hug. "Or just me. You have no idea what you're getting yourself into. You'll *need* help."

"And that's exactly why we have to do it alone," I'd whispered back. It hurt so much to meet his eyes and see what I was doing to him, but I refused to spare myself by looking away. "We have no idea what we're going to find and I—I can't risk you like that. Or Niko. Whatever's in those mountains, I can't let it have you. You would do the same, if it were you and Niko instead of us, all tangled up in something this terrifying and invisible. You'd *never* let us come with you. You know it."

He kept his teeth clamped tight against everything he wanted to fling at me, his fists clenched on the bar top. "Okay, then," he said finally. "Fine. But is there anything I can do for you? I need—just something to do, Iris. Anything."

"Could you tell Jovan that we had to go, please? If we say good-bye, he'll never let us go, he'll have the police hold us if he has to. Maybe if you could tell him that we found something to do with Jasmina, with the people who made her—he'll know what that means—and that we had to follow it all the way to the end. Maybe it'll give him some comfort."

"Of course it won't. But I'll do it, and we'll see him through this. I promise."

He nodded one last time, then caught me in a fierce hug. I could feel the hammering of his heart against my cheek. It would take me a long while to forget the carefully curated devastation in his eyes, especially because of how completely I deserved it. I'd let him down and broken his trust in every form, and now I wouldn't even let him do the only thing he'd ever wanted—just to help me.

Still, whatever was waiting for us in the mountains had to be cordoned off from everyone we loved, no matter how much those left behind us hurt.

ABOUT AN HOUR and a half in, it was the ribbons that woke me fully.

I peeled my face from the glass, squinting into the glare. My cheek was both numb and hot, and I'd left a charming snail-smear of drool on the window. Beyond it, the day was crystalline, a pennant of clear sky above even greener mountains on either side of us.

We'd worried about what we'd even do once we got to Žabljak, but as we looped around the hairpin turns that seemed impossibly narrow for the unwieldy lumber of the bus, I could feel the ribbons surging against my scalp, glowing with a sweet, lovely warmth nothing like the spitting-cobra tingle I'd felt at the churches.

It must have been a slow burn, like the gradual turning of a dial, because neither of us could tell when it had begun. But now it felt purely wonderful, like the pull of home after such a long, long time away. Like the idea of crawling into your own bed after the hardest day.

We didn't talk about it. Lina could hear that I felt what she felt, a madcap thrill strong enough to revive me from my stupor. As the bus groaned into its Žabljak stop, we were the first to pile out and rush into the station. A leathery woman with windburned cheeks and wiry hair signed a yellow Fiat into our custody without even bothering to check my license, though her eyes narrowed as she scanned our faces.

Outside, a single shared glance confirmed that Lina would drive. I'd gotten the most practice with Luka, but there was no way I could have managed it, not with my limbs still feeling like kindling. As she pulled carefully out of the lot, easing back into the motions of driving stick, it didn't seem to matter that all we had was a tourist guidebook and map the woman at the station had given us. The ribbons didn't just warm and soothe; they tugged in a gentle, possessive way, like fingers wound lovingly into our hair, massaging away the qualms. Straining like a compass needle. We were going *home*. And maybe there, we'd finally find our mother again—or at least understand enough about what had happened to her to learn how to let her go.

We drove past the Žabljak township, bare of people in its off season. We passed empty streets lined with domed streetlamps, wooden chalets with long, slanted eaves that shed snow during the heavy winters, and ski hotels shaped like wedges for the same reason. For a while, a sheepdog puppy trailed the car, barking like a beast, his coat shaggy and his eyes a startling, milky blue. We reached a glacier lake ringed with soaring pines—Zmijsko Jezero, I found on the map, the Lake of Serpents—and still we climbed higher into the dense, evergreen woods.

"This is the way, isn't it?" I asked her. "You feel it, too?"

"Oh, yes." She jiggled her shoulders with pleasure. "It's definitely the way."

Checking the guidebook, I pointed out the mountain summits silhouetted above us as we drove deeper and higher into the forest. The humped outline of Veliki Medjed, named "Big Bear" for its bear-snout shape, roared into the sky next to the crisp, near-perfect triangle of Savin Kuk.

When the forest finally widened into a clearing that held a dark, massive chalet the size of a hotel, the ribbons pealed like soundless bells, all homecoming and jubilance. As Lina pulled us into the gravel driveway, neither of us had any doubt that we'd arrived.

We stepped out into the clearing together, the chalet looming in front of us, hewn from deep mahogany logs. It was at least five stories tall, its eaves nearly brushing the ground, wide glass windows opening into what looked like a ballroom. The clearing itself looked like something out of a fairy tale, the kind that Malina and I had read to each other once Mama could no longer be bothered. Clouds of midges whirled like snowflakes in the golden shafts of afternoon sunlight, and silken spiderwebs glinted, strung between the pines. Some even floated through the air in glimmering strands, untethered, clipped from their moorings by the briskness of the breeze.

"It's so pretty here," Malina murmured, echoing my thoughts.

I was still nodding when the giant door swung open on silent hinges. A woman stepped out, and for a moment the world shifted sideways.

In the slanting light, and still shadowed by the inside of the chalet, she looked exactly like our mother.

The illusion shattered as soon as she came forth to meet us, each step delicate and deliberate, like a cat walking along a sill. A jade tulip dress parted above long, bronzed legs, and a simple silver lariat looped around her slender throat. My mind flashed back to the photo of Anais, the smiling girl with the valley behind her. Something about this woman called her up. The bright, curling fall of her sorrel hair, threaded with ribbons like our own, was darker than that fiery copper but close enough, though her jawline was much squarer than the girl's had been, more like Mama's.

"Faisali's girls," she murmured, her frost-pane eyes welling. Her full lips pressed into a smile so much like Mama's that my eyes filled instantly, too, like a reflex. "*Finally*. It's so good to meet you, after all these years."

"Who are you?" Malina asked, her voice trembling.

"I'm Shimora, dear heart. Your grandmother."

Before we knew it she'd drawn us against her, sinewy arms wrapped around us both. She was surprisingly warm and solid, all muscle beneath that silken, amber skin, and her perfume lapped over me like a fragrant tide, like how the air must have smelled in the Garden of Eden. Pomegranate, cinnamon, fig, and calla lily, and something else too sweet and unusual for me to know its name, yet familiar all the same.

"But how is that possible?" I whispered into her neck, struggling to understand how I could believe her so readily when nothing made sense. "You—you're *dead*. You died before we were born. Mama said that our grandfather killed you and her sister, that you died trying to protect our aunt. And even if she lied about that, look at you. You're *young*. You're Mama's age, if that."

Sadness flickered prettily across her face. "Is that what she told you? My poor Fai. She was hurting badly when she left us, and I suppose the truth wouldn't have done, not when she was trying so terribly hard to protect you from it all."

"Protect us from *what*? And do you have her? Do you have our mother?"

She sighed deeply and stepped back, trailing her long fingers down our arms until she held our hands in a warm, smooth grip. From this close, she was somehow even more flawless. A faint spray of freckles speckled the tanned bridge of her falcon's nose, and even that seemed deliberate, a subtle, natural enhancement rather than a flaw. She wore the lightest makeup, flicks of mascara to bring out the ice glint of her eyes, high sweeps of blush on her cheekbones, and a peachy, near-transparent lip gloss. Her hair fell in sculpted curls, loose ringlets that gleamed as if each had been carved from cherrywood, like the mermaids on ships' prows.

From that simple dress to the long muscles in her bare arms, and even down to the nude-painted toes, everything about her was so precisely, near-painfully right. An elegance so sleek and Spartan it felt like the privilege of looking at her must have a price.

That thought drove a tiny pinprick of recognition through the blanketing warmth of her presence and her scent—it reminded me of what Luka had said about me and Malina. That we were *too* beautiful, near unnerving to the eye.

But the slight sense of quailing vanished immediately as she moved back toward the chalet, drawing us with her, stepping deeper into the perfume.

"We'll tell you everything as soon as you're properly back with us," she said, her gaze shifting warmly between us. "Everything you want to know, and everything you need. But you'll let us welcome you first, yes? We've missed you for so many years—and you've missed us even if you didn't know it."

"Who is 'us,' exactly?" Malina asked. "We don't have anyone to miss."

Shimora hummed mournfully, deep in her throat. "Your whole family, of course, dear heart. Will you come inside with me, meet some of your kin?"

I nodded immediately, without thinking. Beside me, Malina took a beat longer before she bit her lip and nodded too. Together, we let Shimora lead us across the threshold.

TWENTY-TWO

FROM THE INSIDE, THE CHALET'S GROUND FLOOR WAS even grander, vast and wide as a ballroom. The four stories above us formed an atrium, ringing a glass-and-steel chandelier strung from the highest eaves, each piece dangling down to a different level—hollow spheres and onion bulbs like Christmas ornaments, and long cylinders scored with patterns, like the metal rolls of sheet music I'd seen inside self-playing pianos. A row of silken white bolts trailed down from the ceiling as well, ends pooled on the floor behind a round dais made of gleaming black marble, forked with veins of amethyst.

All those fascinating patterns, a lattice of glass, metal, and fabric, swam in and out of focus as soon as I looked up, straining brutally to fracture into a mosaic of itself. The gleam bucked inside me as if I'd swallowed a living thing, and I doubled over, eyes squinched shut.

"What's *happening* to me?" I managed, before clamping my lips shut. Words were going to lead directly to vomit, that much was for sure.

I heard Malina's squeak of alarm even as Shimora laid a light hand on the back of my head, rubbing gently until the spasm loosened and the bile stopped lapping at my throat.

"Easy, dear heart," she soothed. "It's that you're back where you belong, is all. The gleam in your blood feels mine, feels *all* of us."

Faintly, I remembered Mama telling us of home. *That's what it's like, when women in our family eat the moon,* she had said. *We're bound to each other, braided together. And when we catch fire, we burn as one.*

"It merely wants you to let it loose," Shimora continued. "And you will, but for now, just breathe. I'll help a little, too."

"Help how?" I gasped.

"I ply scents, the way your mother plies flavor. You've smelled it already, the perfume of my welcome to you both. Scent can mean so many things—it can make one feel, or even see, such a great deal."

As if she could sense my nausea and mental churn, her distinctive perfume shifted by a single note, fresh and cool as a zephyr, and I relaxed before I even fully registered the change.

So that part of Mama's story had been another pyrite fleck of truth, then, I thought as I leaned on my thighs, sipping air through parted lips. Our grandmother *did* make perfumes that swayed the mind, though I wondered if she even needed the physical trappings of essentials and absolutes.

Or if she herself was somehow enough.

"There, that's better, isn't it?" she cooed. "It'll be better still the more you breathe. It's not just me you'll smell in here. It's all of us, the scent of how content we are together. And of how much love there is between us."

I took a few questing breaths. The air did smell powerfully of that unnameable sweetness that suffused Shimora's scent, so rich it must have leached into the building's planks. It still smelled somehow familiar, and I found myself breathing as deeply as I could, until I felt not only recovered but giddy and light-headed from the sweetness of the sting.

Beside me, Malina grinned as soon as I straightened, her lips pink and bright against her teeth, her silvery eyes glazed like glass.

"It does smell *so good* in here, doesn't it?" she said breathlessly. "It's . . . wow. It smells like when I first realized . . ."

"When you first realized what?"

She gave herself a little shake. "Nothing. I—nothing."

I gave her a slantwise frown, but before I had a chance to pry into what she had meant, Shimora trailed her hand over the hobnailed back of a velveteen black-cherry love seat close to the marbled podium.

"Will you come sit, Iris, Malina?" She wrinkled her fine nose a bit. "We'll have proper names for you soon, but we thought the naming and the scenting could wait until after. You have your ribbons already, after all, and that's most important. Faisali saw to that, at least."

"Naming?" I echoed dumbly as Lina and I settled back into the plush contours; there were even two ottomans for us each to rest our feet. "We already have names, too."

"Yes, ones Faisali chose for you, as she chose Jasmina for her common name. But they aren't coven names; they don't capture you as they should."

Coven. The word felt strange in a way "witch" never had when Mama said it. Eating the moon hadn't felt like a coven to me, nothing so formal. It had felt like family, my mother and sister holding my hands while we wove wonder through beauty, on a shared loom beneath summer nights.

Coven was something else altogether. And even with the smell of joyous homecoming filling me to bursting with every breath, the bone-deep sense of hearth and home that I somehow recognized even if I'd never seen this place before, I wasn't sure I liked what it might mean.

"What does that mean, coven?" I asked cautiously. "How is it different from—"

Shimora had moved fluidly to stand behind us, winding her fingers through our hair in a way that sent tingles rushing down my spine. "Let us perform for you, first. All these years without full gleam . . . I can't imagine how you made do without it, or without us. How that loss must have ached at your core, even if you couldn't fathom its origin. I understand why Faisali chose that way, but I swear I don't know how she could have borne it in the end, being so alone."

She bent forward between us, propped on her forearms, her

curls creeping over my shoulder like ivy. Her breath smelled like mint and strawberries when she whispered, "Watch your kin now, if you will. See what you were born to be."

I only had a moment to exchange a seeking glance with Malina before a raw swell of music washed over us, crystalline violins over a thrilling heart-stir of a beat. It was gorgeous and freezing and uncanny, the aural equivalent of a rave inside a palace of ice.

Then the atrium above us shattered into a moving swarm of light.

The clusters of hollow spheres and onion bulbs that dangled from the eaves filled in a moment, some with little sprigs of suspended flowers, others with glimmering insects: dragonflies with whirring wings, fireflies, butterflies with elaborate tigereye designs. Some of the spheres simply held light, amber nuggets that shed a glow without any visible filament. I dug my nails into my palms to keep the shifting patterns from fractaling into a transcendence that would have eclipsed anything I'd ever called up before.

As if she could sense my struggle, Shimora pressed her cool fingers into my nape, and another fresh-breeze waft of calm swept over me. My blood stopped feeling like it wanted to surge free from my veins.

While we'd been looking up, gaping, a woman had stepped onto the slick marble podium, a petite olive-skinned beauty with glossy black hair braided around her head like an elaborate crown, a few spiral curls bouncing free by her temples. Her strawberry face was much softer than ours, with a tiny chin and wide, full cheeks, a lush scarlet pout, and a button nose. She wore something like a catsuit in bands of sparkling red and gold, sheer over the carved muscles of her abdomen and the powerful density of her hips and thighs.

She gave a deep but sprightly bow, sassy as a wink, one small bare foot pointed in front of her and arms spread and lifted behind. Then she spun once and sprang into the air, launching herself into one of the bolts of silk behind her. In the two blinks it took to wind her limbs through it, all the bolts deepened into a velvet blue like the darkest edge of night, shining with constellations so bright the silk might have turned to damask, pricked full of holes and held up to some massive light.

The illusion was so convincing that when the woman spiraled down, unwinding from the silks in a tumbling plummet, she looked exactly like a falling star spun free of the Milky Way.

As she climbed and fell, leaping effortlessly from silk to silk, the bolts changed along the way like a theatrical backdrop to her celestial play. They melted into plum and peach palettes of dusk and dawn, clotted with clouds, trailing her rise and fall as if she were the sun—then a comet—then a meteor hurtling hot through the atmosphere. Then they formed the brilliant sky above a green canopy of trees, and she fluttered easily between them like a tropical bird—before rising upward like a phoenix, against the roaring fire that raged beneath and around her.

"Oh my God," Malina whispered next to me.

"Holy shit," I agreed, just as quietly, my heart racing. This wasn't a gleam but a Gleam, a magic of an entirely different order of magnitude from anything Lina and I had ever done. "How is she doing this?"

"Manipulation," Shimora said. "Of sight, in Ylessia's case. We're all manipulators of the senses, to evoke sensation, emotion, or both. That's the nature of the gleam, to sway perception toward beauty. Ylessia could do it without her silks, if she wanted; she doesn't need to move at all to project a vivid illusion on any backdrop. The elders are always stronger because they're higher, closer to the source." Something like envy tinged her tone.

"But it's so much lovelier with the silks, don't you think?" she continued more lightly. "And that's what we're made for, after all. The striving for beauty in all things."

I frowned at that, but just then an entire universe in miniature painted itself across the bolts, exquisite solar systems and whirlpools of galaxies like an orrery brought to life against pitch black. A supernova pulsed at the center of it all, and when it finally burst—a yellow heart scorching outward into blinding red, blue, and green—Ylessia catapulted free of the silks and landed lightly on the podium, as if the dying star had given birth to a new one in her shape.

I wondered if this was a good time to clap. This was a performance for us, for sure, but it felt somehow both bigger and more sacred than that.

Malina must have had the same idea. She brought her fingers to her lips and kissed them, then held them out to Ylessia, who gave a smile like gilded sunshine with deep dimples on each cheek, dipping into another pert bow.

The pageant continued after that, relentless. I barely remembered to breathe, with the joy clamoring inside me so loud. This was what I'd missed, through all those years of my fading gleam. The ability to steal the breath of the world, to stun, to stab with beauty. To revel in the birthright, wallow luxuriously like these women did.

Though they weren't exactly like us, I realized, as the next took to the podium. She wore a leather corset over a frothy emerald tutu skirt, her feet in matching green ballet slippers laced up her sturdy calves. Her knotted hair was dyed glossy teal, shaved on one side and on the other full of magpie things, feathers and coins, insects made of wire and little chips of colored glass. Her lips were wine-dark and her nose pierced through the septum, and she was round-limbed and curved everywhere, heavy breasts and strong, full hips. Sleeve tattoos raced down both her arms, tsunamis and lightning storms and flowers on tangled vines. I loved it all, but somehow none of it had the razor edge it might hold in real life, on a punked-out woman brushing shoulders with me in the street.

In its way, it was no less studied than Shimora's spare elegance.

I forgot the thought when massive wings spread behind her, raven-black like a fallen angel's and at least twelve feet in span. She spread her arms along with them, wrists cocked and palms held up, the fingers splayed petal-soft. Standing en pointe, she preened in a circle like a music-box dancer, showing them off from every angle. They rippled, feather by feather, from glossy black to dove white, then whirred into iridescent dragonfly wings, two on each side. And then she grew silky, near-transparent bat wings, threaded with fine veins, that she curled around herself, peering up coyly above their bony tips with black sequins glittering above her eyes.

Both Malina and I gasped as she flung them out into dragon wings, so massive that they nearly reached the atrium's third floor, a faint smoke rising from them. But even when she beat them toward us, like fanning a flame, I couldn't see even a slight budging of her frame. They weren't going to lift her no matter what she did, and no hot air stirred toward us, either.

"It's not real," I whispered. "Is it? And why just wings?"

"Seems, like, very specific," Malina said, then added hastily, as if she might hurt someone's feelings, "but gorgeous, definitely."

Shimora sighed behind us, another faint strawberry waft. "It is very specific, and yes, that's all Oriell can do—project illusions directly behind her, extensions of her own frame. Not only wings, of course, she has a surprisingly broad repertoire within her limitations. But this is her prettiest for you. The gleam has . . . honed itself over the years. A dilution of necessity. And Oriell's one of our youngest, only three blood-tiers above you."

"Three blood-tiers?" I asked.

"She's my mother," Shimora said simply. "Your great-grandmother."

Shock yawned inside me again, like a vast pit, but there wasn't time for it.

The next performer already knelt on the podium, strawberry-blond hair drawn back into an austere bun, her face sharp-angled as a Valkyrie's. Her skin was thoroughly freckled, nearly nutmeg against her fine-cut lips. She was naked above the waist, save for silver earrings like chandeliers, trailing demurely over her chest and breasts down to her bare knees. In measured movements, she laid a series of ornate bells in front of her. Cocking her head to the side, she lifted a slim, arched brow, lips pursed into a sultry smirk. Then she spoke a careful litany of words, like picking a path across slick river rocks, ringing a new bell to mark each syllable.

She was polyphonic just like Malina, I realized, before my head fell back, a wave of pure sensation rolling across my skin. I bit back a moan as a thousand invisible, silken streamers trailed with almost painful languor over me at once. She spoke again, a burbling rush this time and with different bells, and I plunged into warm water fizzing with bubbles. It was so real I could feel my hair lifting as if to drift like seaweed around me, even though I could look down and see myself dry.

She didn't really need those bells, either, I thought. Like the winged one hadn't needed ballet shoes, or the falling star her silks. But I was beginning to understand. All these women were like clockwork—like our mother must once have been—painstakingly matching tools and their own movements to their gleam. Every head tilt and loose curl meant something, each bent joint an evocation.

Trained to entertain.

There were others, after. A brunette in the middle of a flighted swarm, butterflies, moths, and bees flitting around her like buzzing clothes as she twined herself through hoops and a trapeze. A bobbed redhead wound her body through slow, snaking contortions as she flung up ground ice that magnified into a flurry twirling lazily around her, fat, lacy snowflakes as large around as basketballs—followed by a handful of sand that blinked into a massive array, a confetti of broken bits of seashells, rock-candy crystals, and polished pink fragments. Another cast shadows like simulacra all around her, black silhouettes that fell in step beside her and followed every rolling tumble that she made.

It was all too beautiful to bear.

"How?" I finally said, when my face was slick with tears. I turned back to face Shimora, drawing my legs up. "They're so young. They can't all be our family, how would that be possible? And what is it all for?"

"That isn't for me to answer," she said, running her finger down my damp cheek. "We just wanted you to truly see it, what a gift it is. How worth it it always is for both, the one chosen and the one who lives."

Dread dropped into my belly like a swallowed ball bearing. Beside me, Malina caught a shuddering breath. "What does that mean?" she barely whispered. "The one chosen?"

"Let me take you to meet Sorai, dear heart. No one but her should tell you."

TWENTY-THREE

I'D SEEN HER IN A STOLEN MEMORY. I'D EVEN SEEN HER IN
the flesh, for a moment, on the bastion's ramparts in the Old Town.

But not like this. She hadn't been so close, then. She hadn't
been anything like this.

Shimora had led us up one of the two sweeping staircases that
winged to the second-floor landing, and from there we'd made
our way to the fifth floor. But as soon as we stepped into Sorai's
chamber—my mind wouldn't let me think of it as a mere room—I
felt purged clean of the casually strewn wonders that we'd seen.
There had been so much, all of it pulsing in my vision, frantic to
fractal: silver platters of cracked-open geodes with winking crystal teeth; vast sculpture-scenes made entirely of stained glass; huge
models of constellations etched bas-relief into the chalet's walls,

precious stones wedged in like placeholders for stars.

None of them compared to Sorai.

She knelt with her back to us, inky hair tinged plum by the dusk creeping in through the series of slanted skylights above her, cut into the chalet's roof. Even without facing us, pure power rolled off her in tremendous waves, like a desert wind, or the clanging of some silent, behemoth bell. The air nearly trembled around her with its force. It was hard to look at her directly; it was as if we saw her through a porthole, elongated from the curving of the glass.

And all around her, the room writhed with black roses. They were glistening and unruly, twining through the air as if they needed no espalier to hold them, no soil in which to sink. Petals, stems, and branching roots were all black and suspended, as if the maze of thorns trapping Sleeping Beauty's castle had erupted into midnight bloom.

Maybe it had, if Sleeping Beauty had once been our mother.

Mama lay on the floor in front of Sorai, her chestnut hair fanned out and shining against the mahogany floorboards. She looked both cold and flawless, as if someone who'd once adored her flesh-and-blood face had carved her exact likeness from snow and ice. A shroud of roses covered her, and it was almost lovely until I realized that their roots and thorns drove into her, piercing flesh and digging deep. The network of veins around each puncture branched out black beneath her skin as if whatever lived in the roses flowed through her too.

Then the roses crept over her entirely, closing ranks like a living, floral casket and hiding her from us.

"What did you *do*?" Malina moaned, half sobbing. "What did you do to her?"

"Nothing, child," Sorai said, in a burred, resounding triptych of voices. Malina and I staggered back as one; I hadn't seen any of the steps it took Sorai to stand and cross the room toward us, the roses parting neatly for her. She'd been kneeling one minute, and in the next she faced us, close enough that I could feel her exhales on my own lips—her breath smelled exactly like that dizzying sweetness that underpinned everything else: our ribbons, Shimora's perfume, the entire chalet. She wore eggshell ivory, glowing pale against all the flowers that nudged and strained toward her like eager children, a long-sleeved, narrow gown that clung to the contours of her body and pooled at her bare feet.

Her eyes were just like ours, but they also weren't, set against the deep, dark skin of her imperious face. They didn't seem like human eyes so much as a window into the soul of winter.

"Nothing," she said again, and warmth spread through me at her voice, a fire-flower of ecstasy unfurling in my chest. "Something was done to her, and now I fight against it. Do you see these roses? They are my will, made flesh. And so I still her with my will, keep her at rest. Until you do what must be done to save her."

"I don't understand," Lina and I whispered in tandem. It was so difficult to think with Sorai's eyes on me, and nearly impossible to fumble for words, my mind smooth and sifting as sand pouring through a sieve. I kept fighting the urge to kneel, to fling myself at her feet. My knees trembled of their own accord.

At some point Lina had taken my hand, and now she squeezed

it, speaking for me as I struggled. "Who are you? Who are *we* to you? And who did . . . *this* to our mother?"

"I am Sorai, the highest, first daughter of Mara." Eyes shifted between us like frost gathering on glass. "And that's what you are, too. Far daughters of Mara the sorceress, called by some the strongest witch who ever lived, the pride of her tribe four thousand years ago."

I barely remembered moving or sitting down, time spinning like a whirligig around us, but suddenly Lina and I sat cross-legged in front of her on crimson cushions. In each of her hands, Sorai held one of ours, though Lina still hadn't let go of me where our fingers were linked. The roses moved all around us like animal things, creeping over our shoulders, brushing our cheeks. They weren't an illusion, unless illusions could feel more real than my own skin; I felt their softness and the sharp potential of the prick behind each curved thorn. I heard the rustling of the leaves as they twined around us both.

"As daughters of Mara and youngest scions of her blood, your names are mine to choose," Sorai continued. "You who were named Malina, and who was born first—your true name is and should be Azareen."

As soon as she said it, I knew it to be fundamentally true, the same way I knew a clap of thunder meant lightning even if I hadn't seen it strike. Deep inside, I'd always believed that I was the oldest, even if we'd had no way to know. But now we did, because those three syllables somehow held all of Malina caught inside them, a spoken cross-section of everything she was. From the lush sweetness surrounding an unyielding core of strength, like the peach around a pit, to the luxuriant certainty of always knowing what she wanted, and quietly having it whenever she wanted it. Such silent disregard for consequence, so easy to mistake for something pliable.

My sister had never truly been anything like soft.

"You see how strong words are," Sorai said. "Such a sturdy vehicle for beauty. And an even better one for will. Even mortals know the worth and weight of phonemes, to string them together for natural power though they can't instill them with their own will. Ask the Arabs of their hamza, almost like a soul-sigh, and they will tell you—it can break a heart all by itself."

"But Azareen isn't a real word," Malina protested, though I could hear from her voice how it had moved her. I had no idea where she found the strength to do anything but marvel at Sorai. "You made it up."

"Of course I did, and of course it is real, and of course it means *you*, fledgling." The purring multilayers of her voice took on a gentle chiding note. "Will you smell this too, and feign that you can't find yourself in it?"

She offered Malina—*Azareen*, my mind railed. *You know her name is Azareen*—a tiny crystal vial, lifting its stopper. My own nostrils flared as I recognized the scent; it was the same as the perfume on Malina's ribbons, though much stronger. Sweet pea, vanilla, apple, and verbena, deceptive sweetness over a sharp, astringent base, with the faintest hint of Sorai's scent swirled in. Just as Naisha's ribbons had conjured her up back in her apartment in Cattaro, the scent filled my mind's eye with Malina even as she sat beside me, her eyes and hands and tumbling blue-black hair, the blinding dazzle of her smile.

Sorai closed Malina's fingers around the vial, then turned to me, fixing me with her gaze like a butterfly speared under glass. "And you, little one, an altogether different thing. Your true name is and should be Lisarah, and you'll use this for your anointing."

It was such a strange thing to hear yourself spoken, in three such simple syllables. Especially when you didn't sound like anything you thought you knew. If Malina was a peach I was a scuffed-up walnut, wrapped in a shell of rough but porous strength. I could take hammers and pliers, even be ground underfoot without cracking—but the meat inside was mild and sweet, all desire to protect and yield and please.

My sister's exact opposite.

My own vial landed gently on my palm and all of me wafted out, top notes of tobacco accord and copper, and beneath it carnation, plum, and cherry blossom. It smelled like the sleek black wing of my hair over one shoulder, my apple cheekbones, the long and sinuous lines of all my limbs.

Abruptly I remembered Mama's bedtime story of coaxing our gleam, the platter of her offerings, the hibiscus flower and the cherry. Maybe this was where it had come from; maybe this was the gift she'd wanted to give us, in whatever form she could. "Did you do this for Jasmina, too? For Faisali, I mean? The naming and the scenting?"

"Of course, when she was old enough to understand and wear the ribbons that bind us together, that connect us to each other's blood and link all the way back to Mara. Among many things, there's honey in each one, harvested on our grounds the day the daughter was born—the birthplace home is as much a part of a witch's soul and heart as anything else. I've done this for Faisali, and your grandmother, Shimora, and your aunt, Anais. For every single one of you, ever since all this began. This is your welcome to our coven, to your true family."

"And what is all this, really?" I said softly, marveling. "How many of us have there been? And how are we—you—all still alive, and young?"

She took our free hands again, opening another current of shocking warmth between us. "Years and years ago, those with blood like ours were half divine, as near to the gods as to mortals. The source of our magic is a place as much as it is an element—the people of this time might call it another dimension, perhaps, or even a universe, above or below or woven through ours."

She waved a dismissive hand, as if she had about as much use for these newfangled words as for the people of this time. "What matters is that all the gods, the old and new: they swim in it, are made of it, and never die. Mortals might reach for it and sometimes find the conduits, take little sips of it here and there, make small ripples of magic happen. But we're born with it already rushing through our veins. We may not live where gods and magic dwell, but we're born to it all the same."

I frowned. "So, we're immortal? We don't die?"

She held up a hand, and I cut myself off in an instant. "No, child. We're long-lived and more robust than most, but of course we would die otherwise. Everything natural in this world does. But all those years ago, another great witch snagged upon a woman in our mother Mara's tribe, a mortal beauty who had won the love of a man this powerful, outlander witch had wanted for herself. The jealous witch grew fat with fury and called upon the old gods to curse the poor woman, such that everyone she loved, including the man, would be dogged by death, given to accident, illness, and injury. And once they were mortally wounded, they wouldn't die but live on in relentless agony, suspended between this world and the next."

Just like Mama. Dead and undead all at once. Pain speared through me, hooked like a harpoon.

"Like Mama," Malina said, echoing my thoughts even as my mind raced ahead. "Does that mean that she—that she can feel the things that happened to her?"

"And what does this woman's curse have to do with us?" I added.

Sorai shifted her head once, just enough to spill her hair over her other shoulder. Even that small movement, the slick, snaking fall, was staggering to watch.

"The curse was vast and vicious," she said. "So colossal it killed the witch who wrought it even as it took hold of that wretched mortal woman and her kin. It would dog her and her bloodline, ruin everyone around her that she loved, lay waste to our mother Mara's tribe. And Mara was her people's healer, their beating heart. She couldn't stand by and merely watch. So she worked her own spell, an even larger one—shifting the curse to herself and her own line. It was a tremendous thing, a blazing sacrifice.

Something only she could have done."

I thought of Mara kneeling naked on that icy plateau from the dream, heat rising from her, those ground bones and powders with their patterns in the snow, blood sluicing down her arms. "What was the sacrifice?" I whispered, roiling with dread.

"Twofold, child," Sorai answered, eyes sliding over to mine. "First, to summon an immaterial force—to give it flesh, make it attend to her—she offered raw material: the burned remnants of my youngest sister, weaned only a few months before. From her ashes, she clothed Death with mortal flesh, made it human enough to reckon with. To bargain with. To be swayed by the temptations of lovely flesh and blood."

"Her own *daughter*?" Malina said. "She killed *her own daughter* for it?"

Sorai's gray eyes held steady even as her voices dipped into a sibilant hiss. "The power we have isn't always kind, child. It demands that we do what must be done, for those who can't do it for themselves. The burden and the gift of the half divine."

The legend of Mara and the spring god Jarilo she had birthed flicked through my mind; this wasn't that, but it was something close. Mara *had* borne something into life, though it wasn't exactly a son.

"Once Death stood before her, she offered it a trade: if she became its helpmeet, its courtesan and lover, Death would keep the curse at bay. When she wore out—for not even a half-divine woman could walk by Death's side forever—a daughter of hers from each generation would take up the mantle. And so, from then on, there would always be two. One to carry on our line, the other to become the sacrifice."

I knew where this was going, could see it, could feel it already. Desperately I scrabbled for anything else to keep the looming truth at bay. "So how are you still alive? Why is everyone young?"

"Because the curse could not be broken—it could merely be waylaid, like damming a river to change its course. Instead of preying on us and those we love, Death would do the opposite and simply pass us by. Whichever sister remained behind would become undying, upon the sacrifice of one of *her* own daughters. No peaceful death for the remaining daughter, but also no agony. We would stay young and hale forever, and Death would have a bride."

She reached out and with a fingertip light as a breath, traced my profile from the space between my eyes down to the crests of my lips. All the wispy hairs at the back of my neck stood on end like lightning rods. "And not just any bride, but a singular one, who could weave magic into beauty. One versed in the arts and sciences, music and games, taught to speak of anything. The most exquisite sample of her kind, the brightest candle until she burned down to the wick. Down to the quick."

"And we all agree to do this?" I whispered hotly. Not even the lapping currents of Sorai's home-love could still this fury, the idea that someone might wrest Malina from me. "We have to give up our daughters and our sisters, and then live with it *forever*? How can anything be worse than that? Why don't we just let it die? Stop having daughters, take the curse to the grave with us?"

"Do you truly think you are the first to have attempted such active problem-solving, child?" she demanded, flat. "We cannot do this. If our line were allowed to die, the curse would simply reach out its barbs and latch onto someone else. It is nearly a living thing in its own right, mindless magic, all hunger and no reason—we thwart it by living. We keep it at bay."

"Then why did Mama run from it?" Malina asked, and I noticed with a start that she was using a fundamental and an overtone without singing, as if in response to Sorai's striated voice. "Why didn't she tell us anything about this? Why did she stop teaching us to gleam?"

"It was as Lisarah says—your mother loved your aunt more than anything. The decision is made within the three, between mother and both daughters, as to which is best equipped to serve. It is a willing sacrifice for all; it must be, for the spell to work as it was wrought. But though they decided together to offer Anais, once it was done your mother could not be consoled. She chose to raise her own daughters outside of coven, alone, with the understanding that she would return you once it was time. She wanted you raised to love each other freely, without knowing that one would have to lose the other. For that, she was willing to sacrifice everything we offer. The safety of the coven, the comforts. The love."

I thought about Mama's furies, the alternating tides of her moods, my insides buckling with the understanding of what she had tried to do for us. She'd tried to give us the little snatch of freedom we could have, and it must have cost her beyond anything

I could imagine. It might even have been worse than what she was protecting us from.

And she had *known*. She had known all that time that she would lose one of us, that we would lose each other. It must have hurt so much to love us as we grew older, knowing what she did. Maybe impossible in my case—always twisting away from her, squirming toward the gleam when all she wanted was to protect me while she still could. When I was so much more dangerous than Malina's music with the glittering firework of my fractals, so much more likely to draw attention.

All of her stories had been distorted, distant, bent like the light from some far-off star. But they had always been true in part, and told from love. And I had let myself sink so far into hating her.

I thought the guilt might choke me.

"And love?" I said thickly, thinking of the story of Anais's death—Anais who hadn't truly died, but who had been lost to Mama all the same. "Is it true that love stokes the gleam?"

"No, little one. Faisali simply didn't know how else to protect you in the outside world. In coven, it is safe for us to gleam as we should—not only safe, but necessary, for us to learn and bloom fully. But on the outside, we must be careful. This world is not one that can accommodate what we are. Faisali could not risk you falling in love and showing some falsely trusted mortal your true nature, for fear of what might happen to you. We can be terrifying in our beauty, outside of the safety of the coven. You could have been taken against your will, to be captured and studied and contained, perhaps even taken somewhere where we couldn't find you once it came time. And then the curse would rage free."

Beside me, Malina gave a hitching sigh so deep I turned to her. She'd gone pale, but her cheekbones burned high, like points of candle flame held beneath her skin. "So why . . ." Her voice caught. "Why am I stronger than Iris, then?"

"Because of Naisha, little one." Sorai cocked her head to the side like some lovely bird of paradise. "Your Natalija, your music teacher. We wanted to respect Faisali's wishes and let her raise you away from us, but once she stopped teaching you, we couldn't risk not having at least one of you fully prepared for when the time came. So we sent Naisha to watch over you, to coax your gleam with her nearness, to instruct you silently with her own grace and bearing. Your gleam, Azareen, was the easier to nurture without drawing more attention to you, more prying eyes."

"That's why you came to check on us," I said, realization dawning. "That time in the Arms Square, years ago."

"Yes. We did not want to ask Faisali to return you to us any earlier than we had to, but at the same time, we could not afford to let your gleam dwindle entirely, Lisarah. I stripped the memory of our visit from you out of respect for Faisali, but allowed the yearning to remain, the desire to seek the gleam, to fan your spark. I made sure you would not forget yourself, even if she could not bring herself to teach you, knowing what it was for."

"The flowers," I murmured. "Is that why flowers would still fractal for me? Even if no one else could see it?"

"Yes. A flower is a natural fractal, a perfect, self-contained emblem of life and beauty—something easy for your gleam to latch onto.

And then once the interloper attacked your mother and we all set out to trap her, it was time to allow you to remember fully—to let you make your way back to us. We could not guide you, could not force you. In Faisali's absence, you had to come to us willingly, entirely of your own accord, in order for the sacrifice to function properly once it was time. Because there are only two of you, every iota of your willingness matters that much more, without your mother to form the third point of the triangle and make a binding decision together."

"So it was Dunja," I whispered, stomach clenching. "Why would she try to kill Mama?"

"She wants what we have," Sorai replied bluntly, all her voices dipping low in a crashing, ominous cascade. "I can find no other reason. We tolerate our immortality; she must covet it for herself. She waited for Anais to burn out, as every sacrifice does—and then she tried to kill your mother in order to break the chain of succession, to prevent the mutual choosing that yields the next sacrifice."

"She's stealing things, too," Malina said. "Icons, a saint's bones, my violin, and one of Iris's sculptures. Why?"

Sorai's face went steely. "The shape of her magic is not known to me. We do not know who she is, or how she learned of us at all. But she is strong, strong enough that I needed to hunt her down myself in order to contain her, and that is a rare thing. It took myself and nearly ten of our eldest to trap her, but we have her now."

I thought of Dunja, that sweet smile, the softness with which she'd spoken to me. "The day I saw her, though . . . she and Mama hugged, before they fought. Could they have known each other, somehow?"

The tight corners of her mouth softened. "Perhaps that was how she learned of us. Faisali would have been fastidious about secrecy, but being closed off from coven is a devastation of loneliness. We belong with each other, and the ache of solitude is strong. Perhaps she slipped up the once, became friendly with this woman, told her about us. In any case, she would not speak when we caught her." Her voice turned to tar. "And now she certainly cannot."

I thought of Fjolar, his stories of his witch mother. Maybe he had been tied to Dunja somehow, wrapped up in Mama's death just like Malina had thought. "Sorai, there was someone else the past few days. A boy. He recognized the gleam, wanted me to do it for him. Is it possible that—"

Her face sank into uncanny stillness. The roses hovering around us froze, then vibrated like tuning forks in response to her tension. "Tell me of him. Everything."

She listened stonily as I spoke about him, a distant storm brewing in her eyes. I explained how he'd asked me to gleam for him, how his presence made me flare stronger.

Finally, she said, "It sounds as if the woman's plan was pronged, and somehow this boy was meant to siphon off your power while she did the rest of her work. It would explain how she managed to elude us for so long, if she was working in concert with another. You said he told you his mother was a witch—perhaps she instructed her son to beguile you, then bring you to her when she was ready, as some final element to her spell. Many spells are blood-fueled; she may have meant to kill you as an offering, to power hers. But you are safe here with us, and we will find him as we found her."

So that was what he had wanted from me. It was stupid, that it should feel like such a burning betrayal. I had barely known him, and he had left me so stripped and weak that last time. Yet it still ached heavily in the pit of my stomach, the idea that he hadn't wanted me in any true way. That he had just been playacting for my benefit, luring me into a cage with blinding smiles and peacock displays.

That he had never thought I was both beautiful and wild.

"And now?" I clenched my teeth to keep my voice from breaking. "What happens next?"

"Now you decide, children, which of you will be the sacrifice. Without the power of Faisali's consent, her willingness to give up a daughter, there must be no wavering between you. You must determine it between yourselves. There can be no cracks between you, not even a hairline's worth of fissure."

My chest felt like a pounded anvil, and beside me Malina dropped her face in her hands and whispered something, a single word that I couldn't make out.

My throat was so tight I could barely breathe. "And if we don't?"

"If you cannot come to an agreement, either between yourselves or by competing against one another in a show of skill, Death will lapse permanently on its end of the bargain. Faisali will wake to endless agony; I can barely hold her quiet as it is, even with my will bearing down on her. And the curse will spread like wildfire to anyone else you love. To anyone that *any* of us have ever loved, if they still live."

Jovan's, Nevena's, and Niko's faces flashed in my mind, one by one.

And Luka, with his quirked half smile, the sun-bleached sheaf of summer hair falling into his hazel eyes.

Then finally Mama, when her eyes were soft, when she was the living, breathing center of every room rather than a mute, rose-smothered mound trapped between deathlessness and agony.

"So how long do we have, then?" I asked her. "Is there a deadline? Some sort of point of no return?"

Sorai spread her hands. "There may be. In the past, the transfer from one sacrifice to another has always been nearly immediate. As soon as one expired, the next one would take her place in a matter of days, at most. We are already past time, and I can only fend off the curse for so much longer until Faisali wakes. And once she wakes, it will be done. Our time will have run out. So be quick about deciding between yourselves, fledglings. Be as quick as you can."

TWENTY-FOUR

SHIMORA LED US BACK TO ONE OF THE GUEST ROOMS, THE atrium echoing with the stony silence between us three. There were others of us here—I could nearly feel them through the ribbons—but they'd all withdrawn. We passed no one else on our way down to the third floor. Malina wouldn't speak or look at me, even as Shimora swung open a baroque bronze door into a haven of pewter and plum. The walls were silvery gray, with a textured, violet accent of velvety fleur-de-lis wallpaper behind the two king beds' cushioned, dove-gray headboards. A dripping crystal orb like a fractaled snowball hung above the bed, shedding gentle light, and I looked away from it as it flickered, eager to split and multiply under my gaze.

Lina perched on the edge of the plush purple ottoman against the footboard, her back rigid, while I slid sideways onto one of the beds, spreading my palms over the impossibly soft, peeled-back duvet, worked with glinting silver thread. Everything was so beautiful here, so forcefully luxurious. How had Mama ever resigned herself to the way we lived in Cattaro? No wonder she had accepted Jovan's gifts despite herself, and labored so intently over her tailored dresses. After growing up in this silken cocoon, our whole world must have seemed so ragamuffin to her, all uneven seams and stains.

"Where does it happen?" I said stiffly. "If we—once we decide to do it, where would we go?"

"Into the Ice Cave. It's in a fold of stone near Bobotov Kuk, the highest point of the Durmitor range. Over eight thousand feet up." She nodded her chin out the window. "You can see Bobotov Kuk from here, that wedge of stone like a pyramid balanced on its end."

I didn't look. Instead I tilted my head back against the soft give of the headboard, wishing I could sink through it. I felt like a whole cairn of stones had stacked up inside me, so heavy with grief and resignation that I couldn't imagine ever standing up again. I knew we had to do this; there wasn't a choice.

And it would have to be me. I'd spent so long testing myself against our mother, flinging myself against the rock of her until it left me first bloody and then scarred. Even if I was softer inside than I had ever thought, most of me was tough as resin, scorching and malleable as the gather of my molten glass. I would last, and serve for years and years, as long as I could.

Especially if it meant Malina would live.

It had to be me.

Tears welled hot, pooling in my lashes. I dashed them angrily away, taking deep, slow breaths as Shimora lingered in the doorway of our room. "Is there anything else I can get you?" she said, stroking the sculpted fall of copper curls over her shoulder, her nude nails sparkling in the chandelier's light. "Anything you need? Anything we can—"

"What is it like?" I broke in. "What happens to the sacrifice?"

Shimora drew her glossed lip between her teeth, shaking her head. "I wish I could tell you, but I don't know. None of us do. The chosen leave their bodies behind in the cave, fall into a deep sleep from which they never wake. When their service is over, they simply stop breathing. And during the sleep, though they don't age, their bodies change. Their hair and nails grow, their muscles even strengthen. We cut their hair for them sometimes, when it grows too long."

"Their muscles *strengthen*? Wouldn't they atrophy? Isn't that what happens in a coma?"

She gave me a wistful smile. "It's not a coma, dear heart. The chosen's mind and soul are elsewhere, and wherever they are— whatever the essence of her is doing—it changes the clay of her body. That's all that I can tell you. It's all that we know."

We fell quiet. With a little nod to us, Shimora slipped out and gently clicked the door shut behind her, leaving us alone. Malina and I sat silently together. Everything felt impossibly vivid, and just as impossibly slow. If we'd had an hourglass, I thought that we'd be able to track each grain's descent, and that each would take an hour to fall.

And then I said, "It's going to be me," at the same time as Malina said, "I'm not letting you do it."

She whipped her head over her shoulder, and we stared at each other. Her lips tightened, a muscle in her jaw twitching, and then she sprang up, fists clenched. "I *knew* it," she spat. "It's just like you to go ahead and decide for the both of us, as if it doesn't even matter what I say."

"That's not fair," I protested. "You're making it sound like I *want* to do this."

"You do want to do it," she accused, "because it means you can keep on being Iris the Martyr. Because, what, you think you know everything? You think maybe you deserve this somehow? I think you bought into all of . . . all of Mama's bullshit over the years. I think you really believe you're worth less than me."

"That's not—I can't believe you're saying this to me." My entire face was tingling. "I just want to protect you—"

"I never *asked* you to protect me!" She stalked to the center of the room, turning in a furious little circle. I'd never seen her so frantic before, like a doll wound up too tight. "We're twins, Iris! You're not even my older sister. *I'm* the older one. And I'm the one who . . ." She took a shuddering breath, wringing her curls with one hand. "I'm the one who got to have everything I wanted. I'm the one who always let you take every fall."

I bit down to keep the tears back, but I couldn't stop my lips from quivering. "What do you mean?"

She turned her back to me. "I thought it was my fault," she said, muffled. "My fault that my gleam didn't go when yours went, even after Mama stopped teaching us. Because I fell in *love*, Riss. I fell in love, and Mama never even punished me for not fading like you did. She never tried to break me down, to make me hate myself. To make me feel unworthy of anybody's love. I think she thought she didn't need to, not like she did with you." She huffed out a bitter half laugh. "She thought I was the *safe* one."

"I . . ." Something like a firestorm began boiling inside me. "What? You fell in love? Was it—" I clenched my fist against my mouth, thinking of all the stolen glances between Luka and Lina, the way she'd stepped effortlessly into his arms to hug or dance, the way he'd kissed the gleaming top of her head. My insides quivered like they might cave in. "Was it Luka?" I finished, in a dry whisper.

She whirled around to face me. "Of course it wasn't Luka! Luka loves *you*, he has since we were little."

Love.

Luka *loved* me.

It felt like I'd spent years trying to remember a word that was always poised on the tip of my tongue, yet just the slightest bit out of mental reach. It had been the secret center of everything he'd given me—every gift of an exotic flower, every math lesson that allowed me to translate a fractal notion into glassblown life, every warm imprint of his hand on the back of my neck—and I'd always averted my gaze, let it settle in my blind spot, dubbed it best-friendship. I had known it, but I couldn't let myself know. Because I'd sworn to my mother and sister that I wouldn't. So I'd let myself live in that gray with him, in the shaky middle ground from which I wasn't technically betraying anyone. But gray was gray. He'd been offering me color all that time, and I'd spent all that time turning it away.

How could I have done that to him, along with everything else? How could one person hurt another in such a full, wide spectrum of ways?

Lina's face softened at the look on mine. "I know, Riss. I know you wanted to love him back, so bad—I could see it every day. It made me want to die, how much it hurt you. But you listened to Mama, you actually did what she wanted. Even while you fought her about all the things that didn't matter, you did exactly what you were told. You wouldn't *let* yourself love him, or anyone. You were always alone, except for me."

I crossed my arms over my chest. "What are you talking about? I may not have been allowed to have him, but you didn't have anyone, either. That was how it was. You and me, alone together."

"I *wasn't* alone!" she shot back. "I had Niko!"

"I had Niko, too. We weren't best friends, but still, that's not the same as love."

She groaned in frustration. "God, Riss, *listen* to me for once. It is the same, it's exactly the same. I love her, okay? I've loved her since I was fifteen. Longer than that, really. And she—she loves me, too. We . . . we just told each other a few days ago. Really, finally said it, for the first time."

The shock was so numbing and intense I felt like someone had rung some massive church bell inside me. On some level, I found it hilarious that this should rock me more than anything that had happened so far, but there we were. I actually shook my head, as if that would clear it. "You—you and Niko? You're in *love*? Why . . ."

I scrubbed my hands over my face, stretching it tight over the bones beneath. "Why wouldn't you tell me that?"

"Because I felt so guilty for betraying all of us," she said softly. "Falling in love, sharing my gleam with Niko, singing for her every day. Doing all the things that Mama said put us in danger, when you didn't get to have anything. Not love, not magic. And also because you're so much like her, sometimes."

"Like who?"

"Like Mama. All that control, all the time. You make your mind up about things, and it's like concrete setting. Whatever impression gets left, whatever indent, it's there forever. The way you think I'm a coward because I don't want out of Cattaro like you do, for one. Because I don't think about Japan like it means freedom and salvation and everything Montenegro doesn't mean for you. Don't shake your head, I know it's true. I've heard you feeling it at me. And I don't mind that you think those things about me—we're not one person, Riss, we can feel different things—but Niko . . ." She glanced up at me, suddenly tentative. "I didn't know what you would think of us together."

I couldn't believe the notion had never crossed my mind before—that the reason Malina barely noticed men might be that they genuinely weren't interesting to her. I'd thought it was growing up around Mama that had done it, the endless castigation, the relentless shaming. Of course, that had been meant for me—Mama hadn't seen the need to chisel away at her more malleable girl, or maybe couldn't bring herself to do it to us both—and it had worked.

I'd never fully given anyone my heart.

But Lina was my sister, my twin, the first thing I'd seen when I opened my eyes in our shared womb. I'd held her by the hand before we were even thrust into this world. I should have felt the need to look deeper, to think of her as more than the most vulnerable extension of me, a weaker limb I needed to favor. Especially when that was so far-flung from the truth.

"I'm sorry I didn't know," I said softly. "I shouldn't have needed you to tell me. But if you had, I would have been happy for you, Lina, I swear."

"And you don't care? That she's a girl?"

"Of course I don't. Does Luka care that his sister's with a girl?" I replied tartly, as all the furtive half gestures, the bit-back sentences, fell into place.

She winced. "He wanted to tell you. And he almost did, a bunch of times. He thought it was wrong of us to hide it from you, but Niko made him swear he wouldn't say anything until I did. Only because that's the way I wanted it." She huffed out a little breath. "She hated hiding it, so much. And you know how hard Niko can hate things. I spent a lot of time paying penance by watching horror movies with her. A *lot*."

"So what were you waiting for? What did you think I was going to do?"

"I'm not sure. I didn't want you to judge me for being so indulgent, for letting myself do what I wanted. And sometimes . . . sometimes you make things bigger than they need to be. I was a little afraid you'd, I don't know, be loud about it once you got on board? Throw me a one-person parade, just so you could fight anyone else who judged me for it."

I took a shaky breath. "I might be Iris the Martyr, but this does make you a bit of an asshole, Lina."

She sputtered out a little laugh. "Yeah. I guess it does."

"What is it really like, though?" I twisted my hands together in my lap. "Being in love, I mean."

She crawled over the bed to meet me halfway, then laid her head tentatively on my shoulder. I wriggled down farther to rest my cheek against her crown. "I don't know if I can tell you about love in general. But I can sing you what it's like for me. Being in love with her."

I nodded once. I could feel her smile against my shoulder, and as I closed my eyes she began to hum the fundamentals, overtones layering in. Usually her singing transcribed directly into emotion, but this time it was even more vivid, images blooming on the insides of my eyelids, as if she were showing me what she'd seen as well as felt. Maybe being here was making her stronger, too.

I caught a mosaic of glimpses, little glittering stained-glass pieces that each reflected some part of Malina's love. There was Niko in a white triangle bikini top, her slight midriff taut and brown beneath it, a jewel winking in the shadow of her navel. A sarong was draped below the tuck of her waist, and she danced for my sister, the slim flare of her hips rippling to some beat I couldn't hear, each dainty foot perfectly placed. Her silky hair fell over one sloe eye, but the other was large and dark and heavy-lidded, narrowed with her smile. I could feel the exact way it had made my sister's heart race.

Then Niko breaking the water's surface, her chin tipped up and mouth opening for breath, slick hair glossy as an otter's, water trembling in her lashes.

Niko feeding my sister a dewy, amber slice of peach, laughingly pulling it out of reach before she finally let Malina have it, sealing it with a kiss.

Niko's face drawn and blurred with tears, her little hands clenched into furious fists before Malina caught and uncurled them, brushing her lips over the knuckles. When had that been, I wondered vaguely; maybe after her and Luka's mother died.

A hundred flashing glimpses of Nikoleta Damjanac, and then a hundred more, of her swimming and laughing and dancing with my sister, their fingers always entwined.

And then a final image of Niko's sleeping profile: the pert outline of nose and lips against the pillow, her lashes fanned like a paintbrush, her fist baby-curled beneath the chin. And with it, the first swell of love my sister had ever felt, the moment in which she realized that this was the girl who held her heart. That was what the smell downstairs had made her remember, this precise moment of falling.

The devastating and glorious yielding of all control.

"That's lovely, Lina," I whispered, my voice thick. The illusion fell away as Malina's singing fractured into tears, until she sobbed into my shoulder. "Shhh. Don't."

"I don't want to leave her, Riss." Her voice shuddered. "She'll hurt so much without me. But I can't let you go, either. You should have your chance to have that too, to feel how much you're worth.

I've already had it, so many years of love. It's your turn now. It's time for *you*."

"No." I could feel the resolve hardening within as I said it, like cooling glass taking on its final shape. "She can't do without you; I could feel that much. You'll have each other, and Luka—he'll find someone else. It should be me who goes."

Lina struggled upright, balling her fists against her thighs. "I won't let you. Not this time. And even if I were willing, think what it would be like for me. I'd have to have *babies*, Riss, to carry on our line. How could I do that to Niko, drag her into all of this, make her watch me groom my children—ours, maybe, if she were still with me after all that—for sacrifice? Would she even stay with me? And if she did, how could I live and watch her get old, die in front of me? I won't do it, I won't. I'll go—you stay. You have all the things you've never had."

I drew away from her, unsteady. An ache began building in my center, growing outward, until it sank through my skin and bowed my skeleton down toward the earth.

"Really?" I whispered. "After everything you just told me, everything you've already gotten to have that I didn't—you won't even let me make this one choice? After all that fighting I did, all the struggling, all the barbed-wire *shit* that meant nothing while you hid in plain sight? Now you won't even let me be the one to sacrifice, if that's what I want? I don't *want* to be the one to stay behind."

She shook her head, her eyes pooling, pale and clear as spring water. "You're not taking the hit for the both of us, not again. Not ever. I'm the prepped one, anyway. I'm the one they groomed just in case, you know?"

Resignation thudded over me, heavy as soil dropped on a casket. "Then I suppose we'll see what sort of contest happens when sisters can't decide."

"ONE DAY TO prepare," Sorai said through her teeth. This time she stood as we knelt before her on the cushions, the roses wheeling around us. Her eyes glittered with tamped-down fury, and the skin beneath them was dusky with fatigue. "That is all the time I can give you foolish, self-indulgent fledglings—my hold frays already, the curse bucks beneath my will. Faisali has tried to wake four times since I saw you last. Four times in two hours."

Guilt poured over me, prickly with panic, and beside me Malina made a low sound of distress. We were putting so much at risk because we couldn't come together the one time it truly mattered. But there was no splitting the difference here. I wouldn't let her go willingly any more than she would let me.

"Death will be your judge, and you will agree to abide by the decision. There can be no dissent once that is done, do you understand? Not even an inkling of it."

"I do," I said softly, my throat tight. Beside me, Malina nodded silently. We weren't holding hands this time.

"Then go to bed, rise early, and begin. I will send someone for each of you. If you truly wish to fight each other for this, you will do it tomorrow night."

"What . . ." I cleared my throat. "What will it be like?"

"After your lessons, you will be readied for the ritual banquet, where you will then perform. Everything done to you—and everything you do—shall be in the service of beauty. That is your work now; make yourselves lovely. Azareen has the advantage here, Lisarah. She has been learning from Naisha since she was a child, where you have been given far too much free rein. So, you will do everything in your power tomorrow to smooth all those jagged edges—in which you seem to take such pride—into something fit to be beheld and beloved by Death."

Even though I'd decided to do this, committed myself fully to fighting to win, everything in me bucked in protest at that imperative. In my lap, I curled my hands into tight fists. I could do it, if that was what it took to save her. I could force myself soft.

"What about me?" Malina asked quietly.

"As I said, you are already primed to win. But your sister has been fierce like you never have. Where she should learn softness, your challenge will be to grow truly bold; now is the time to shed that meek veneer, show us what truly lies beneath."

"Can I . . ." Malina's voice cracked. "I'd like another bedroom, please. If you have one to spare, I mean?"

I could feel my insides splitting, cleaving in two. So this was heartbreak. At least now I knew what that felt like.

TWENTY-FIVE

EVEN WITH THE BONE-DEEP EXHAUSTION OF THE PAST FIVE days turning my marrow into lead, I hadn't thought I'd sleep at all without Malina breathing beside me. But Shimora had kindly scented me into some semblance of peace, stroking my hair while waves of her perfume lapped me into sleep like some gentle tide. In the early morning, my heart still throbbed like a rotting tooth, but otherwise I felt more awake than I had in days.

We had breakfast in a massive, sunlit dining room, at a polished table so long it could easily have seated fifty people. A row of iron chandeliers swung above, square cages nestled within cages all the way down to the minuscule, metallic birds trapped within each. Shimora sat between me and Malina, like a buffer; there were about thirty others of our family there. I wasn't even sure what to call them, all these grandmothers so many "greats" removed. Relatives? Kinswomen? "Grandmother" felt jarringly strange when they were all so youthful, that ripe, full bloom of Mama's age. So many pairs of mothers and daughters, indistinguishable from each other without the telltale indicia of years.

I recognized falling-star Ylessia from the night before, smiling at me as she forked burstingly sweet heirloom tomatoes, brined feta cheese in olive oil, and curls of salty Njeguši prosciutto onto her plate. All the food was so perfect and simple it tasted lavish, an elegance that made me ache for Mama. Oriell was there too, the teal-haired ballerina, and the Valkyrian bell-ringer named Xenia.

Despite a nearly tangible undercurrent of tension—they all clearly knew that everything depended on us, and that we couldn't align; it was obvious in the sidelong traded glances, the hushed whispers down the table from us—they all flocked gracefully to us between bites, eager to greet us and skim our cheeks with affectionate hands, as if we belonged naturally to them even after years apart. After so much time with just Lina and Mama, it felt impossibly surreal to be surrounded by these gorgeous, ageless women, so hemmed in and awash in family. I could feel the kinship of their gleam, twining and curling fondly against mine. It was beyond wonderful, a warm web of joy and belonging. It made me wonder again how Mama could have ever snipped herself loose from it.

"Where's Natalija?" Malina asked. "Naisha, I mean. Shouldn't she be here?"

Shimora glanced around, brow furrowed. "She wasn't feeling

well earlier this morning, I believe. But yes, she is here. I'm sure she'll find you later."

"And where is everyone else?" I asked Shimora as I washed down a bite of oil-soaked, divinely crusty bread with a tangy sip of yogurt. "Four thousand years of us, and never dying—there should be more, shouldn't there?"

"There are," she confirmed. "With a new pair of daughters every twenty years or so, we're over two hundred by now, scattered all over the world. We have other strongholds like this one, though we began here, built this one first for ourselves. There's also a lovely little palazzo in Venice, and a castle in Spain belongs to us. Quite a few others, too. With so many years to ourselves, why not roam as we please—especially if we can do it together? We have companions, too, of course, for as long as we choose. We live however we like, and we always have each other to return to in our little enclaves."

"How?" Malina asked quietly. "All this is so . . . grand. Where does the money come from?"

"Clever investments, for one, with so many years to accumulate profit. And we're consummate performers, exquisite ones. What we do can be easily reframed as a spectacle for the wealthy. As long as we're careful to keep it in the proper setting, contained within the trappings of mundane entertainment. You can imagine what we can charge, performing together."

"Like a circus," I murmured. "Only we're real."

"Precisely." Shimora dabbed daintily at her mouth and rose in one smooth movement. "Now, will you come? Azareen, Xenia will take you." The freckled Valkyrie from the night before stepped next to her, her smile restrained but warm. "Though everyone else will soon be here, it will take too long to wait for one of our melodic empaths to tutor you today. And you're already well on your way, besides."

My stomach clenched into a fist at the throwaway mention of Malina's greater strength. They all thought that she would win. "And me?"

"Ylessia will teach you. She doesn't have the infinite bloom—what we call your fractals—but only one other of us has that gleam variant in any case. It's one of the rarest forms. And . . ." She hesitated for a beat, and I glanced at Malina out of habit for her reaction; she was staring intently at Shimora, her nose slightly wrinkled the way it did when she was listening avidly to someone. "And she's much too far away. Let us not waste time while Sorai struggles."

BACK IN MY bedroom, Ylessia sat across from me like a yogi, cross-legged with one calf tucked over the other and foot pointed in a display of flexibility that made my inner thigh ache in sympathy. Other than the pale eyes we all shared, she looked nothing like Malina, Mama, or me, especially with the riotous froth of her black ringlets bouncing freely to her waist, rippling with ribbons. She reminded me of the South American tourists we sometimes saw in Cattaro, tanned beauties with tiny noses and impossibly full lips, round faces and prominent bones very different from my own jutting angles.

She pursed her lips at my scrutiny, dimpling. "Have I passed muster, Lisarah?" She had a sweet, lilting accent, and her voice was surprisingly deep and musical for someone so small. It reminded me painfully of Niko. "Or shall I hold myself captive for you a little longer, until you've examined me at your leisure?"

Hearing her speak so formally jarred me. There was such a disconnect between that young face and the almost archaic structures of her speech that belied her true age.

"I was just wondering where you were from, if that makes sense. You look . . ."

"Foreign?" A curved brow arched up. "Unusual?"

I dipped my head, a little embarrassed. "Typically those apply to me."

"Understandable," she said simply. "You're magnificent. Even by our standards. Faisali made a very wise choice with your father, whoever he was."

"What?"

"We cherry-pick fathers for wit and beauty, those of us whose . . . burden is to carry on the line. Once a sister is chosen to sacrifice, the other must get with child as soon as possible. Each chosen one only endures twenty years at the very most, and when she burns out, the next generation must be ready to serve. Jasmina waited nearly a year to have you, which is far longer than we normally take. But she was grieving badly for the loss of Anais. We understood the time she took."

I thought of Luka, and the uncanny valley. He'd been right, to a degree. If this was true, Malina and I were human and born, but we were made, too.

I bit the raw inside of my cheek, thinking how awful it must be to have to even consider it, to think of designing your own children in the wake of losing your sister. What a desperate, miserable thing.

"It sounds terrible, does it not," Ylessia said bitterly, as if she could read my mind. "And it is, at times. We, all of us, have lost a sister and a daughter, and the pain . . . the years erode it, but do not erase." She turned her hand over, moving it until the tiny crystal caught between her veins sparked in the light. "That is what these are for—once we fulfill our final obligation and give up a daughter, this diamond locks us into place within Mara's spell, the counterweight to the curse."

"Why diamonds?"

But even as I said it, I remembered Luka's lit-up face as he told me how diamonds could be used for quantum computing, how the tiny flaws within their atomic structure could hold over a million times more information than silicon systems. Something about nitrogen pockets, maybe. I'd tuned out as I sometimes did when he turned the nerd dial to ten, but now that I might never see him again, I wished with such a fierceness it bordered on yearning that I could remember exactly how his voice had sounded as he said it.

"Because they're what we're made of, in a static state. Carbon in its purest form, a natural conductor for magic."

"Can I touch it?"

She held out her wrist to me, presenting her hand as if it were a gift. I ran my finger over it, a tinge embarrassed of my clammy hand. The hard surface lay flush against her satin skin, as warm as she was. "Did it hurt?" I asked softly, tracing its facets, peering into the tiny, yellow flickers of flaws in its depth.

"Yes." Her voice was husky. "When the spell spears through you for the first time—it feels like I imagine dying might, which I suppose is only fair." She cleared her throat. "Let us begin."

The parquet between us was littered like a three-dimensional found-object collage. Trays and bowls held bolts of snakeskin gleaming with a liquid sheen, strings of rainbow beads, glittering crushed powders, piles of multicolored stones, spiderwebs glistening with dew pinned between sheets of glass, birds' nests with eggs, even what looked like a heap of preserved butterflies with nearly transparent orange wings.

"Go on," she said, gesturing toward it all. "Begin."

"But I don't know where to start trying," I protested. "There's so many."

"Don't start 'trying' anywhere." Her eyes were level. "'Trying' won't make you the one who wins. Do all of them, at once, with everything you have. You're back in coven now; your gleam might not be honed and precise like your sister's, but you should be near to full strength, as we all are when we are close to each other. It's been paining you to gleam fully thus far, because you were not taught how to do it properly, and it stunted you. But now I'm here to guide you. Now it will be a glory, so do not be afraid of it."

I dug my nails into my palms and began—and as soon as I did, the whole of the room kaleidoscoped between us, shattering into a behemoth fractal. And as Ylessia had said, now that I was no longer holding back or panicked, it felt like my human insides had been replaced with an endless, surging flood of light, a rushing river of pure relief.

Diamond trails of green snakeskin blazed everywhere, crisscrossing one another like reptilian bridges, while helices of multicolored beads spiraled through them. The powder grains whirled around each other like miniature tornadoes, near blinding in their brilliance, and as they multiplied, the piles of different stones bathed the room with light—agate, violet, periwinkle, crimson, a spectrum of my own making.

In the very middle, a writhing column of dead butterflies rose up like an organic Chihuly sculpture, surrounded by a chain link of nests with endless arcs of speckled eggs.

And the dew-flecked spiderwebs stretched out around it all, anchoring every corner, encompassing the whole of it like a dangling dreamcatcher.

"Beautiful!" Ylessia whispered, low and fierce. "Now stand. Walk among what you've created. Hold your head up and be *lovely*."

She stood along with me, moving as I moved. I kept the fractals fracturing, shuffling them like some glorious tarot deck, even as I stepped between them delicately, ducking my head beneath the floating snakeskin arcs, slipping my hands through the pearled strings of the beads, stepping over glowing stone paths that looped around our feet. Ylessia corrected me with light touches as I walked through the world of my own making—lifting my chin, shaping my limbs, guiding me toward grace.

"Be strong, yet soft," she whispered into my ear. "Be fierce, yet so fastidious. Remember what all this power is for—to serve, and play, and always please."

Another ripple of rebellion stirred hot in me; I could do all this, whirl the world into orbit around me as if I were a sun, and I had to be *soft* while I did it? I could whip this gorgeous fury into motion all around me, tug it toward me with my own gravity like a black hole, and I was supposed to be *fastidious* about it?

That couldn't possibly be right.

And then I heard Malina's song.

She could have been rooms or even floors away, and it didn't matter; it sounded as if an entire army of angels had crashed calamitously into the earth. This wasn't just a fundamental and an overtone, or two, or even ten—it was an orchestral score from some hybrid of heaven and hell, so staggering and celestial that hearing it crushed my fractals with its aural weight, dissolved them into motes of sparkling dust.

It sounded like the world's most epic victory march.

She thought she was winning. She was *going* to win.

I couldn't let that happen.

I forgot about Ylessia and her instructions; I closed my eyes to the materials outside me and reached inside myself, as if I were striving to close my fist around my own heart. I thought of Sorai and her black roses—and like flinging a javelin from deep within myself, I flung out the repeating pattern of branches and flowers that made a massive wisteria tree, a living, thriving fractal in the shape of my own will.

Ylessia was screaming something—it might have been something like *stop!*, or *please!*, if I'd had even the slightest room to care—as slim branches and pink and purple blossoms surged all around us, in the most delicately dangerous headlong rush. They funneled toward the center of the room, where they collided, building a waterfall arch of wood and flower like a wedding wreath. In their center they formed a portal, opening into somewhere I had never seen—a pale, pastel night sky cluttered with stars, as seen from beneath the stony overhang of a sea cave, neon streaks of aurora borealis reflected in the placid water beneath.

I could actually see the splash of the Milky Way, like a sparkling cream dissolving into the thicker liquid of the night.

I moved toward the opening almost without thought, wanting to step through, into what I knew would be the warmest salty water. Ylessia swiped uselessly at me as I walked, foot in front of foot; my sentinel wisteria wound itself around her, tucked her into a distant corner of the room and held her pinned against the wall. There was nothing she could do to me. Her gleam was thin and empty, just an illusion of a dream—mine was whatever I dreamed made flesh, through the sheer pounding force of my own will.

Then black roses flooded over everything, in a fragrant, crushing tide. They slithered swiftly over my flowers, choking them at the vine, and I could feel Sorai's arms close like a vise around me from behind.

"Enough, child," she whispered almost under her breath into my ear, and still the many layers of her voice tore through my mind so loudly I thought they might have made my brain bleed. There was fury in her tone, and fear, and beneath it a puzzling, pulsing pride. "You have shown quite enough. No one here could possibly teach you, that much is more than clear. Nothing tamed can curb what grew unfettered. So let us hope that Death has acquired a taste for such wildlings as you are."

TWENTY-SIX

THEY DRESSED ME IN FLOWERS, AND WOUND ME IN THORNS.

"Wild as she is," Sorai had said, "she may as well look like something that clawed up out of the dirt on its own."

Ylessia had bathed me in water scented with meadowsweet, her cheekbone eggplant-bruised where one of my branches must have whipped her in the face. "I'm sorry," I whispered to her as I clung to the edges of the tub, bobbing in the froth of bubbles with my skin flushed and slick. "I didn't mean to do it. I didn't mean to hurt you."

But she wouldn't answer, or even look at me. Even when she finally caught my eyes in the mirror as she dressed my hair, I couldn't quite decipher her gaze. There was an awestruck sort of terror there, that much I could see, but beneath it . . .

It looked like a vast, scorching vat of jealousy.

When she was done I looked like I'd crawled naked through the world's primordial forest, dressing myself only with what I could pick or pluck. Gossamer-green folds wound strategically around me, as if a spider had spun a web of silk and leaves, laced together with curls of ivy. My hair was braided loosely up and away from my face, beneath a crown of purple morning glories and their heart-shaped leaves, with wicked little berry sprigs tucked in here and there. Torques of thorns surrounded my biceps and my wrists, and something like barbed corn silk twined around my calves, like the straps of the gladiator sandals I'd worn in what felt like someone else's life.

And my eyes were blackened with such a dense, matte liner that my irises all but glowed, like something that crept silent and hungry behind the night-rustle of leaves. Even my lips glistened a diluted red, as if I'd licked them with blood still lingering in my mouth.

It was the most beautiful I'd ever been, everything so tailored to me I might have grown it from my body, but I couldn't quite tell why it all felt so wrong.

"There," Ylessia said flatly, stepping away from me. "As lovely as you'll ever be, if we can call it that."

I reached up to touch the deceptively simple tangle of my hair; my hand sparkled violet and green where it caught the light, from the shimmering minerals in the lotion she'd rubbed on me. It smelled too sweet for something just meant to moisturize; curious, I brought the back of my hand to my mouth and gave it a little lick.

It tasted like the candied violets Mama used to make as a garnish for her spring sunset sorbets.

"You *sugared* me?" I demanded. Somehow this was infinitely more terrifying than anything had been so far, this proof on my tongue that I wasn't myself any longer, but an offering. And that was the fount of all the dissonance, I abruptly understood. They may have decked me out like something that could sting or prick, but that was purely for show. I wasn't meant as a thorned rose but as a lychee fruit, all tender sweetness once the spikes peeled back.

And I had not just volunteered, but fought so hard for this.

It would be better, I reminded myself. It would be worth it. Whatever happened, it would be to me and not to my sister.

"Not to worry, Lisarah," Ylessia replied tartly. "Nothing can truly sweeten all those years of brine beneath. I assure you it will not sink in too deep."

I held her eyes in the mirror until she dropped her gaze. "Is there any particular reason," I began, girding my voice with steel, "that you've now decided to be such a spectacular bitch? It's not really the quality one hopes for in a great-great-great however-many-times grandmother. Especially not when getting ready to step willingly off a cliff."

Her face softened a measure, and she opened her mouth as if to say something before closing it with a neat click of her teeth. "It isn't your fault," she finally said, low. "You're right, you don't deserve this from me. Especially not now."

"So, what is it, enlighten me. It might be my last request."

She shook her head once, and turned away. "It'll be another few hours yet," she said quietly. "Sorai must ready herself for the ritual, as well, along with the rest of us. Enjoy what you can until then. Enjoy all of it."

I sank onto the ottoman as she left, feeling more desperately alone and scared than I had ever been.

I COULDN'T THINK what else to do, so I made myself eat as dusk gathered outside, dousing the mountain peaks that had burned bloody with the force of a high-altitude sunset. I wasn't really hungry, even with six days of barely considering food since all of this had begun, but if I did it—if I won—who knew if eating was something I'd ever get to do again.

And if I lost, I couldn't see how I would want to ever eat. Or live. Even though the choice wouldn't be mine by then.

They'd left me a silver catering cart loaded with delicacies, like some sort of decadent prisoner's last meal. There were fat strawberries, hollowed out and filled with white chocolate cream; I ate those first, swallowing them nearly whole. Then tiny glazed doughnuts spread with foie gras and sweet, gritty fig; beef tartare topped with a trembling orange yolk and spicy buttered toast points; miniature brownies with truffle shells tucked inside that burst and bled hazelnut cream when prodded with a fork.

After what felt like a lifetime of refusing Mama's food to make the most pointless point, once I got going I couldn't get enough. I washed all of it down with whole glasses of cold water, flavored sweet and tart with an elderflower cordial.

I might have eaten myself to bursting if one of the wrought-iron inlays in the wall hadn't shuddered, then swung open like a seamless panel to let my sister in, and Naisha right behind her.

Lina and I gaped at each other for a silent moment. Her hair was pinned up in elaborate curls, beneath a slim, gleaming circlet like a halo. She wore a gown cut low over her creamy spill of cleavage, a metallic black bodice above a full skirt like chain mail—if every link were a perfect feather worked intricately from platinum. Bracelets shaped like feathers circled each wrist, too, and though her eyes were lined as mine, it was precise, the black swooping into curlicues toward her temples. Her cheeks were dramatically flushed, and her lips gilded.

"Are you meant to be channeling a *bird*?" I said, just as she asked, "What even is that, like sexier Poison Ivy?"

We burst into tears at exactly the same time, and she flung herself into my arms. Above her shoulder, I saw Naisha wipe at her narrow, finely chiseled face, her eyes swimming with tears.

I could think about what that meant in a moment.

But first I held Malina tight, cheek pressed against hers, both of us bubbling with sobs and laughter. "I'm supposed to be a dark angel, I think?" she said. "You know, because I, uh, sing like one? It would be a little hilarious if only I could breathe."

"Right, of course, and I'm a very dangerous wildflower. But an edible one, that's the important part." I sighed deeply into her hair, breathing in its warm scent. Everything in me loosened, as if a terrible coil tightened around the barrel of my insides had been cut free. "I'm so glad you're here with me, Lina. But what are you doing here? I didn't think you'd—I didn't think we'd even see each other, before."

I jerked my chin at Naisha, who looked like Eve before the apple: a floor-length cream sheath clinging to her fine-boned frame, her platinum hair loose and festooned with flowers and glistening strips of snakeskin along with the scent-ribbons. "And why are *you* here? Were you Lina's fluffer? I really drew the short straw with Ylessia, I will say that much."

Lina drew back away from me, her face shuttering as she shook her head. "No, it was Xenia who *readied* me." She nearly spat out the word; clearly she had enjoyed it about as much as I did. "Naisha came to see me after that, Riss. Something's happening here—it's not what we think. It's not what they told us. They're lying, they all are. And especially *her*."

The ribbons in my hair nearly writhed in protest at the maligning of Sorai. "What do you mean? Why would she lie? And wouldn't you have heard it before now, if something was that wrong?"

"I *have* been hearing something off, ever since we got here, but it's all so . . . everything's so muddied, there's so many of them, it's hard to hear properly. I still don't understand what's happening, exactly, but Naisha has something to show us. While they're all still busy."

I crossed my arms over my chest, hugging myself. Everything in me thrashed against doubting Sorai. Even listening to Malina was beginning to become physically painful, like a fit of ague.

"Why are you doing this?" I asked Naisha. "Why are you betraying *her*, if that's what this is?"

She pressed her rosy lips together, her eyes huge and mournful. "Because I watched you grow up," she said simply. "Malina, mostly, but you too, Iris. I watched you be free, and saw the happiness you managed to find in the world despite all your limitations. With your own names, without being molded into Lisarah and Azareen. Without being curated like the rest of us. So I want to—I want to show you something. I don't belong to her like I once did, and I won't again for a while yet. I still remember myself from all those years, enough to want to give you a choice, a true one, while I still can."

I frowned at her. "I don't understand. What are you trying to say?"

"I can't—" She smacked a fist into one palm, groaning in frustration. "I can't go further than this. If you want to know, we have to go now. We're running out of time."

Lina took my hand, squeezing hard. "I don't think she can say anything more, Iris. But I trust her; she *sounds* right. So I'm going to go with her, but you don't have to, because this time it *is* your choice. Trust Sorai, or come with me and find out whatever it is." She spread her hands, eyes guileless and bright. "Whatever you want to do."

I took a long breath and let it out in a quivering rush.

"I want to go with you."

THE CHALET WAS practically a warren, a terrarium of secret passageways carved into its walls. I wondered how the whole thing didn't collapse onto itself, riddled as its foundation was with holes, and whether Sorai knew of all or any of these.

I followed the metallic swish of Lina's feathers, which caught the little light there was, and the clink of the rattling key ring Naisha carried. We bore sideways and down, taking winding, narrow stairways until we reached what had to be the basement, the air drafty-cold and smelling of dank, pressed dirt.

There, Naisha paused in front of a weathered wooden door, bolted in three places. I could hear her hitching breath as she worked three different brass keys into the locks, grunting in a very ungraceful fashion at the effort of turning them.

"Come on, come on, come on," I whispered behind her and Malina, frantic, bouncing on the balls of my feet. "What if she knows we're here? What if she knows that I'm—that I'm betraying her like this—"

"That's the ribbons talking," Naisha whispered back, leaning into the final lock. "I took a few of Malina's out, so it's not quite so bad for her. That's why I could come to you at all before I rejoin the others. Mine were taken out while I was posing as Natalija; they're too much bright magic to be cloaked by my gleam, even under a masquerade glamour as complex as mine, and your mother would have seen them through it. So, I had time to get to know my own mind a bit. Unclouded by all the love."

"Why wouldn't you have known your own—"

The door finally screeched open, and I caught my breath.

The room was full of glowing ice, a giant block shot through with the black roses of Sorai's will. They streaked through the expanse like a network of oily veins—or like prison bars for the woman trapped within. She had frozen in a half crouch, leaning forward, her arms flung up with fingers splayed and white hair flaring around her like the sun's corona. Her dainty little jaw jutted forward, and her eyes were open wide and unmistakably full of fury. She was so close to the ice that I could make out the creases in her delicate lips, the individual golden threads of her eyelashes, and the silver striations in her gray eyes.

It was Dunja. And like all the other women here, she also had our eyes.

"She's one of us," I whispered, pressing my palms against the ice. It was blisteringly cold but didn't leave my hand damp or stick to my skin. It wasn't real ice, any more than the roses were actual flowers, but instead another manifestation of Sorai's will, of her desire to hold this girl captive. Because she *was* a girl, maybe only a little older than us, if that.

"And not just that, I think," Malina said softly, leaning forward until the tip of her nose nearly touched the ice. From that vantage point, I could see the shocking similarity between her profile and Dunja's, the identically gentle slope of their noses and the sharp double crests of their upper lips. "Look at her, really look. Do you remember that picture of Mama's sister, Anais? It's her. The one who was supposed to be the last sacrifice; the one they said had burned out right before all this started. Her hair is white, but it's *her.*"

We both turned to Naisha, who gritted her teeth and screwed her eyes shut, then gave a single flinch of a nod.

"Why would you all have lied about that?" I demanded. "And why would she have tried to kill our mother?"

Naisha shook her head miserably, her mouth opening and

closing without sound. Her face was leached of color, save for two spots burning overbright on her cheeks, and beads of sweat shimmered above her upper lip. She looked like a tubercular Victorian bride in her last gasp.

"I don't know." Lina laid her own hand flat against the ice. "Naisha clearly can't say, look at her. But I think it means they lied about a lot of things. And I don't think she was the one who tried to kill Mama, either."

"Why would you say that?"

She turned to me, her face bathed in the reflected glow of the ice, as if the woman inside was luminous somehow, shedding her own light. "We only think it was her at all because that's what Sorai told us, right? But we know Mama saw her twice, even went to visit her at that hotel. And more than that . . . this is Mama's *sister*, her own twin. Would you ever have tried to kill me, Riss? Because nothing you did could bring me to that. I would cheat and lie and steal to keep you safe. Kill, even, if I had to, but never you. And I think you'd do the same for me."

Swallowing tears, I remembered the way Mama had hugged this woman, clung to her. The way they'd whispered into each other's ears. And I believed her; I believed my sister.

"What do we do now?" I asked her.

She set her jaw. "Now we set her free, and then we see what happens."

"Are you sure you want to do this?"

"Yes. Are you? Because it'll have to be you who does it. I can't sing to something that can't hear me, I think, and Naisha told me what you did with the fractal wisteria. Maybe you can try it again, whatever you did that time."

The doubts still spun like a maelstrom inside me, even with the evidence of lies right before my eyes. And it was that, more than anything, that somehow made me want to do it—the fact that I couldn't even trust my own mind. I could see Naisha's struggle now—she'd wrapped both arms around herself and shook in place like a last frail autumn leaf, her mouth twisted in a rictus—and remembered her face all those years ago in the Arms Square when she stood next to Sorai, her features so smooth even as *don't tell me what to do* resounded beneath them. If she had fought so hard to bring us here, we owed it to her to forge ahead.

And if this really was our aunt suspended in front of us, the least we could do was hear what she had to say.

I closed my eyes and pushed into that inward reach, struggling to frame what I wanted, to force it outward into the heart of the world. It was harder this time, without Malina's song to goad me, to make me certain of what shape my will wanted to take and what my goal was—and feeling my faltering, she began to sing. The battle march of it fortified me, stealing into the crumbling cracks of my own foundation like ivy twining through a building and shoring it up.

"What is that?" I forced out through my teeth.

"It's defiance," she said. "It's what you used to sound like when you and Mama fought."

"I sounded like a bagpipe war song? Could be worse."

Fragile little buds of wisteria unfurled from where my palms touched the ice, and with another fierce push that made all the veins in my body expand with the effort—*free this woman, free her, let her loose, want it more than anything*—I drove my will into the ice block's weakest points, the ones emptiest of Sorai's roses. Cracks raced through the surface as if it had been tapped along a faultline with a chisel and a mallet—and without warning the whole of it shattered, raining winking crystal particles that vanished before they hit the floor.

Lina and I had both reflexively flinched away, shielding our faces from the fallout, while Naisha cowered against the door behind us. When we turned back, Dunja stood free, blinking slowly like something ancient and predatory waking from a long sleep.

Despite myself, I pressed my back against the wall as she picked her way toward us, hips rolling, precise as a tightrope walker. This close, I could see all the finer details of her face. Her eyebrows were as white as her hair, and her face was shaped sweetly, exactly like my sister's, with the same cherry-cleft lower lip.

"Iris," she said to me in that low, rich voice. "Malina. Quite absurdly trussed up, the both of you, but still so very lovely. Which is to be expected, but still—no harm in admiring my nieces." Her eyes slid behind us, over to Naisha. "And I see you have a partially willing accomplice. Which is better than none, I suppose. Even if she might collapse at any moment, by the looks of it."

"Please tell them everything," Naisha whispered. "I . . . I have to leave. I can't hold on much longer, but I swear I won't—I swear I'll keep this secret until you get them out. That much I can do for them."

"Do it, then," Dunja snapped. "And keep as far away from *her* as you can. Blend with the others. She can't see you quivering like this, or she'll know something's afoot."

Naisha nodded once and, throwing a last plaintive look at me and Lina, fled back into the corridors.

Lina's hand sought out mine; our aunt wasn't frightening, exactly, but she had such an aura of power to her, of a different breed entirely than Sorai's. It crackled like ozone in the air before a rainfall, sharp and anticipatory, prickly on my skin. Still reeling from the effort of will that had freed her, I struggled to think what I wanted to ask her, where to even start.

She was examining me now, head tilted and eyes narrowed. "You set me free, with the infinite bloom. I thought only *she* could use that, and I've never seen any but the first nine tiers actually manifesting will. I wonder what makes you different. . . ."

"Why aren't you dead?" Malina broke in. "Or with Death?"

"I *was* with him," Dunja said, her tone laced with such longing my stomach knotted with sympathy. "And I should have been the final one. That was what your mother and I decided, between the two of us. That it would end with us, that we would be the last. That there would be no more sacrifice."

"But how?" I strained to understand. "One of us would have had to take your place, to keep Mara's bargain with Death. To counterweigh the curse, so that no one we loved would die without dying."

"Is that what they told you?" Her face went stark and bitter. "That there was a curse of some kind, that we do this for some *noble* purpose?"

Malina and I glanced at each other, then she nodded. "Sorai told us that—"

Without warning Dunja's head whipped up, arching her throat, like an animal catching a high-pitched, distant sound. "It's starting very soon," she said grimly. "Not yet, but soon. They'll come looking for you within the hour, perhaps less. There's no time now for explanations at your leisure. I can explain it all once I have you away from here. Away from *her*."

"But if one of us doesn't go tonight, Mama will wake up to agony, and the curse—"

She flashed forward and caught me by the jaw, her grip like steel, but so precise it didn't hurt. "There's no *curse*, sweetness," she said through her teeth. "Just Mara's simple bargain with Death: one daughter every generation, in exchange for her own immortality and that of all her other daughters. Your mother is only undead because Mara herself attacked her, and then suspended her in a deathless loop—to give both of you reason enough to offer willing sacrifice, without the requisite years of being brainwashed by all her poisonous love. Unlike you, daughters raised in coven don't need to be incentivized. You've seen them all; you've seen what it took from Naisha to rebel. They're trained from birth to be pliant, lovely, flawlessly obedient."

Still held captive in her hand, I stared into her crystalline eyes. They seemed to go endlessly deep, made me think of the infinite lattice of carbon in diamonds. I could feel the wisp of her breath on my face, and it somehow seemed uncanny that she even needed to breathe. "How is that possible, when Mara was the first sacrifice? Her daughter, Sorai, said—"

"It's entirely possible, on account of that being another whole-spun lie for your benefit. Your 'Sorai' *is* Mara—that's the honorific we all used for her. The highest, the first mother, the one who begat us all and then ensnared Death into letting her sell us to him."

"She's not lying," Malina said, her voice abstracted with concentration. "She sounds like glass rung with a spoon. Nothing muddy here at all."

"I'm honored to offer my fetching cadences to you, little pretty," Dunja said dryly, dipping into a mock curtsy. "And I'm glad to know you can even hear me, with that love-struck garbage in your hair. I assume it's because you've only had a few days with it, it hasn't taken root properly. You may want to please her terribly, but you don't yet *have* to do it; entertaining the notion of revolt doesn't make you feel as if defiance or betrayal would tear you apart from within. The ribbons are dipped in your soul perfume, and each of our scents has a drop of her wretched come-hither blood in it. It's the first way we become tied to her, an open conduit through which she compels love. That's how she can sense you through them, beckon you toward her."

"Why would Mama have put them in for us, then?" I asked.

"Oh, try to keep up, baby witch," she snapped at me. Her porcelain-doll face was so unsettling from this close up, the youthful delicacy of our own age paired with those deep, distant eyes. "Of course she didn't give you ribbons—that would have been one of the coven, to set everything spinning in motion before they tried to catch me. Your mother was attempting to hide you as best she could, all these years. After the monumental failure of having had you in the first place, that is."

Malina let out a distressed little sound next to me. Dunja sighed, her face warming over a fraction. "I'm sorry, sweetness," she murmured. "No need to say such barbed things to you, you who asked for none of this. Might we agree I'm perhaps a tiny bit on edge? Of course, having you wasn't truly Fai's—Jasmina's fault. We never even considered that it might play out as inevitable, just like everything else. Like the proverbial spindle, as it were."

"Lina," I said miserably, "how do we know to believe her? I still feel it, all this . . . devotion. It makes me feel like we'll be hurting Sorai. Mara. Whoever she is."

Lina turned to me. "We'll believe Dunja because I can hear her, and I *know* she's not lying, Riss. She sounds entirely pure, unlike any of the others. The sound of her truth is stronger than what the ribbons make me feel. I believe Naisha, and I believe her."

She searched my eyes with that beloved, familiar clear gaze. My sister's eyes were so much like my own, but not the same. "I know I've let you down before, but remember Fjolar. Remember that I knew not to trust him. This is my 'I told you so' moment, sister. Crappy timing, but here we are. Can you trust *me* enough to be strong for the both of us, to let that be our foundation?"

I wavered, my hands over my face, desperate to hide. I didn't know how to do this, when I wasn't the one being strong.

"I could sing you into it," she said gently, tugging down my hands until I could see her again. "But I'm not going to. Again, this is your choice."

Looking at her, I remembered that I'd once read how twins,

after four or five months of sharing a womb, reached for each other every day, held hands and touched each other more than they touched themselves. My sister and I had been together as little tapioca clusters of cells, bumping against each other as we swam in salty amniotic seas. No matter who else I loved—real love, not the false kind Mara had foisted upon us—I would never love anyone as much as my sister.

And if I loved her like that, it stood to reason that I could trust her when I couldn't even trust my own instinct or judgment.

"I know," I said finally. "I choose you. I trust you."

Malina folded me to her, then pressed a fierce kiss to my forehead. "Thank you, Riss. We'll get through this, I promise, okay? So what do we do now?" she asked, turning back to Dunja. "How do we get out?"

"I won't be able to fight through them if we come at them head-on," she said. "I'll need the ambush advantage. And I'll need the two of you."

My mouth sucked itself dry. "The two of us to do what?"

"To compete, of course, as she means you to. To keep her occupied. To play your parts to perfection until I can make my way toward the center of her web, and then get us out of here in as few pretty pieces as I can."

TWENTY-SEVEN

DUNJA LED US BACK THROUGH THE PASSAGEWAYS, TO MY bedroom, before taking a branching route away from us. We spilled out of the wall to find the door still shut and the room empty, and after a crushing hug, Lina melted back into the corridors to make her way to her own room. I sat on the edge of the bed to wait, my hands shaking so hard I couldn't even drink any of the elderflower water to calm myself. Why couldn't they at least have left some wine, those miserable bitches? Presumably taking the edge off might have diminished the beauty.

By the time Shimora came to collect me, I had flung the windows open and was leaning halfway out, taking great gasps of the brisk mountain air—cool pine and the sweet green exhales of closing plants—trying to fortify myself for the onslaughts of perfume that I knew were coming.

"Lisarah, it's time," she said. "Come. Azareen is already here with me."

"Just a moment," I told her, swallowing hard. *Please*, I thought into the night, unsure of who I meant the plea for. Sorai had said there were gods made of magic; if that was even true, maybe one of them would hear me. *Please, no matter what happens, don't let me lose her.*

Shimora had become even more stunning since we'd last seen her, in a midnight-blue sheath overlaid with black lace, her hair pulled back tightly into a tail that fell high from her crown, each shining section held fast with a silver band. Her scent was both mellower and spicier than before, allspice, mint, and something Christmasy like chocolate-dipped oranges—a heartening, celebratory smell that made me want to relax my shoulders, let excitement seep into my belly as if we were headed to some sparkling, joyous occasion instead of being all but led to a menhir for sacrifice. I let the scent soak in, but bent it to my own purpose, a bolster for the performance I was about to put on. My heart quickened as I fell into step with her, sharing a warm, furtive glance with Malina—*I trust you*—before we both shrugged back into the guise of sisters at the worst kind of odds.

Keeping marked distance between us, we followed Shimora out onto the balcony overlooking the atrium. The ceiling fixtures were aflame; the globes and onion domes cupped fire without any kind of fuel, varying in shade from electric blue to ruby red. They snapped with sparks that glimmered oddly, and with a closer look

I saw that each flame flung off a perpetual shower of tiny crystals as it burned.

Shimora caught me looking at them. "Do you know, dear heart, that the tiniest of diamonds are born even in a candle's flame?"

"No," I said quietly, taking note of it for later. "I didn't know that."

Below the chandelier, candle sconces flickered over a hall filled with our family. Some wore clinging cocktail dresses, while others billowed in tiered ball gowns, full relics of satin and lace from another era. Many danced together, arms looped around each other's waists as if they'd been apart for long enough to fiercely miss each other, while some stood in chillier clusters, by the long glass table that held cut-glass wine decanters and goblets that would take two hands to cup.

And at the center of everything, I saw Sorai. Or Mara, rather, our witch-queen in the flesh. Dazzling and regal and very much alive, the room around her billowing with waves of her undiluted scent.

She sat on a throne of glass and metal, her black hair still shining like a firelit river. Her dress was just as sleek and dark, flaring out into an oil-spill train that pooled all around the base of her chair. For once her arms were fully bare, and now I saw they were cluttered with diamond piercings, connected by lines of ink into complex constellations. Somehow I immediately understood, now that Dunja had told us the truth—the shape of the spell itself was pierced and inked into her skin, so it could run freely through her. As if she were a lightning rod.

I would have bet anything that she had exactly as many diamonds as there were daughters sacrificed.

Her hands rested on the scruffs of two lionesses sprawled beside her, and as I watched they glimmered in and out, human to animal, as if beneath a strobe light. Her honor guard, maybe. From the first nine tiers Dunja had mentioned, whatever that meant. And all around her dais, tiny bonfires burned in bronze bowls, hissing and sparking, circling her with fire. I wondered what they were for, if they were purely ceremonial. Or if they reminded her of her younger days, those dim, prehistoric times when fire meant the difference between being safe and being devoured.

The entire room went silent as Shimora led us down the staircase that spiraled to the banquet room. I felt as if I could sense the weight of every pair of gray eyes on me, and now that I knew what I was looking for, the spectrum of emotion behind them was visible, the triumph and jealousy and pity. Many of these women still served Mara; maybe most. But some, I thought, did not.

We followed our grandmother toward the throne, the sea of beauties parting before us. "Kneel," she murmured to us. We did, the floor cold beneath my gauzy skirts, the room so silent I could hear the metallic feathers of Malina's dress scraping against the marble tiles. The seams between them bit into my knees, and it made me want to shift a little, rearrange my weight. But I could feel the stillness of Malina's form beside me, and I wouldn't run the risk of seeming any less composed than she was.

In front of us, Shimora fell into a curtsy so deep it brought her to her knees at Mara's feet, bare beneath the hem of her dress. Mara laid her hands on Shimora's shoulders to lift her up. I could see the shudder that traveled through our grandmother's body at her touch, the involuntary arching of her back.

Tipping Shimora's chin up with a curled finger, Mara leaned forward and brushed her lips in a chaste kiss.

"Do you present these daughters for the choosing, Shimora?" our blood-mother crooned. Her words were wrong in the most enchanting way, burred and dark and flat, like a fossil record of the language we spoke. Tonight she seemed more feral than ever, as if the occasion wouldn't allow her to hide any more of her true nature, her real age. "In the absence of their mother, you are the closest of their blood kin. Would you stand now in Faisali's stead?"

"Yes, Mother," our grandmother said. "I present them to you." I could hear how the love caught the breath in her throat, the tremor of the weakness in it. Then I momentarily lost the scornful thought as Mara's eyes fell on me, and I swam inside the cool, fathomless sea of their gray until she shifted her gaze to Malina.

"Such beauty," Mara murmured, its echo resounding again and again, as if the banquet hall had become much larger than it was—as if we knelt in front of her in that original plateau beneath an ancient sky, surrounded by the soar of mountains singing back her sound. "Like flowers grown in dark jungle depths. Look at this one's hair, black and blue and even threads of red, like surging seas beneath the breaking dawn. Look how well she holds her wrists. And the other one, the fearless bones that shape her face, the fretwork of that collarbone, like a birdcage for her heart. Are you ready, daughters? Are you ready to gleam for us?"

I wished desperately I could reach for Malina's hand, but I forced myself to not look at her as I nodded once.

Mara tapped one of her flawless nails on the armrest; once, twice, three times. Each click thundered through the hall like an avalanche, and that distortion around her gathered in density, like a dome of molten glass. She fairly reeked of power, and though she wavered like a mirage behind the thickening, I could see her glance up and to the right, as if someone invisible now stood by her shoulder.

Unseen but unmistakably there, the true holder of the stakes, the one who would claim one of us.

Death. The way she looked up at it was almost fond, like they were friends who'd kept each other company through the endless years.

Then she turned back to us.

"Azareen," she boomed. "You who were born first to Faisali, who is lost to us. Rise and begin."

For the first time, I shifted enough that I could look at Malina. Her eyes were closed, her face nearly serene and almost alien with the swooping patterns drawn with kohl winging away from her lids, her lips glittering and cheeks vivid with blush. Even just the cameo perfection of her profile nearly broke my heart.

She took her time raising her chin, and when her eyes finally opened it was with languor, slow blinks like an invitation—as if she had all the time in the world, and was preparing to invite some-one to share it with her. She lifted one knee and then the other, rising to her feet with weightless grace, and when she spread her arms as if through water I remembered that she'd had something I'd never had—Naisha's tutelage, years of being invisibly nudged toward beauty.

Then she began to sing, a slow, sweet summoning, with the underpinning power of that tremendous, angelic chorus she'd found within herself. *Come find me*, it said. *I'm worth it. I was born for you.*

As her voices crested and rolled in multitude, she moved along with the song; not dancing, exactly, but simply following its currents, stepping gracefully along the path of its flow, the metal feathers shimmering around her, the tops of her breasts and her fine shoulders glowing like silvered snow above the black bodice.

I'd heard my sister sing of true love, of Niko, but it hadn't been like this.

This song was pure passion, and a kind of aloof sensuousness I'd never known Malina even possessed. It made me think of enchantment, of being mesmerized by a sylph. Of following her through a forest as she leaped ahead like a doe, wearing something wispy and trailing with lace and ribbons, glancing coyly back over her shoulder above the froth of her hair. It made me think of her resting in a stream with her arms above her head and her back against smooth stones, water soaking through her wedding nightgown until it clung to her skin, near sheer.

Her cherry lips glistening and parted as if she'd drunk fresh from the sweet stream. As if her mouth would taste of it.

Come get me, the song called out. *Come claim me, lover, and have me for your own.*

It was so sensual it made me want to squirm out of my skin, that something like it should come from my sister, but it didn't. Because right now, she was someone else. Not Malina, but truly Azareen. Someone distant as a star, as far from me as other galaxies, and infinitely more beautiful than the sky in the clearest night.

Where are *you, Dunja?* I thought desperately. *We need you.*

Because if she didn't come for us in time, I was going to lose my sister. Because how could I ever compare to this.

Malina finally completed her slow circuit of the hall, and with a final parting trill of song—like the sweet, guileless thrill of fingertips pressed to lips, a kiss blown toward a lover to be borne along the wind—she settled back next to me on her knees with a heavy head, dropping her chin. Now that she was near me again, I could see the toll the song had taken. Her chest still heaved with labored breaths, and the hollow of her throat had pooled with sweat. Single tracks of tears silvered her cheeks, and I thought how much this must have cost her, betraying her real love like this. It had been far from effortless, and the sight of it made a sinkhole of fear gape in my belly. She'd given everything she had, because she thought this might be real. That Dunja wasn't coming.

Mara made a pleased, humming sound, like a queen bee glutted and secure in the confines of her hive.

"Lisarah of Faisali," she purred at me. "Born second, but no less bold for it. Rise, and begin."

I came to my feet, not bothering with feigning grace. It wasn't built into my limbs, and I didn't think now was the time to try plying artifice. For a moment I just stood with my eyes closed, letting myself breathe; feeling the gossamer folds of leaves and ivy draped around me, the thorns that circled my skin, even the thick black around my lids. Thinking of the way my pale eyes would flash when I finally opened them.

I wasn't some elusive maiden-sprite flitting, mesmerizing, through a copse of trees. Nor was I cool, trickling streams, or lips parted expectantly for a kiss. So what was I? What could I be to save her, to win us this?

"Lisarah," Mara began, a stratum of something like uncertainty glinting through the ancient, limestone layers of her voices. "Will you—"

Without answer, I snapped my head up, and shattered the sky.

The constellation of chandeliers and baubles dangling from the ceiling may as well have been designed to fractal. I let loose all the gleam at once, splitting and multiplying them without mercy—glass and metal into endless, massive rows of domes and spires, the trapped butterflies and iridescent beetles bursting into a shimmering, winged army that looked like it might conquer us like a locust plague. The entirety of the ceiling grew like stalactites striving in fast-forward, into a celestial city built of crystals, like a heaven of my own making.

As I pulled at it with all I had, it came rushing down the atrium toward us, as if this crystalline new world might crash-land onto ours.

To meet it, I turned my gaze to the ring of flames around Mara's dais, and began blooming them one by one. Tongues of fire swirled around one another like blazing prayer wheels, and as they overlapped they formed a scorching, spitting wall of orange, red, and gold, a hellfire that rose to meet the heaven I'd built from above. Within the flames, those diamond-sparks I'd seen before magnified into a blinding shimmer, until the entire inferno glittered like a hellscape contained inside a ruby. Together, ceiling and floor obscured Mara entirely, trapping her behind the fire and glass.

I didn't move with it like Lina had, and I couldn't have even if I wanted to—it took all I had simply to hold this marvel, and then some to keep it spinning. But it didn't matter, because this showed everything I was.

That I was wicked.

That I was wild.

That I would not be curbed.

Dimly I could hear the gasps of wonder, the shrieks from the lionesses beside Mara, even delighted, raptured laughter from others in the crowd. And I began to think that maybe I could finish it this way, that maybe I could simply close the fractals around her. Trap her and Death both inside this cage.

Then those three clicks again—Mara's fingernails on steel—before she snuffed my bloom out in the space of a breath, the ceiling retreating meekly back to where it hung static, the flames diving back into the confines of their bowls.

"ENOUGH," she boomed. "ENOUGH, MY WILDLING. THE WINNER HAS BEEN CHOSEN, AND IT IS—"

Then Dunja landed neatly in the center of the hall like a fallen star, between us and Mara, and the world froze around us all.

She stood poised so perfectly she could have been a statue rather than breathing flesh, en pointe with one leg swept high behind her head. Both her arms were flung up too, curved above her in a soft oval, fingers nearly interlaced. Her head was tilted so the snowfall of white hair could spill freely down her back. Her spine arched like a bow, and the muscles in her bare midriff stood out from strain, above billowing harem pants and below the slip of beaded band that covered her breasts.

She launched into a series of movements, a flawless finesse that defied anything we'd seen in the pageant the day before. Barefoot steps took her through effortless flips, arms and hands and the tilt of her head sketching the shapes of another world, as if she were painting with her body. The trappings of the ballroom blurred and then fell away, until she danced on the surface of water, beside an abandoned ship that had grown a tangled forest from its rusted iron innards. The chandelier—the atrium itself—had been replaced by a blue sky with a slender row of clouds above its horizon.

The desolate beauty of it was so intense it ached. Nothing I'd seen so far could have compared to the immensity of her dance, the illusion she conjured with every movement.

The women all around us were caught, rapt, in poses of fascination. Dunja swept by them, whirling and swooping, and even when she dipped so close her passage stirred their hair, none of them moved—eyes wide and lips parted with wonder, some with hands clutched to their chests.

She dropped into a mocking bow as she finally reached Mara. The lion-women beside her were simply women now, on their knees with faces mesmerized. "I don't do well on ice, Baba Mara, you should know that much," she said. "At least not since you left me gathering frost in that godforsaken cave."

Mara trembled with the effort to move, the tiny muscles in her face quivering, but only her eyes shifted to track Dunja as she whipped forward, looped a lock of Mara's hair around her little hand, and ripped it out by the root, then tucked it into her pocket.

With an enormous, straining yank, all the tendons in her neck and chest cording like rope, Mara tipped her head back and shrieked like a banshee. The dance-illusion shattered at once. Ship and sky and water vanished like mist, and the candlelit room snapped back into place. The baubles of the chandelier knocked hard against one another, cracking and raining down over her and Dunja in a shower of glass. A tangle of black roses began snaking from Mara, transparent at first and then blushing full and dark, rounding into existence. The rest of the coven began shaking themselves free from their stupor, as wave after wave of love rolled off Mara, pungent and irresistible.

Destroy the usurper, the scent urged. *If you love me true, strike her down where she stands. DESTROY HER.*

The urge to leap to Mara's defense was so overpowering I was ready to spring at Dunja before Malina actually snatched me by my hair and wrenched me back.

"No, Riss," she managed, between panting breaths and snippets of defiant song. "No. You don't really want to do that."

Next to us, Dunja's eyes flicked back and forth, assessing the ranks descending on us. "Well," she said mildly, "this won't do."

She leaped away from Mara and the throne in a neat, airborne somersault. As she landed, she brought one foot down with a crack-ing *boom* that reverberated through the hall. It echoed over and over, spreading away from Dunja in nearly visible ripples, and each wave brought down the advancing women as if it were a physical blow. They collapsed over one another, tumbling to the ground as if they'd been struck.

Only the two of us and Mara, near Dunja's epicenter, were unaf-fected. Lina and I flinched back, hands knotted, as Mara swept to her feet, teeth bared like a wolf's and chest heaving beneath the dress's sparkling mesh, hands curved into claws at her sides. Yet her words sounded like a caress. "Come now, daughter," she said to Dunja, sweetly through clenched teeth. Every fine hair on my body stood at attention. "Would you do this to me, your old blood-mother, the one who gave you such gifts of love and life?"

"You might call it love, first mother," Dunja said, rolling to readiness on the balls of her feet. "I call it something more like slavery."

She spun on her heel like a whirlybird, flinging herself around the axis of her own body before delivering a massive backhand to Mara's cheek. Mara's head snapped back, and the force of the blow swept her up and away from the throne, until she rolled to a stop in a tangle with her lion guards.

Dunja wiped the back of her hand against the silk of her pants, than hawked and spat in Mara's general direction. She searched for me over her shoulder, eyes blazing as they met mine. "Now, Iris. *DO IT NOW.*"

I reached out and squeezed Lina's hand until I heard her

indrawn hiss; I needed her to galvanize me again, to spark that primal, indomitable instinct to protect her above all else. Once I felt it roar to life, I turned inward and unspooled the wisteria of my will, letting it loose in a flood like a river choked with petals, a crashing tsunami of branch and blossom that rolled over everything. It rushed over Mara's throne and the women in the banquet hall like a living net, a floral cage that pinned and trapped them even as it cleared a path for us.

Dunja grasped both of our hands, and the three of us ran together, heading toward the massive chalet doors and then out into the night.

TWENTY-EIGHT

WE BOUNDED THROUGH THE DARKENED FOREST, BETWEEN tree trunks and past fallen, moss-furred pines. Moonlight poured between the trees, bright as headlight beams. On the lower levels, where the sun couldn't reach during the day, the branches grew bare of needles, instead curved and sharp like thorns. Forest mulch, a mix of fern, pine needles, and bursting mushrooms, squelched beneath our bare, pounding feet.

Far ahead of us Dunja flashed between the pines with white hair whipping behind her, following no route that I could see, fleet-footed and agile as a deer. My own breath had already grown ragged and Malina kept tripping beside me over the hem of her ridiculous metal-feathered dress. Dunja had paused in our headlong tumble only for long enough to unweave the ribbons from our hair, her fingers flying inhumanly fast before she plucked them all out and dropped them on the floor, grinding them viciously underfoot. After that, it had been running and running, until my knees felt like aspic.

"Could you possibly move an iota faster, pretties?" Dunja tossed over her shoulder. "She'll cut herself free soon with those sharp old claws, and once she does, she'll rouse the others."

"Would you like to carry us on your back, *auntie*?" I called back between pants. "Because we don't get any faster than this."

We finally burst into a little clearing, choked with mud and massive, weathered logs. A battered white van was parked there, backed against the logs. Dunja unlocked the doors and we piled into the crowded insides, scrambling over stuffed animals and threadbare pillows. There was a collection of pots and pans in the farthest back, along with a carton of provisions, dried meats and fruits, juice boxes, and canned vegetables. It smelled like baby powder, chili pepper, and soap.

"Where did this come from?" Malina asked her. "This looks like someone's home."

"I bought it from some American tourists after I left Perast," Dunja replied. "A traveling family, I think. With children."

"And they just gave it to you? Along with all their things?"

"I may have stolen it a bit," she admitted vaguely. "But I left money in its place, I think. Learning to drive it properly was the larger problem, though everyone emerged from that relatively unscathed."

Malina and I exchanged uneasy glances as to what *that* meant as I tucked a matted-haired Barbie into the seat pocket to make more room for us.

"We'll be staying in the woods for a while," she continued as she fired up the ignition. "Now that your ribbons are gone, Mara won't be able to track you through them any longer. But Žabljak is too small for us to hide there properly until all this is over, however it all ends. The coven is known there, the chalet a 'retreat' for rich eccentrics. Someone might tattle on us for the right price."

"How exactly will 'all this' be over?" I asked her. "How did it even begin?"

"With one of you fair ladies falling in love, I believe," she replied as she shifted the van into gear. The engine sputtered alarmingly, but turned over. "That was when you first drew his notice. Like I said, Jasmina and I had sworn an oath to each other: the one chosen would love Death so fiercely he wouldn't want another, and the other would run and hide from the coven, live freely and never have children. So I told him I'd be the last, and he believed me—you two were the first to ever grow up outside of coven, disconnected from Mara. He couldn't feel you through his connection with her, didn't even know that you existed. And he was so happy with me, content enough he even claimed he *wanted* me to be the last. Because after me no other would compare."

I looked over at Lina, whose hand was at her mouth. "Mama told us never to fall in love," she said faintly. "Is that why?"

"That's why," Dunja confirmed. I watched her in the rearview mirror, her lips twisting with sadness. "When he felt one of you fall, he just couldn't help himself. He had to see you, to go look for himself. He's like a spoiled child that way, drawn by each new thing. No matter how much he claims to love the one he has."

A lightning shudder of chills flashed through me, a tingle of familiarity. *A spoiled child, drawn by each new thing.* I knew a bit about what that looked like. In fact, I knew *exactly* what it looked like. "So Death really is a *person?*"

The car lurched as she turned onto a rutted semblance of a road. Some little forest animal dashed across the path in front of us, its brushy tail disappearing last as it plunged into a thicket of fern and wild strawberry.

Dunja tilted her head back and forth sinuously, considering. Even that simple gesture was hypnotic to watch. "He certainly seemed so to me, though I don't believe that's entirely true. Mara's spell forces a communion, a bond between the embodied essence of an immaterial force and the soul of a material creature. He only agreed to it because she beseeched the old gods to lend him flesh and then made him love her enough to be willing to grant immortality, in return for such prizes as her daughters are. It's all beyond true comprehension. But it felt like . . ."

She gave a wisp of a sigh, and the softness of it was unmistakably wistful. "It was like the most vivid fever dream, yet the truest dream I ever had. Truer than the small, faint flicker of a life I lived before it. It's almost hard to hate her, for all she stole from me— from all of us—when being with him was the singular glory that it was. It might be a terrible wrong, a craven evil to breed daughters for such a selfish purpose. But I won't lie and say it wasn't the happiest I've ever been."

She missed him, badly. There was a terrible longing beneath the bright surface, like the hottest heart inside a star.

"What did he look like?" I asked her, my heart still pounding.

"He appeared to me like a boy I'd once admired—a form that was particularly pleasing to me. I couldn't tell you if that's how it always works, but I suspect it might be. We're as much a part of the pairing as he is; his flesh echoes whatever we desire, whatever is best to incite and seal in the love."

My stomach churned with bile. Fjolar had always seemed so familiar to me, almost remembered, and now that original, underlying memory struck like a spearhead. I'd watched a boy once, many years ago, walking along the Riva. A Scandinavian tourist, the most handsome boy I'd ever seen, jostling along with friends who'd never be brighter than they were in his shadow. He'd looked at me and smiled admiringly, the smile spreading wide across his broad and bony face, lighting his gas-flame eyes.

He'd seen me, liked me, enough that I never forgot. And everything else Fjolar had been—the eyeliner, the bracelets, those jagged, lovely tattoos; even the story about a younger brother, a cruel mother, the similarities in our names—had all been designed to appeal to me.

Malina may have been the one who fell in love, but I'd been the one he'd sought out, and wanted for himself. Did that mean I could have saved Lina, no matter what? Did it mean I might even have enjoyed it? And at bottom, what did that make me, that I'd been so ready to dive into him at the expense of anything else?

"How did you leave at all?" Malina asked Dunja. "It doesn't

sound like that's a choice the 'offering' would have."

"Once he was gone, his kingdom couldn't hold me any longer," she said simply. "It's like a trapped bubble, a pocket between our world and the next, dependent on its occupants. A space he and Mara made together—a bit like you blowing your glass, Iris, forming new space with your breath and solidifying it—as a haven for him and each companion. Without him in it, it means nothing, and so I woke—to find him, and to bring him back."

"And how do you plan to do it?"

"By stealing Mara's spell from her and shifting it to me. Though the spell flows through her, it needs the pinions of her other daughters, the ones who also become undying after they offer up their own. Like an electrical grid. I want to close the loop with just him and me inside it. No more succession; no more immortality. Just he and I forever in his kingdom—and freedom for the two of you."

WE DROVE DEEP inside the forest before we stopped, tucked high up in the mountains for Dunja's comfort. I was swimming with fatigue by then, and beside me Lina was swaying on her feet. Though Dunja seemed impermeable to the night chill, both of us were nearly chattering with cold. We'd traded in our flimsy outfits for some plain T-shirts and shorts we'd found in the back, and sneakers too big for both of us, but it still wasn't enough to shield from a mountain night.

"You're cold," she said, almost a question. "And near dead on your feet. Of course. I remember about that. There's sleeping bags in the back, why don't we put those out for you?"

"What about you?" I asked as we unrolled them, the puffy blue material ballooning. "Do you get tired? Do you even sleep?"

"I haven't tired since I returned, so I'm not sure—perhaps it will come, in time? Everything looks different than I remember, and I can feel—I can smell and hear and taste too much. The air itself has cloying flavor when I breathe, at times so I can barely stand it on my tongue. You've seen the things I can do, the way I'm strong. Whatever I am now, it's far from human anymore."

She made a faint sound, barely above a whisper, but I felt the pain of it like a knitting needle down to the soul. "It's as though I spent so much of myself on him, that what's left is this body forged of strength, run by the barest paucity of spirit. And when I try to sleep, all I see is him. It's less torment to keep my eyes open, though I'll lie down with you."

We set up the sleeping bags into a Y, our heads together at the center. Above us the pine branches crossed each other, carving up the night sky into a puzzle of star-pricked pieces with wind whistling through them.

"Strange," Dunja mused, staring at the sky, "that they should call fighting death 'raging against the dying of the light.' As if so much of light itself weren't already dead, shed by corpse stars long since passed. And as if he himself weren't so bright. Incandescent."

"I'm sorry you lost him," Lina said, her voice faint. "It was me, you know. I'm the one who fell in love. If it hadn't happened, would everything have gone the way you and Mama wanted?"

"No, sweetness. Perhaps it could have, if Jasmina had managed not to have you at all, but as it was, as soon as Mara found her again and discovered the two of you, there was no question what would happen. You merely sped things up a bit. Otherwise, once I burned out—and I would have in another year or two, he couldn't spare me from that; I would have stopped being able to dance for him, disappeared from his world just in time to die back in my own body in the cave—Mara would simply have claimed you one way or the other."

"Why didn't she just take us to begin with?" I wondered. "She knew where we were for years. Why did she let Mama keep us at all?"

"I imagine it's because the sacrifice must have a willing component in order to function—the mother's sacrifice of one of her daughters is the fuel for the spell itself. Mara would have hoped that Jasmina would come around once she tired of the constant battle it was to have you and to hide you; that would have been easiest for her. And if Jasmina refused to the bitter end, well, Mara would simply have woven a different web of lies to entice you to sacrifice, for each other and for your mother. That's why she let you come to her. So that every step you took was a testament to your free will."

Like a snake charmer, singing the song that wound our inevitable way to her.

"How do you think she found Mama in the first place?" Malina asked.

She flicked one shoulder in a delicate shrug. "I'm not sure. Jasmina would have known to shed her ribbons and not take her scent with her."

So that was why she'd had Koštana craft her the Scent of Home as a substitute, I realized in a flash. To evoke the feel and scent of coven when she missed it most, to indulge as safely as she could.

"But perhaps she still had some dab of it on her somewhere," Dunja continued, "we all wore it every day. And she had to run quick, while they were distracted with offering me, so she might not have been as thorough as she needed about washing it off. Even the slightest bit of Mara's blood still on her skin might have been beacon enough."

"What awful bullshit this all is," I said, clenching my fists against my thighs. "Mara said the sacrifice was mutual, agreed on between the mother and daughters. We were only going to compete against each other because we couldn't agree."

Dunja snorted. "Hardly. She knew you couldn't possibly agree, the way she set it up for you. There's *always* a contest between daughters—it's part of the appeal the bargain holds for him, the thing that strikes his fancy. Two beauties vying so mightily for his hand. Then once he chooses between them, Mara sparks that daughter's love to seal the bond."

"He sounds kind of like a raging bastard," Malina noted. "No offense to you."

"Oh, he is, no mistake," Dunja agreed mildly. "But also devastating, charming as the summer day is long."

We went silent for a moment, listening to the life stirring in the ferns and foliage around us. Something snuffled curiously before rushing off with a high-pitched call. I wasn't afraid; there was nothing here we couldn't fend off, between the three of us.

"I'm sorry if I've got this wrong," I began. "But you seem to miss him, and it sounds like you were happiest when you were serving. And then Mama would have lived forever, if she'd stayed in coven and given up one of us. So why is it all so terrible? The chalet is gorgeous, and Shimora said there were others all over the world. It seems like it could be a lovely life."

"Because there's no choice about it," Dunja said, flat. "No consent in anything. We're taught how to walk, to talk, to move, to think. Only to be beautiful, and amusing. Mara doesn't strip us of love for each other, of course; I'm not sure even she could go so far. So there is that. But so much forced molding empties out the gleam, makes it hollow. Like anything else, magic takes freedom to thrive. That's why you two are so different, I think. Because you grew up free."

"What do you mean?"

She shifted in her sleeping bag, rustling, stretching out her arms until her hands tangled in my hair. She ran it idly through her fingers, stroking each long strand just like Mama had done when I was little. Maybe the two of them had done that for each other. I wondered if she was still in that room, trapped by roses, on the precipice of death. Or if Mara had already let her die now that the charade was over. It strained my heart to think that nothing we could do would save her, but at least if we managed to break free, we would be doing the one thing she had fought so hard and miserably to do herself. We'd be forging a new kind of legacy for her.

"Mara's line were all true witches once," Dunja said. "The first nine tiers still are, with a weakening in every generation. The gleam is meant to be a vehicle for the bearer's will, in whatever form it takes. Instead, all our training turns it into no more than a parlor trick, empty flash and glitter with no true strength behind it. Women like us were leaders, once, healers and warriors and priestesses. Before Mara turned us into living dolls."

The wind picked up her hair, and it drifted above us like moonlit spider silk. "That's why the two of you are still so strong, reared to all that freedom. And you, Iris, have something none of the rest of us have had: the infinite bloom, the ultimate culmination of the gleam. Though the first nine can all impose their will upon this world through the gleam, only the infinite bloom lets you grasp hold of space and time, fling your will so far and wide that you can even call upon the gods. Only she has ever been able to do that."

I remembered Ylessia's churning jealousy, the envy in Shimora's voice when she talked about elders with more strength. "It gets worse as the years go on, doesn't it?"

"It does. When we're little, we don't know any better, and the ribbons make us pliant, eager to please her. But once we're older, after we've lost both a sister and a daughter, and she no longer needs to hold us back from the outside world—it becomes impossible not to see all that we gave up and all that we're missing. All the things that we could be, out there. Especially now, in this new age with wonders so accessible, it's becoming harder for her. I think that was what happened with your mother and myself—by the time we were born, the coven had reached some critical mass."

"What do you mean? What changed?"

"There were simply too many of us, maybe, for her to maintain a proper hold. Salia, who taught me to dance when it came clear that movement showcased my gleam best, let me watch videos of the Bolshoi Ballet. And I thought—I could be that, go out there, dance for anyone I wanted. Or even just for myself."

I remembered the alias she'd chosen for herself, for her brief stay in the Hotel Cattaro. Nina Ananiashvili. The woman my aunt had wanted to be when she grew up.

"Salia encouraged me a little when I shared the thoughts with her, very quietly, even started taking my ribbons out bit by tiny bit."

"Until you and Mama swore that it would end with you," Malina said.

"Oh, Jasmina hated it even more than I did. She railed to me against it all, the naming and the scenting, that nothing could be chosen by or belong to us alone. She was the one who named us in secret when we were still little, so that we would have something of our own. Jasmina and Dunja—*dunja*, for sweet-smelling quince. A sister flower, and a sister fruit."

"But then she fucked it up a bit," I added.

Dunja hummed a chastising little note. "She was so racked with guilt over everything, when she came to see me. She barely remembered how it even came about; a year after she'd made her escape, she simply met your father and *wanted* him, with disregard for consequence or any promise she had made. Like a fugue state of the will. And once she was pregnant, she couldn't bear not to have you—it matters little if that was a result of the spell or her own loneliness, the ache for coven. It was all such slow torture for her, from then on. Tamping down your gleam so Mara would never hear of you or find you. Forbidding you from loving so that

Death would never look your way. Rendering you unlovable so you wouldn't even be tempted."

"How fucking terrible," I whispered, thinking of the many years of battling her, how it must have ground up her insides even as it ground mine. The pain twisted like something alive trapped inside me. The ache might have been less, if I couldn't still see the look in Mama's eyes that last night when I'd slept in her bed. "Why didn't she just tell us all of it? We could have listened, hidden together. She didn't have to fight completely alone."

"She was afraid you might prefer the coven life to life with her, no matter the cost of the sacrifice," Dunja said softly. "Immortality is a powerful lure, not to mention wealth. And if she gave you that choice and you chose Mara over her, then she would have failed me twice."

"Or she could have trusted us," Lina said bitterly. "Given us a choice, like no one ever gave her."

"She was trying to make it right," Dunja chided. "When she came to me, she was the one who suggested a mortal's spell—a friend of hers had been a magic worker, and taught her a little of a different way. She told me to begin gathering those artifacts; that was why I met her at the café the morning Mara descended on us, to see how we would carry on. Neither of us knew that she'd already come to stalk us by then."

"So what do we do now? How do we cast it?"

"I wish I had the first notion, sweetness." The admission took all the breath out of me. "I know nothing about this brand of magic, or why it should even work at all. We'll have to find someone who does, as quickly as we can, with Mara on our heels. My thought was that this practitioner, Jasmina's friend, could help."

Malina and I sat bolt upright as one. "She's dead," I said, my heart pounding, part dread and part sheer, swelling joy. "But there *is* someone. We do know someone who could help. Could you get one of us to a phone, in town?"

TWENTY-NINE

NIKO AND LUKA WERE THERE BY MORNING; THEY MUST have driven all night, set out as soon as we called them. Dunja had picked them up in town with the trundling van so we wouldn't have two cars to conceal; as they piled out nearly on top of each other, I clasped my hands behind my back so they wouldn't shake.

Niko flung herself at Lina like something propelled from a slingshot, the chestnut pennant of her hair flying in her rush. I nearly thought she'd knock Lina over, but my sister swept her up easily as if this was something they'd done many times before, spinning her in a little circle before setting her down and tucking her close, her cheek resting on the shining crown of Niko's head.

"You fucking asshole, Lina," I could hear her rasp against my sister's chest. "You do not ever, *ever* do this to me again. Hear me?"

"Hear you, princess," Lina whispered, drawing back so she could tip up Niko's chin. "Do you think you're going to punch me this time, too, or can we maybe get on with it?"

Niko glowered for a moment, then melted into a smile like sunrise, reaching up with both hands to pull my sister's face down to hers. Blushing a little, I turned away from the private fervor of their kiss.

In the meantime, Luka waited for me by the van, his eyes hooded. His face was pale beneath its olive tint, his hair tousled from lack of sleep, jaw tight the way it was when he hoarded words like a living vault. I approached him slowly, penitent, wondering if he would keep me locked out—but as soon as I lifted a hand to touch his shoulder, he circled my wrist with his long fingers and pulled me to him, crushing me against him so tight he lifted me off the ground. It wasn't exactly the most comfortable thing, dangling in his arms with my toes just barely brushing the grass, but I'd have let him hold me like that until I died.

"Thank you for coming," I whispered. "Thank you *so* much."

"I'll always come for you, Missy." I felt his heart beating steady against my chest. "Always, anytime, anywhere. Though I'd rather just be there to begin with. You should really know at least that much by now."

I'M NOT SURE what I'd expected from this spell. A cauldron, maybe, bubbling over a low flame. Pickled nightmare nuggets bobbing in glass jars. Fingernails, teeth, black candles, and bloody runes. And nighttime, at the very least.

What I hadn't expected was to be standing at a lapping lakeshore in broad daylight, staring at the glint of my glasswork bougainvillea, which perched like a diadem on top of the unlikely pile of things we were about to burn.

"So how, exactly, are these bits and bobs supposed to work?" I asked Niko, sweeping my hand at the pile.

"We know Mara bound Death to her through a love ritual, though we can't know exactly how it worked, and we aren't her, anyway," Niko said.

We'd spent over an hour explaining everything to her and Luka. I'd expected more pushback, more incredulity. But then there was Dunja beside us, gazing narrowly at the pile. She should have looked absurd, barefoot in the forest with her snow-fox hair and harem pants, sunlight sparking off the sequined band that covered her breasts above the bare expanse of navel. But she didn't. Instead, she looked like something precious from another world, too queer and beautiful to be human. Like something that had been born in a realm a sideways step from our own.

"This gathering should act as a reversal," Niko continued, ticking them off on her fine fingers. "The tapestry from Our Lady of the Rocks is a symbol of boundless love, the willing sacrifice Jacinta made for her husband—her labor and eyesight, in exchange for the hope that she might bring him home. The opposite of Mara's forced-labor love."

"Not only that," Dunja broke in. "That island was meant to be consecrated to Mara, a gift in her name. The brothers who discovered her figurine on that first stone kept it; and Jacinta sought it out, ground it to bits, wove the fragments into the tapestry. Her will—a mortal's will, but still, not to be dismissed—was that Mara's power of love help save her husband, the chosen of her heart. It therefore connects directly to our witch mother, but with a purpose equal and opposite to the spell that she wrought. Subverted by one woman's choice."

"And Malina's violin and Iris's sculpture," Niko continued. "They represent you, the gifts you inherited as Mara's daughters so you could be fun and pretty for Death like the spell demands. And Mara's hair, and Dunja's, link this ritual to them, specifically."

"They used to call her Black Mara when she was truly young," Dunja said, her eyes distant. "She was always proud of her hair. That was how they caught me in the first place; I had to risk getting close enough to her to steal some for this, and they swarmed me, trapped me before I could take it."

"What about the bones?" Malina asked, choking a little over the last word.

We knew now what Dunja had taken: the remnants of the saint's right hand, wrapped in a torn-off bit of the velvet raiment. She'd called it his "righteous hand," and I hadn't been able to tell if she was being sincere or sarcastic. I wondered with a shudder if there'd still been scraps of tendon attached to it, if it had come loose at the lightest tug, or if she'd had to snap it free like chicken bone.

"From what you've said, the Christian canon doesn't agree with Mara, not if she's bound to much older gods," Niko said. "Christianity doesn't exactly play well with others, particularly witches. That's probably why you had that reaction at the Ostrog monastery,

Iris. Those bones are holy, and they rebel against Mara and her blood. Their burning should release that aversion, and that'll be our fuel."

Luka spoke up for the first time. He sat with his back against a pine trunk, the color finally returned to his face now that he was sure I wasn't going to vanish on him again. "So, basically, you're just doing what the legends in Mama's book say. You're trying to burn her—and then drown her, I assume, since we're by the water."

Niko raised her eyebrows at him. "That's right. Do you object?"

"I don't *object*, gnat," he tossed back. "I'm just not sure we're going about this the right way."

"And why not?"

"Because you're acting as though it's an algorithm, and all you have to do is plug in the proper values for it to spit out the result you want. That's not how spellwork goes. A collection of symbols isn't enough by itself. There has to be something—something more. Active intention, maybe. Even I know that much from Mama's stories."

"How would you know? You hated her stories."

"I didn't hate them," he forced out. "And I *always* listened. And I'm just . . . I think something here doesn't add up properly."

Dunja moved so quickly I barely had time to gasp. One moment she'd been facing the lake, and in the next she'd streaked over to Luka, where she crouched balanced on the balls of her feet, violence radiating off her like a wildcat with a swishing tail.

"Maybe that's true," she said through gritted teeth, "and maybe it's not. Either way, I don't remember asking for a critical analysis from doubting Thomas. And unless you can present us with another solution, why don't you consider not undermining your sister before she even begins?"

He met her gaze, his hazel eyes even. All of us held our breath as she considered him for a moment longer, eyes dangerously narrowed, then sprang up and spun on her heel.

"Um . . ." Niko turned to Dunja, warily. "It has to be you who does it, actually. You're the one trying to move the spell, right, shift it from Mara and onto you? So the intention behind it has to be yours. You should be the one who sings, too."

Silence settled over the four of us as Dunja stalked off to fetch the jug of gasoline that had been bumping in the back of the van beside the pots and pans. She doused it over the objects and the bristle of kindling that surrounded them. I felt a piercing pang for what would be lost. That singular tapestry; the bougainvillea, the gift I'd given my mother made with my own breath; the violin that my sister had used to play me everything I'd ever felt but couldn't say, since she was barely old enough to hold it properly. Even the idea of burning the saint's hand felt like sacrilege.

Still, there was a quivering sense of expectation in the warm, early-summer air, the sunlight dense as amber as it fell over us and broke itself into the ripples of the lake. The world beyond us and the lake seemed to have receded entirely. The van was tucked into a secluded campsite about a mile away, far from where tourists usually gathered, and it was still too early in the season for hikers and wildlife enthusiasts to be making their pilgrimages to the Black Lake.

I wondered if the name was why Dunja had chosen this place—yet another connection to Mara, besides its obvious and staggering beauty. A perfect ring of pines surrounded the water, reflected in its sky-blue surface; one of the pines had died, and stood white and bare next to its green neighbors like a lingering ghost.

Dunja stood still in front of the assemblage, gathering herself. She splayed and flexed her fingers a few times, the only sign of nervousness I'd seen her show so far. When she began singing, her voice was clear and lovely as a lyre. Probably all of them were taught to sing, along with everything else. Just in case that was something that he liked.

> *Her bones are of nightmares, her face cut from dreams,*
> *Her eyes are twinned ice chips, cold glimmering things,*
> *Her hair is the scent that will drive you to death,*
> *Her lips are the kiss that will steal your last breath.*
> *Kill her in winter, so she can birth spring.*

Reaching into her deep pocket, Dunja withdrew a plastic lighter, small and orange, the kind you could get at any gas station. It didn't seem like the kind of thing that could set us free from an ancient magical binding, but then again, what did I know.

As if she'd caught my thought, Dunja hesitated, dancing the lighter through her fingers like a magician's coin. Then she strode over to the leftover pile of kindling and found a slim little branch, rolling it between her palms as she strode back over to the pile. She dropped to her knees and angled the stripling against a central hank of wood. It whirled between her palms into a blur; one moment there was a bright ruby glint of sparking and a single thread of smoke, and in the next, flames raced over the pile like a conquering army. Dunja leaped neatly away as they whooshed together into a massive, roaring fire.

I bit my lip as my fractal bougainvillea charred and then melted, wilting in on itself like a true flower. Below it, Malina's violin and the tapestry threw off a shower of sparks.

We watched it burn for a while, the smoke and fire smelling uncannily of winter against the sunlit day. Dunja's eyes were closed and her face intense with concentration as she sang the next stanza.

> *To chase out the winter, build her to burn her,*
> *Make her a body, the better to spurn her,*
> *Build her of twigs, and of scraps, and of sticks,*
> *Then build up the fire, and sing loud as it licks,*
> *Kill her in winter, so she can birth spring.*

Once the fire settled into a steady, almost homey crackle, Dunja reached for the pots and pans she'd filled with lake water earlier, and began tossing them over the conflagration. The flames hissed like a tangle of snakes, and the stink of wet wood rose and filled the air.

> *Strip her arms bare of glitter or silver,*
> *Choke her and flay her, force her to deliver,*
> *Drown her in lakebeds, or quick-running streams,*

Dunk her in pond scum to smother her screams,
Kill her in winter, so she can birth spring.

As soon as the fire subsided, Dunja began picking up the objects and flinging them into the lake. Some still smoldered, and they'd have burned me to the bone if I'd tried to do it, but her movements were so deft and quick that once she was done, the few streaks of soot on her silk pants were the only signs that she'd even been close to the flames.

Then, under the water, the remnants of the objects all caught on fire again, as if they'd never even stopped burning. As if the water was made of alcohol.

I caught my breath, and beside me, I could hear Malina's gasp. It reminded me of images I'd seen of oil fires raging unchecked on ocean surfaces, but these continued blazing as they sank, like the ruins of some catastrophic shipwreck. Smoke from them funneled through the water, and spat up black and oily, spinning into the sky like a sooty tornado wreathed with veins of flame.

"Oh shit," Niko whispered. "Is that what it's supposed to look like?"

"Would we know?" Malina asked. "Would we feel it if it was?"

"Well, *something* has certainly transpired," Dunja said, so dryly I nearly laughed. She swiped the back of one hand over her cheekbone, leaving a trail of char. "In either case, we cannot stay here. This will hardly have escaped her notice, whatever its effect. I need to get you all away from here immediately, back to our camp."

"Why camp?" Luka argued. "Why can't we leave, right now?"

"Because if this isn't over, we will need some other way to finish it," Dunja said. "And there is nowhere in the world for these two to go, where she would not eventually flush them out like prey leaving a bloodied trail."

WE ATE WHAT we could forage from the back of the van. I wrestled open a jar of cocktail hot dogs that had seen better days, or possibly years, and we roasted them over a little fire banked with stones. Luka had lit this one; Dunja had been oddly willing to let him take the reins, and now she perched on a massive stump across from us, huddled in a tasseled black pashmina that had also come from the van. She looked like a bird that had drawn a sheet over its own cage. Maybe she was finally tiring, I thought. Or maybe she just missed him.

Malina sat with Niko on a log a little ways away from us, far enough that we couldn't hear their conversation. Her head rested on Niko's shoulder and her arm draped across Niko's legs. Even exhausted, and with all the danger we were still in, my sister looked happier than I'd ever seen her.

I teased a baby hot dog off its stick with a pair of cheese crackers, and offered the makeshift sandwich to Luka. He took it without looking at me, making sure our fingers didn't even brush, muscles twitching madly along his jaw in the firelight. He'd barely spoken a word to me since we got back here, and I could almost see the fury simmering inside him. It scared me. We'd been friends for almost ten years, and in all that time, I didn't think I'd ever seen him fully angry. At least not like this, with it boiling so close beneath the surface.

"What's wrong?" I whispered to him. "Why are you being like this?"

He gave a tight shake of his head, then stood. "I'm going to take a walk."

I looked down at my hands as he left, picking at my fingers, my insides raw with pain.

"It's not you he's angry at, sweetness," Dunja said. The firelight painted flickering shadows across her face, until she looked like a jungle cat peering through foliage. "He's furious with himself. You can see it from a mile away."

"Why would he be?"

"Because he doesn't think it's working, and he doesn't know how to protect you. And that's the one thing he yearns to do."

I hesitated. "Dunja—I think I know him. Death, I mean. There was a boy I met, right before Mama died. Right before this all started. You haven't said so much about him, but I think . . . I'm afraid it may have been him." I took a shuddering breath. "And I wanted to say I'm sorry, for anything that happened with him. I didn't know he belonged to you. And having known the best of him, even for just a little bit, I know it must hurt so much that he left."

She unwound the pashmina from her shoulders and rose, stepping neatly over the fire and to me. Her movements were so precise the air barely stirred as she dropped into a crouch in front of me and took my face into her hands, thumbs brushing over my cheekbones. I leaned into her touch.

"He hurt you, didn't he, sweetness?" she whispered fiercely, her pale eyes holding fast to mine. I could feel the outraged flare of her protection, even beneath all the love she had for him, and it was too much to keep from crying. "We aren't meant to serve him with beauty outside of the magicked confines of that bubble kingdom; our living bodies are simply too frail to withstand the burden. So he pushed you too hard when he shouldn't have, didn't he, because he was eager to see how far you could go? Demanded more than you could give. Am I right?"

A tear slid hot down my cheek. "Yes. I mean, I wanted to do it—I was happy with him—but it just—"

"Let me tell you something your mother wished so desperately she could have told you, little niece." She cupped my cheek. "Not everything is your fault. And certainly not anything he did. You don't always need to be so brave."

Tears stung my eyes. "What do you mean?"

"You know what I mean. Go to that boy." She skimmed her fingers down my throat, hovering them gently above my breastbone. "Tell him what's in there. Or what *would* be in there, rather, if you weren't so hell-bent on keeping it out. There's no need for that anymore. Not when you could have the true luxury of love."

I'D NEVER KNOWN such a complete silence. Down by the sea, there was at least the sound of water, and from our apartment, we could always hear the faraway rush of the cars on the Adriatic Highway, the lonely bark of stray dogs, the shuffling and muffled voices of neighbors around us. But here, the hush was nearly perfect, broken only by the high *skree-skree* of some sole insect in the ferns. Even the birds were settling in for the approaching night.

I followed the path back to the van, my ears full of quiet and the rushing of my own blood.

He wasn't there. "Luka?" I called out softly, counting my heartbeats in the silence. I was up to seven when he replied.

"Up here." I followed the sound of his voice until I saw his silhouette above me against the gathering dusk. "Be careful. There's roots, and loose stones."

I picked my way gingerly to the incline, hauling myself up the slope toward him. The little hillock overlooked the liquid glimmer of the Black Lake below, and across from us, the great humped summit of Veliki Medjed and the triangle of Savin Kuk hulked against the purpling sky. The cherry of his cigarette flared when I reached him, and my palms tingled again. I knew he only smoked when he was unhappy.

"Hey," I said. "Can I talk to you?"

Another smoky exhale.

"I don't know, Iris. Is there anything to say? I'm never sure, with you."

I placed my palm on the rough trunk of the pine between us, stroking it like a pet. "Maybe I can start, then. I know—I know you're angry. I'm not sure why, and if you don't want to tell me, that's all right. But I don't know what's going to happen after tonight."

Silence, but I could see him nod. I traced his chiseled profile, the well-hewn lines of nose and lips that were so delicate on Niko but fine and strong on him.

"If it didn't work," I continued, feeling the well of tears in my throat, "I don't know what's going to happen. Mara will keep hunting us, and I think—I'm afraid that she might win, somehow. And if she does, I can't let Lina go. It has to be me. I'll go willingly, if I have to."

"No." The word sounded so raw it may as well have been ripped from his throat. "Lina will hate you forever if you do it."

I shrugged, leaning my cheek against the scrape of bark. "And that's why I'll do it. Because she might hate me for it, but she'll get to live. Sometimes that's what real love takes, I guess. A sacrifice on both sides, doing for the other person what they can't do for themselves."

"That's funny you should say that," he bit off, swiping the back of his hand over his mouth. "Because I've been trying to love you for as long as I can remember, and you've never let me give you *anything*, no matter how much you needed it. That's what all those flowers were for, you know? I ordered them online from a rare-flower distributor in Belgrade, I may as well tell you now. They were the only thing you'd ever take from me. I thought the price was worth it."

I pressed my lips together. "I loved those, Luka. But they weren't the only thing you ever gave me, please believe that. You were always *there*. It meant so much. It meant everything."

"And what about now? I can't give you anything. I can't even put myself between you and her."

"It's not your fault," I said softly, laying my palms lightly on his chest. He jerked beneath my touch, and I could feel the fire-heat of his skin beneath his shirt, and a matching, incremental melting inside me. "Just the fact that you want to is so wonderful to me. I feel like I've spent my whole life fighting, sometimes maybe even when I didn't need to. But even still, why did you never try to tell me? Anything about what you felt?"

It was so hard to look at him like this, full-on and unblinking, with nowhere to hide. I'd spent so much of our time together with him by my side that I wasn't remotely prepared for how facing him would make me quake.

"Because I didn't want to push you into anything," he said, eyes steady on mine. "I didn't want you to feel like—like you owed me anything. Like you were supposed to love me just because I loved you. That's not how it should be. That, and I deserved more, Riss, than to keep banging on the door of someone who refused to ever let me in."

My fingers trembled against his chest, and I swallowed before I went on. "I didn't let you in, you're right. Not just because Mama told us both not to; obviously that never stopped Lina. It also felt safer keeping you right next to my heart, so close. Because if I let you inside, I knew the only way to ever get you out again would be to crack it all the way open. And that's not . . ." My voice broke clean through. "That's not something I'd survive."

His hands crept over mine, and his palms were so warm that I couldn't stop the tears. He gave the deepest sigh—as if he'd held that single breath for years, a genie stoppered in a bottle. His eyes glittering in the dark, he took my hands and brought them up to his face, pressed a soft kiss into the center of each of my palms.

Then he cupped them over his own cheeks, so that I held his face with his hands above my hands. "So why now?" he whispered, low and rough, tilting his forehead until it met mine. "Why tell me now?"

"Because if it turns out I have to be the one to go, I can't"—I choked back a barbed sob—"I can't do it unless you know I *do* love you, too."

I hadn't been prepared for the fierceness, either. Over the years, I'd thought about how this might go—of course I had—but the scenarios I'd played out had been tender, coaxing, and cautious.

Instead, Luka slid his hands up my arms and spun us around, pressing my back hard against the trunk. I opened my mouth to gasp and he covered it with his own, lips warm and expert as they caught mine. He tasted so good, sweetness and salt with that slight, smoky underlay of tobacco. I sighed into his mouth, hands sliding up his chest to wind around his neck. He caught them and pinned them above my head, one hand wrapped around my wrists. I pressed against his grip despite myself.

"Let go, Missy," he murmured, tipping my chin up with his free hand. "Just let go, for once. Let me."

I did, melting fully against the trunk, the bark rasping against my head as I tipped it back. Whatever I gave him would be the right thing. I could trust him with not just the best, but with all of me.

He trailed kisses down my neck until my entire body burst with tingles. Everywhere he skimmed his fingers, the inside of my skin ignited. I remembered how sometimes, in mining cities, the coal beneath the earth caught fire and burned for years without ever going out, because it couldn't be extinguished. That was what I felt like when his hands ran over me, as if he were drawing out veins of ore I'd never known I had. Even my cheeks felt like they might glow with heat as he brushed his lips where my tears had dried.

He set his teeth delicately into my neck, and I shuddered against him, shock waves spreading from the suck and flutter of his lips and tongue in the hollow of my throat.

"Oh, that's going to leave a mark, my Missy," he breathed against me, ringing one of my wrists with his fingers so he could feel my racing pulse. "How do you feel about that?"

I licked my lips, trying to gather myself. "Um, I feel very *yes* about it."

"Good," he purred. "Because if I'm going to be yours, I want the whole world to see."

He drew back for a moment as I tried to catch my breath. Strands of my hair had gotten caught between my lips, and he gently smoothed them free. "There," he said, leaning in for a kiss that startled me even further with its softness. "Now you're perfect again."

"Perfect?" I challenged. "Or uncanny?"

He let me go to smile into my face, teeth glinting in the dark as he slid his hands over my waist. "Both, of course. Exactly the way I love you."

Nothing Mara had ever done could have touched what we had then.

THIRTY

A FEW HOURS LATER, I WOKE NOSE TO NOSE WITH LUKA, snug in the sleeping bag we'd somehow managed to cram ourselves into together for a nap. As soon as my eyes opened, he smiled, blinking himself languorously awake.

"Your eyelashes are ridiculous," I informed him, nuzzling the tip of my nose to his. "You look like Bambi's hotter brother. It's completely unfair, and constitutes much of what's wrong with the world."

"And you have pine needles in your hair." He gave me another slow smile, shifting against me. "It looks real pretty."

"Oh, I can tell you think so. They're not only in my hair, either," I added, squirming.

He grimaced. "That can't be good."

"It was *well* worth it," I murmured, leaning in for a kiss.

Dunja popped up above us like a bad-omen crow, the black pashmina rewrapped around her head and shoulders. "So the children have consummated their tendresse," she said. "Thank the gods. The tension was about to give me a migraine, and I didn't even think I could get those anymore."

Luka and I scrambled apart, to the extent that two full-length individuals confined to a sleeping bag can scramble any distance. "Sorry to have imposed on you," I muttered.

"Not to worry." She gave me one of her quick, brilliant smiles. "I'm a staunch supporter of young love. Your sister is somewhere nearby with her lady; I've been keeping watch and nothing has come for us. I think, perhaps, that we might be safe."

Luka and I squirmed our way out of the sleeping bag after that, and Lina and Niko wandered back over to rummage with us through the van's supplies for snacks. Lina gave me a sly look through her lashes as I handed her a packet of dried apricots, humming something that sounded suspiciously like "Peaches and Cream."

I fought back a smile. "You're the worst, you know that?"

"What, *me*? When I'm not even judging you for being such a copycat? Just remember who had their own Damjanac first."

Still, I saw her slip a subtle high five to Luka as she passed by him, and the sight of it warmed my insides much more than it should have. I felt generally tender, as if the clay casing I'd packed around my heart for years had finally cracked open, and what was beneath it was so raw it felt even the slightest, passing breeze of emotion.

Or maybe that was what it always felt like, knowing you might lose everything when you'd only just discovered all there was to live for. The sheer brilliance of the light against the darkness was almost too much to stand.

I was sitting on the ground between Luka's knees, with my back to him, when Dunja returned from one of the perimeter checks she had been running periodically; I could feel his legs tighten around me as she finally appeared from between the trees like some gorgeous, unlikely nun, the pashmina hiding her hair.

Her flawless face was bleak as she reached our clearing. "They're coming," she said grimly. "I can hear them gathering, the ground carrying their sound. It's all of them now, full coven strength. Whatever we did yesterday must have accomplished something, and now they come to hunt us. I can hear Izkara baying."

Luka dug his hands into my hair, as if he could feel the collapse of my heart in my chest. "*Baying?*" I asked faintly.

"Izkara is one of the first nine tiers. Mara's great-great-granddaughter. She can gleam by taking on animal form, any combination that she dreams to life. Like a sphinx, or a griffin, but without limitation. Whatever menagerie suits her will."

"Like Naisha?" Malina said.

"*Not* like Naisha. Her gleam is hollow, a pretty fancy, while Izkara's is ancient enough to be real. If she grows claws of any kind, you had better flee before you think to test whether they can rend you from stem to stern."

Niko twined her arms around Malina's neck as if she had no intention of ever letting go, from where she sat tightly snuggled on my sister's lap. "So, what do we do, then?" she demanded. "*Now can we run?*"

Dunja closed her eyes, and even in that inhuman, altered face, I saw the leaching of her stony strength. "I don't know what to do. Jasmina—what we planned, the makeshift spell, that was the only hope. And now there's nowhere to run from them."

"How much time do we have?" Luka asked above my head.

She tilted her head, considering it. "An hour, maybe. Perhaps a little more. It'll take them time to mass, and with so many abreast, they'll have to scour the forest on foot."

"So dance it for us," Luka said above my head. I tipped my chin back, craning to look at him. His face had fallen so still and furious that it was terrifying, like rage somehow carved into rock. "That's the one thing you haven't done. Show us all what it was like, between you and Death."

Her face shuttered. "Why would I do that?"

"Because it's the one thing we're missing," he said. "You're the only one who's been there and back. Maybe there's something we could learn from seeing it."

"You can't ask me to do that," she spat back, lips skinned back from her teeth. "I nearly couldn't stand it when he left me for the first time. I'll have to feel it all again to dance it for you. I have to do it all a second time around."

"Then maybe that's the sacrifice you have to make," Niko said. "For Lina and for Iris. Because if you abandon them now just to spare yourself that pain, when there might be another way, then you're no better than Mara herself."

Dunja hid her face in her hands, and for a moment she was just a girl again, nineteen years old and cold and lost. "How much do I have to give up," she murmured into her hands. "Just how much."

Then she gathered the final remnants of her poise, and stood.

Between one breath and another, Dunja went so still it was as if she held herself separate from the air, so even the breeze couldn't touch her. The only sign of life was the pretty pulse beneath her chin, and with her head held high, I could see it ticking like a clock's second hand beneath her skin.

When she finally began to move, it was in a single smooth, explosive moment, a lily unfurling in fast-forward. A series of delicate steps, ball to heel, took her out of our little campfire circle, where she became the centerpiece of a diorama against the pines—a glittering ice sculpture with flowing, snowy hair against the backdrop of brown and green. A glistening strand of a spiderweb came loose from where it spanned two branches above her, drifting lazily down until it settled into her hair.

"Sing with me, little niece, if you will," she said to Malina. "I could use the accompaniment."

She splayed her fingers once, and then again. Then she arranged her hands in front of her, back-to-back like a butterfly's wings, to begin her dance.

SHE WAS ALONE when she woke, and the waking hurt. A cave loomed all around her, its stalactite teeth thicker than her arm, ice sparkling inside its every cranny from the faint light that filtered through the entrance. She hurt so much inside that as she rose up on her forearms, she expected them to quake beneath her weight. But they felt strong; so did her legs. Strong, and almost perfect, even when the furs—*the ones they'd wrapped her in, after they'd climbed her up the mountain*—fell away from her. She should have felt the cold, but there was no trembling, no spray of goose bumps, no feeling to her skin. Even the furs she clutched to her as she stood, rabbit and fox and ermine, felt like nothing as she held them.

At least Jasmina would never know any of this. Perhaps she was already well away, having fled as they had planned, while the others carried Dunja to her casket of ice.

She wandered the cave with pelts trailing behind her, feeling nothing beneath her feet. And nothing under her palm as she ran it over rough and frozen rock, then palmed the curves of fat, white icicles. At the entrance, she leaned outside into the gale; even the swirling white of icy flurries wouldn't lash at her face.

The wall felt like nothing against her back, when she slid down against it to draw her knees up to her chest. And yet inside she felt just like herself, afraid and stubborn and so alone; and at least when she leaned her cheek on her knee, she could feel her own skin and how it was warm.

He was meant to be waiting for her here, she thought. He who had chosen her. But the cave was empty save for herself, and the stone pedestal on which she'd had her rest. Still, as her gaze swept through the corners, in one she caught a flickering she hadn't seen before. There, right there, the air seemed bright and blurry, like the shimmering of a heat mirage above an asphalt road.

As she watched it, it gathered more unto itself, until she made out a silhouette. It seemed to her like a shadow play, the way it grew and shrank and changed its shape. But the closer she looked, the more it seemed like something—someone?—that she knew. As soon as she'd thought it, color flowed into form, and the flicker became a breathing boy.

"*You*," she said, and her heart began to race. It was nice to know it could still do that.

"Me," the shadow-boy agreed, and stepped from the corner in full flesh. She wove her hands in her lap and cowered against the nothing stone. He crossed the cave to crouch in front of her, dark curls falling over his brow.

"You're just like I remember," she told him. He'd been so staggering, so unforgettable, that day Salia showed her the Bolshoi Ballet. A Russian boy with near-black eyes and a patrician face, cheekbones like facets and a cleft chin. He was tall and broad-shouldered, dancer-slim. "But how can you be here?"

He offered her his palm, dark eyebrow raised. She laid her fingers on it, and he was so warm and there her insides quickened again. He wrapped his long fingers around her hand and brought it to his lips, tracing their crests with her own fingertip.

Even as her eyelids went heavy she jerked her hand back, frowning at him.

"Too forward?" he asked, one side of his mouth quirking. "I've been known to rush. Usually in the sense of 'untimely,' but I don't like to limit myself."

"You're not that boy," she concluded. "Even if you do look like him."

He laughed out loud, rich and deep. "No, I'm not. But you do know who I am, you who danced so well for me. You who won me fully with your dance." He watched her warmly, brow furrowed. "I could hardly wait to have you here."

The thought of his anticipation made her giddy. "And how long *have* you been waiting for me?"

"Two days, and forever," he said. "A very long time, all things considered."

She put her hands on his knees. It felt outrageous, to do so to a near stranger, but this boy belonged to her already. "What do we do now?"

"Well, you're meant to be my gift." He gave her a broad grin, his teeth straight and very white. "So, I expect you'll woo me, show me all that you can do."

"Is that so?" She pouted at him, tilting her head. "Perhaps it won't work that way, this time. Perhaps *you're* the gift, meant to be mine."

"Then, maybe, if I'm going to be your gift," he said, drawing so close their foreheads nearly touched, and she could smell the warmth and boy of him, "you should tell me what you mean to call me."

SHE WOULD CALL him Artem, like the boy who danced. She knew it even before he brought her to the strangest desert she had ever seen.

"Is it real?" she asked, turning in a circle. The sand wasn't any color it should have been; the dunes around them blazed with

rainbow bands of turmeric yellow, magenta, lilac, violet, and ver-
milion. In the distance rose rich, green mountains, surrounded by
what looked like the tangle of jungle. She couldn't remember how
they'd gotten here. He'd touched her, maybe, in the cave, cupped
her face and told her to close her eyes.

Or maybe not. It didn't matter.

He reclined against one of the dunes, all in white, a loose shirt
and pants that looked like they kept him cool. It seemed like it
should be hot here, though of course she didn't feel heat anymore.
"Certainly it's real. At least for me, and now for you."

She looked down at herself. A white band sparkled over her
breasts, as if the ground dust of diamonds had been woven into
the fabric, throwing icy facets of fire from the sun. The pants that
ballooned around her legs, cuffed tightly at her ankles, were silk so
fine they felt like water on her skin. "Where are we, then? And did
you pick this"—she gestured at herself—"all this for me?"

"These are the Seven-Colored Earths of Mauritius. I thought
you might like it here." He ran a hand through his hair, haloed by
the midday blaze. "Makes a nice change from all that cold. And
no, I didn't pick your clothes for you. That was what you wanted.
Seems to me you like to shine."

She narrowed her eyes at him, raising her chin. "You don't
know me."

"But I'd like to, if you'll let me."

"Seems to me I have no choice."

He laughed again, that deep, warm rumble, and she liked the
surprise that washed like waves across his face. He wasn't used to

laughter, then. That was something she could change.

Then she danced the desert for him, painted its dunes with a brush of flying hair, its colors with each flick of the wrist, and with the skin that she laid bare. She should have felt the sharp grains under her soles—arcs of color sprayed with each sure step, so she knew that they felt her—but it was as if she danced on nothing at all.

As if all the world slept around her, and she its dancing dream.

When she finished and dipped into a bow, he clapped like a child, his face bright with rapture-glow. "How beautiful," he whispered. "None of the others danced quite like you, before."

You see now, a dark voice rilled coolly through her mind. *I bade him love you, just like so.*

She shrugged it off like an unwelcome cloak. She could do it all herself, make him love her on her own. Keep Jasmina safe and free wherever she was, far from here in some new home.

"Do you want to see another?" she asked, dropping lightly to her knees before him. "I'm not tired, not at all. You could take me elsewhere if you wanted."

"So, have you decided, then?"

"Decided what?" She wanted to stroke his hair, his face, but it was still too early yet.

"What you want to call me." He smoothed her hair back from her temples, and she nudged his palm like a cat. She would let him touch her first, she thought. She could live with that.

"I'll call you Artem," she said.

Artem, who's mine.

But she didn't tell him that.

IT WASN'T UNTIL later that she understood. They were real, the two of them. It was the world that was the dream.

HE TOOK HER to a sere mountaintop, a cradle for three lakes that couldn't keep their color. One was the brightest teal she'd ever seen; another green, the other black. But as the sky sped over them, from dawn to dusk to velvet night, she saw them shift their hue like lizards into brown and red and blue.

"Are you *sure* you didn't make this for me?" she asked. "This place can't be real."

"Oh, it is," he assured her. "Real, and very deadly, too. Those are the Kelimutu lakes, and all three will eat you to the bone."

"They'll eat someone else, maybe," she called over her shoulder as she stepped into the blue one. The water pooled around her, darker than the sky above, and she didn't feel a drop. "But not me."

She didn't notice, at least not yet, the streak of her hair that had begun to turn.

AFTER THE LAKES, he took her under the ocean, into the heart of a drowned Lion City. There she danced for him in a banquet hall filled with water, and found, as her hair floated and bubbles rose around her, that she no longer needed breath.

They never slept. She danced place after place for him, never needing rest. After the ocean, he took her to a village of houses with blue walls and inner dunes of sand. She danced this inside desert for him as he chased her from room to room, his laughter echoing when she hid-and-sought from him.

"If you like games, foxfire," he said when he caught her, "then I know just where to take you next."

It was a vast, abandoned amusement park, choked with weeds and red with rust, beneath the ancient ring of a Ferris wheel. She climbed its metal spokes and danced its shape for him, swinging from cabin to cabin without fear even as the metal groaned beneath her feet.

"And you like the rides, too, I see," he said. "Let's look for bigger ones to find."

People left all sorts of things behind, she found, as she wound her way through roller-coaster tracks that sprawled over whole empty miles, while he watched her, clapping, from the ground. Even a domed ballroom beneath a lake, its walls water-stained and windows leaking dappled light, guarded above the surface by a hunched Neptune with a spear. And forts on spindly telescope legs stranded in the sea, and stained-glass train stations with curling ivy but no trains, and stone mills that sprouted grass instead of grinding grain, and peeling wooden houses like matryoshka dolls in Russian forests.

She didn't need to eat. She didn't need to drink. She only needed herself, and him.

The love was becoming her own, and real.

And still her hair was mostly red.

"I want to see what you do," she told him once, taking him by the hand. "Helping them all die. Making them die. Whatever it is, I want to be by your side."

"It doesn't work like that." He pulled her close, tucking her head beneath his chin. "It's happening right now, and in every other moment. It's not a thing I do, but the thing I am. All the other parts of me that you don't see—that's where they are instead of loving you."

"You and your *multitudes*," she teased. "But why can't you take me with you, then? With all the rest of you?"

"Because if I did that, my foxfire love, then that would kill you, too."

"Is that why we never see anyone else? Why it's always just you and me? I'm just forgetting what other people do, a bit. And maybe I wish that I could see them."

"And I would give that to you if I could, my heart. But this is the way she willed it to be."

"Take me somewhere else, then," she said, "where we can really be alone. Somewhere far away from here, where no one's ever been before."

THERE SHOULD HAVE been no light inside that tree. But she could see it perfectly, how its trunk was like a vault around them, wide and silent as a church. Bright beetles with green and pearly shells climbed the inner skin; they would have terrified her once. Now she wished, with part of her heart, to feel their tiny feet scrabbling against her palm.

"It's the biggest banyan that there is," he told her. "Is this much alone enough for you?"

She laid her hands on his shoulders and pressed him down until he sat. "It is."

"But why—"

"Just watch," she said. "I'll show you what I meant."

She danced for him inside the tree, but the tree wasn't what she danced. She showed him how she'd stroke him with her hair, trailing her hands like vines, how she'd like to feel the warmth of him pressed against her from behind. How she'd wrap her legs around his hips, tilt her chin and arch her back; how she'd let him kiss her until she wept, and even more than that.

Much later, she rested her chin on his bare chest and watched him watching her. "What is it, foxfire?" he said. He had a very darling dimple, she'd found, when he smiled at her this certain way. "What's in those she-wolf eyes?"

"Do you love me, Artem?"

He frowned. "I've always loved you. I've told you a thousand times. Do *you* love *me*?"

"But you could say that for all of them," she argued, "the ones who came before me. And if that's true, then what's the use in me loving you, too? It doesn't matter. It's all the same. Unless you chose to choose only me, then all this is just *her* game."

"I did love them, yes, that much is true," he said carefully, feeling her tense against him. "When Mara offered this to me, beauty and love in place of solitude, these became the rules. But you—you're the first, in all this time, who made me love her to the soul. I wouldn't lie to you, my foxfire. That's the full truth that I hold."

"If only you could die for me to prove it," she teased. "Too bad you're not allowed."

"That would indeed be a drastic measure," he agreed. "But for you, I would. If you demanded it of me, at least, and if I found I could."

"And what about me?" she pressed him. "What about when I'm gone? You'll take up with the next one? You'll just carry on?"

"I'll mourn you for an eternity," he whispered. "I'll howl for you in the hearts of mountains, and weep for you into the lakes."

"An eternity and two days, you mean. Until the next one takes my place."

They were quiet for a long time, and so still, that a long coral snake slithered over her feet. It might have made her shriek and shudder once, but now she could barely bother to take heed.

"What would you have me do instead?" he asked her. "What would please you more?"

"That you never take another, of course," she said. "And never let me go."

"I can't, my lover. I wish I could, but she bound me with her will." He ran her hair through his fingers, braiding the white streaks with the red. "I'll lose you, and you'll leave a space behind, a space for a new daughter to fill."

She pulled away from him fiercely, and drew up her spine, and tried to remember how it felt to be brave. "Then don't dare say you love *me*, because you don't," she spat. "You just love what you happen to have."

Still he said nothing, and she rounded on him, forcing them face-to-face. "The one who comes after wouldn't be some stranger; a daughter of *my* blood will take my place. And this is what you'd offer her, my successor and my niece? False love and empty places, no kind of choice and this vacuum of peace? If you love me, then prove it. Don't look for another, for I can tell you, there will not be one. Once this is over, all of you and me, all of this will truly be done."

"I'll be alone then, after you, if that's what you want," he said, and she could hear the tears beneath his voice. "Darkness entire, no more beauty, or love—but if that's what you ask, then that's my choice."

"You won't be alone, because I'll love you, even once I'm gone." She climbed onto his lap and kissed him hard, and he clasped her against his chest.

But when she looked up at him, he'd lifted his head and his eyes were only halfway there—as if he were searching toward the next.

THEN HE ASKED her to dance him the tides of the oceans, and vanished while she danced.

THIRTY-ONE

RIGHT AFTER THE BURST OF MOVEMENT THAT PAINTED HER waking—eyes springing open and mouth shaped into a gasp— Dunja fell to her knees like a doll whose strings had been cut.

Lina and I rushed to her side. She was breathing hard and sharp, as if every breath cut deep, and tears streamed down her face. I wrapped my arms around her without a second thought, like I'd done for Malina a thousand times before, and she clutched me back tightly, hot face tucked into my shoulder. I'd never been close enough to smell her before, and beneath the scents of grass and pine and old fire, her skin and hair smelled so much like Mama's.

"It hurt to wake back in the cave," she whispered through the tears. "Like knives and glass and poison inside me. And I was still strong, so strong, but everything hurt. And I *hate* him and I miss him, I miss him *so* much."

I rocked her back and forth as she sobbed, shushing into her ear. I wanted to murder Mara for doing this to her, and him—him I wanted to suffocate with my bare hands. "You really loved him, didn't you? You really wanted him for your own."

I could feel her ragged breathing slow a little. "It was Mara's doing first, and then I did it for Jasmina. But then, I truly did, for myself. I still do." She gave a little hiccup of a laugh. "And I would never wish him upon you, ever."

"I understand," I murmured back. "I don't particularly think I'd like to share, either."

This time, I startled genuine laughter out of her, full-throated and musical even with the tearful tinge. "We *are* greedy," she said. "All of us, starting with her. Always wanting the fullness of things, everything to its extremes."

But wasn't that true of most people? I thought. Why else would we wage war and fight for freedom and kill each other over the true name of God? Because we all wanted everything, and for everything we wanted to be right.

"So after you woke up," Malina said gently. "What happened then?"

Dunja blinked away the last of the tears, wiping delicately at her face. "There was someone in the cave with me, I think she'd come to trim my hair. Denari, Mara's great-granddaughter. She was rearranging the furs when I woke all the way up. I scared her, and she attacked me and I—" She swallowed. "I threw her hard against the wall, like she weighed nothing. That's how I knew how strong

I'd gotten. Then I made my way to you."

"Reverse engineering!" Luka announced triumphantly.

Dunja, Malina, and I all turned to frown at him in such a synchronized way that we must have looked like real family for the first time. Even Niko, sitting beside him, gave him a dubious squint, squinching up her nose.

"That's what we were trying to do," he said, and I recognized that tamped-down glow, the restrained ember of his excitement when he delved to the bottom of something. "With Mara's legends. We were trying to literally undo the spell by breaking it down into components, and creating an equal and opposite ritual to what Mara did. But the problem is that you were imitating her. Mimicking. And you were using the wrong set of tools to do it, a different kind of magic."

Luka sprang to his feet like a coiled spring, and even though I still had no idea what he meant, watching him pace as his mind whirred so quickly made me want to back him into some trees myself.

"It's freedom," he said suddenly, looking up at us with blazing eyes. "*That's* the opposite. True love is freedom, loving someone enough to do what's best for them—to let them go, if that's what they need. Mara's love is just another kind of slavery, a falseness, a perversion of the word."

"But what then?" Niko asked. "What do you *do* with knowing that?"

"It would have to be an effort of will," I said slowly, my heart beginning to pick up speed. "Maybe that's how she sealed this deal in the first place, by casting her will so far and wide that it set this cycle in place in perpetuity. And that's what I've been doing, isn't it, with the infinite bloom? Imposing my will on things? Isn't that what you said, Dunja? That the infinite bloom is the ultimate gleam, imposed on space and time?"

Dunja's eyes sharpened on me. "Yes. Exactly so. The infinite bloom is the basal gift, the one that lets Mara cast at her highest order of magnitude. It lets you bind far past yourself, to bind the universe to your will."

"So why do I have it now, when I never did before? I mean, I could always make things bloom, but I couldn't do what I did with the—with that wisteria that comes from me. It's like Mara's roses, I assume, but why can I do it?"

"You've never been so desperate before, most likely, and you've spent your life weakened, away from coven and suppressed by your mother. To apply your gleam fully to the infinite bloom, you have to cast from truest yearning. The deepest desire of your soul. The thing you want more than any other thing, perhaps even than to live."

So that was it, then—it had always been protection. Every time I had summoned the wisteria, it had been because I needed it badly, to shelter Malina. To put myself between her and whatever was coming.

But maybe I could want to save myself, too.

"So, maybe . . . maybe we could all go bigger," I said slowly. "I think I already did it once, Dunja. I opened a portal to somewhere—somewhere that might have been his kingdom, even.

Because I wanted to beat Malina. I wanted to will myself to be the one to go, to save her."

"That's it, then," Luka said. "It must be. Because that's what fractals are—an expression of infinity. You can see it, Iris. And if you can see it . . ."

"Then maybe I can touch it," I finished. "But even if I can, what am I supposed to do once I'm there? I knew what I wanted, the last time I did it. I wanted to make sure I was the one who went. But this—I'm not sure I know how to want this, properly."

"You'll have us," Malina replied. "To help you. Mara sold us into slavery; maybe we can do what Luka says, and break those bonds by turning them into freedom. I could sing it. Dunja can dance it."

"But where do we do this? In the cave?"

"No." Luka shook his head. "The Ice Cave is hers—that's still playing by her rules. We need to take it up another level. Set it all up above her. Go even higher."

Malina groaned. "Oh, I was afraid of that."

Niko's head snapped up. "There's not going to be enough room for me and Luka," she said flatly. "Is there."

I shook my head, biting back tears. "No. Not if Dunja will be dancing."

He set his jaw. "I'm not going to leave you. I want to help."

"You already did—you let us see all this in a different way," I answered gently. "And that was what we needed. But I think you know it, too, that we need to do this alone, the three of us."

"Princess," Lina said gently as Niko struggled before melting against her. "Please. Don't make this so hard. Come say good-bye this time."

Luka crouched down next to me and cupped my face with one hand, curling the other tightly around my neck. I inhaled at the force of his kiss, the taste of him, the warmth behind it. The full heat and fervor of his love, as he kissed me on each cheek and between my eyes. And even before he said so, I knew he'd do it. He'd leave me alone to this, because that was what I asked of him.

"Don't you dare think these were good-bye kisses," he said when he drew back. "It was just to tide me over. And because I love you."

"I hope so. And I love you, too."

EVEN IN THE twilight, the world spread below us was stunning from this high up. For a little while, I hadn't even thought that we would make it. The earlier stages of the ascent had been almost pleasant, green and winding paths up the mountain that zigged and zagged to bring us higher without the impression of terrible danger. But the last leg of the climb had been so steep and severe—just scree slopes with hand- and toeholds you had to feel out carefully to find, that should have required actual climbing equipment if we'd had the time for that—that Malina had simply frozen against the mountain with her face pressed against the still-warm stone, whispering that she couldn't go farther, she just couldn't.

Eventually, Dunja and I had arranged ourselves beside and below her against the cliff face, and carefully moved her hands and feet for her as she clung to the side like a limpet. I'd never been very afraid of heights, but the little fear I'd had seemed to have dissipated. Instead I felt a vast, yawning sense of awe inside me, as if my soul had opened its mouth wide to breathe all this in.

"Bobotov Kuk," I said as we scrabbled over its lip and onto its face. "Holy shit."

The summit pyramid of stone was larger than it seemed from the valley below, but not by much. There was enough room for the three of us to huddle toward its center, with a ring of open space around us. The summit stood between two slightly lower peaks—the Nameless Peak and the Maiden, Dunja informed us—and together the three made a jagged mountain wall to the west, dropping off into a plummeting slope toward the green-fuzzed Škrka Valley and the glacial pools of its two lakes below, one massive and one small. Beyond them the rest of the Durmitor range soared, mountain after mountain like the earth's own stone fractals, into the fall and fire tones of the dying day on the horizon.

"I know I was full-throttle about this," Malina gulped, "but I'm very, very scared right now. We're so high up, and it's—I could fall—I don't know if I'll be able to sing anything other than that."

"I would never let you fall," Dunja said, sliding a hand down Malina's hair. "I promise you. And once I start the dance, you'll pick up the thread from me. It'll be all right."

I sat down cross-legged next to her, giving her leg a squeeze.

The three of us simply sat together, quiet, until I could smell and hear things I never could before. The breeze was cooling with the advent of night, and the air smelled of pine sap and moss and ferns, the rank sear of a fox from somewhere far below. I even thought I caught the alkaline tang of water from the lakes in the far, low distance, and I could hear the stirring of the needles with the wind, the brush and rustle of birds and insects in the trees, maybe even the lumbering shuffle of something hungry, big, and hidden.

At the very base of the mountain, we could see the coven swarming. They were tiny from up here, but there were so many, and they moved so fast, like insects engulfing a carcass. Soon they would be up here with us, and then the reckoning would begin.

At some point, I realized that we'd settled into a rhythm, inhales and exhales like a tide, breathing slowly with each other. I thought I could even feel my sister and my aunt, the bright pulse of each of their minds, the slow and steady throbbing of their hearts.

Dunja moved first, but the stirring didn't break the spell. She unfurled all at once, twirling as she stood; her white hair drifted as though it were gravity defiant and alive, something lazy and languid with its own mind. With her first step, I had a sense of scorching sand and translucent veils, as if she danced for a sultan in some baking desert.

That would be one of her freedoms, I suddenly realized; to dance all that beauty for someone else, because she'd chosen not to hide it.

Malina felt it too, the freedom of it, and she began to sing in pursuit.

We shifted then from the desert sands, the peaks and cliffs around us melting away like a spun-sugar confection, until Dunja danced on a minaret's onion dome—above a flat-roofed, baked-brick city stretching beneath a blazing sun, her arms wide and hair whirling like a platinum halo. Then there was a jungle, so dense and lush its canopy was almost solid; she took us with her as she danced upon it, leaping from glossy palm leaf to branch to vine, and all the while Malina's song followed. From beaches to villages to waterfalls, to roaring, white-frothed rivers and skyscraper cities and masquerade balls.

We could go there; we could be there; we could choose warmth and life instead of ice.

Anywhere was open to us, anywhere that we chose. And I thought of Luka, and how he would let me go.

Come on, little witch, I heard Dunja urging in my mind. *Make this the truth for us. Make choice and anywhere the* only *truth.*

Even as the sky unfolded a plumage of stars over us, I focused on my wisteria, watching pinks and purples fracture and multiply, blooming and unfurling and stretching with no end. The branches made overlapping bridges, and the blossoms endless whirlpools; together they formed ladders that could have spanned farther than from Earth to moon. And I pushed them harder, climbed them with my mind, strove to touch where they were going like I never had before.

But it wasn't enough.

My head was pounding as if it would split apart, and I could feel warm rivulets come sluicing from my nose. And there was something—something more—beyond the kaleidoscope of freedom that spun around us like a top.

I could feel her rather than see her, crawling up the cliff like a spider. Whatever bond we'd woven, Dunja and Malina and I, Mara could feel it too.

"She's coming," I whispered, then—"I think she's here—"
And then the first wave of love broke terribly over us.

LISARAH MY DAUGHTER, LISARAH MY LOVE, it roared
in my ears and bones and mind, WOULD YOU UNSPOOL YOUR
MOTHER IN THIS WAY, WHO LOVED YOU AND SACRI-
FICED SO YOU COULD HAVE LIFE?

"You're not my mother," I hissed through clenched teeth. "And
you *don't* love me."

The assault continued, and now I could see her hands and the
scraggly, singed leftovers of her hair as she clawed herself up and
over onto our summit. *I LOVE YOU THE MOST, THE MOST
OF THEM ALL, AND EVEN AFTER EVERYTHING YOU'VE
DONE TO ME, I WOULD GATHER YOU IN MY LAP AND
HOLD YOU AGAINST MY HEART. WOULD YOU TRULY
STAB ME IN MY BREASTBONE, LISARAH, DAUGHTER?
WOULD YOU TRULY WATCH ME DIE?*

Now she stood at the very edge, still in the black dress she'd
worn the other night, tattered and ripped from her hillside climb.
The entire surface of her skin was burned; that was what our spell
had done, latched onto her and roasted her alive while leaving
her own spell intact. Beneath the scorch, a network of black veins
like worms had risen to the surface of what had once been skin,
but somehow even with that she was still beautiful, all sleek and
exposed sinew, reaching hands and that perfume of love. She could
dance like Dunja too, I saw, only disjointed and somehow inside
out, sparse hair thrashing and limbs bending in an unlikely, backward way, as if someone had thrown a strange and gorgeous thing

under a strobe light so it stuttered.

And behind that dance I saw something I remembered: a vast, endless field of black roses that glistened wet under a dim sky, so tangled and thorny they reached the dark, distant dregs of creation before doubling back, like a serpent of flowers swallowing its own tail.

So that was the shape of Mara's will, then.

Well, it wasn't the shape of mine.

The flowers I had in front of me—they were a beginning, but they couldn't reach far enough. But there was one that could, one that grew in my father's soil. Because it was his, it was also mine. It didn't matter that I'd never seen it in person. I could grow it in my mind.

Slowly, as if I were gathering molten glass at the end of my pipe, I snaked a massive underground root system in my mind. Its reaching tendrils grew into a twisted trunk, then burst into a vast profusion of branches, gnarled wood giving way to wisteria waterfalls that bloomed for miles. My hands were clenched into fists so tight I could feel the piercing sink of my nails into my skin, the hot blood that welled around them. And I could hear myself screaming with the strain, but still I pressed forth with my freedom tree. Its flowers twined and wove like living things, over and under the bramble of Mara's roses, shooting up and away from me like the sparking threads of my own synapses.

This was the framework that supported her will—the only way to end was overwhelm it, make it mine.

YOU ARE MINE, the roses shrieked in Mara's ancient voice

as they withered on their vines.

No, I am mine, I told them, as I strangled them with rushing fireworks of purple, pink, and white. *Not yours, old mother, but always mine.*

We were so close I could have kissed her, though she didn't touch me; just faced me with her burned, seeping hands hovering over my shoulders, looking into my eyes. I could see her then as she had been so many years ago, a beetle-browed child with dark hair, improbably lovely and kneeling by a stream. Hauling slick fish in baskets, skinning felled game that steamed in the icy air, curing hides in stinking cauldrons. And watching so many of her sisters die. She'd had six of them since she remembered herself, but four had died bearing their children, one from a wound gone putrid, and the sixth from pains that ate away all her insides.

Until she was the only sister left. The only one left of her whole line.

And then she had her own children, and they died too, a girl, a boy, another girl.

I could feel the roiling fathoms of her grief, see her hone her manifold gifts, the way she could wield love. And once she had more daughters, the fierce and burning need that drove her, to never lose her own again—to never die, nor let her own die young.

Something else flickered deep there, too, so far beneath that all I could see was a trailing shadow, like a passing shark swimming miles under the sea.

"But what about us?" I whispered to her. "The ones who you gave away. Was it really worth the price?"

"Everything is give and take, my blood," she rasped. "You can only pay for life with life."

More images of her times washed over me, and I could feel myself softening toward her, even as my wisteria coiled tighter around the rose mesh of her will. I could hear her howling sobs as she cradled a stillborn baby to her chest, the sweeter croon of her lullaby as she stroked a living daughter's fluffy hair.

And I wanted that. The cradle, the stroke, the lullaby. I wanted all that mother-love.

"*Iris!*" Dunja shrieked at me. "*Break it, break it now! There's no more time!*"

I tore my eyes away from Mara and looked to my sister and my aunt. Dunja was flinging herself through frantic arabesques, her floating hair blazing with starlight, and Malina's face, contorted, was bathed in the same pale light. Behind them, others crested the peak—those would be true witches, of the first nine. My aunt and sister wouldn't be able to stand against all of them.

Rage kindled inside me, the roaring urge to protect them: these two who truly loved me, not the false mother with her lies.

I turned back to the oldest of all my kin, our ancient, greatest grandmother, with her blistered face and bottomless eyes. "I'm sorry," I said to her. "I wish I'd known you back then. But I think, now, it's time to stop."

I bore down on all my flowers, forced them to choke and cover tighter, until the roses beneath them nearly breathed their last. But as I came to the breaking point, I discovered that it would take even more than I'd thought it would take.

Strip her arms bare of glitter or silver, I thought desperately. That was it. It had to be.

Her will was not merely flung wide, but anchored in her skin, and it wouldn't succumb to me until the last pieces were plucked out.

"Dunja," I forced out, as if through a howling wind rushing down my throat, "her diamonds. *Get. Them. Out.*"

I could see her eyes dawn bright with understanding, and the next arabesque brought her behind Mara. She locked her arms around our first mother, as Mara had once done to me, and pinning her flailing, black-streaked arms, Dunja began to dig and pluck with blinding speed. Mara thrashed against her like something primal caught in an iron-maiden vise. Her voices droned into a hellmouth clamor, tinged with a terror so pure it nearly wrested the flower reins from me.

"LISARAH—IRIS—DAUGHTER, *DON'T*," she shrieked, her eyes and mouth impossibly wide. "WHAT I DO IS MORE THAN YOU COULD UNDERSTAND—REMEMBER HOW YOU DID NOT EVEN KNOW YOUR OWN MOTHER'S MIND—"

I thought of all the things I'd heard of Mara, the legends and rumors and lies. She wasn't a goddess of nightmares and winter. Nor was she a selfless savior who'd offered herself and her own for the sake of her people. And she wasn't what Dunja thought, either, a grasping, greedy monster bent on never dying, no matter how many of her daughters she had to sell.

And I thought of the way she had her sacrifices cared for in the caves, sending her other undying daughters to trim their nails and hair and see to them. She didn't have to do that; she could have simply left them there. But that effort, even if it went unrecognized by the offering herself, was still a choice she'd made. Like the overtures, maybe, that my own mother had made toward me, and that I'd just either failed to see or chosen not to see.

Nothing was ever simple. There was no such thing as the one and only truth, and that too was a freedom in itself.

I bore down just once, a single exhale so brutal and sharp that I could smell the last gust of perfume as the endless black roses died. There was nothing left but the infinite lattice-breadth of my wisteria, the dripping blossoms stirring in the mountain wind, and the branches meshing together to form an arch—and within that open space, a distant star-struck sky above a sea.

And Fjolar, stepping through it.

Dunja gasped, then flung Mara away from her, like a child bored with a doll. Mara curled sobbing in a heap, cradling her shredded, bleeding arms against her chest. "Oh, *daughter*," she whispered brokenly to me, her eyes sliding closed, and though her voices were still many they'd been wrung of all their power. "You have no *idea* what you've done."

The dread on her face rocked me like nothing else I'd ever seen from her. I had a sudden overwhelming, terrible sense, like drowning in tar, that I'd gotten everything wrong.

Dunja reached Fjolar but locked in place as if she'd hit a wall before she set even a foot over the wisteria threshold. He cast her a wistful, dismissive glance. "Not you, my love," he said. "Not anymore."

She let out a single, rending sob, and collapsed to her knees. "But *why?*" she wailed, white hair wind-whipped across her face and sticking to her lips. "You loved the dance. And I gave you *every-. thing.*"

"You did," he said simply. "And thank you for it. But I chose her, already." He looked up at me, glowing eyes shadowed by the overhang of his brow, and held out a hand. "You ate our wedding cake, my flower girl. Don't tell me you forget so quick."

The tang of skyr and crushed smear of blueberries flooded through my mouth, and suddenly I found myself standing before him, my hands folded in both of his. His breath blew hot across my face, and he smiled into my eyes. My own wisteria pressed me forward, sending me tripping into his arms. Between us, I saw something like the opposite of an abyss—a crowded, choking sea of relentless light—and knew I'd have to survive it before I even stumbled into the sea that lay beneath his kingdom's stars.

The last thing I heard as he pulled me through was Malina calling my name, before her voice cut out as fully as if it were sliced clean through with glass.

EPILOGUE

Malina

I COULDN'T HEAR MY SISTER.

All my life I'd heard her, steady as the rush of blood in my own ears. Iris had sounded like the rain. Sometimes storms, sometimes light patters, sometimes the sweet, lashing gales after a long drought. Sometimes even the kind that came with rainbows. The kind you wanted to feel on your face while you held the rest of your body underwater in the summer sea.

Rain could be so warm. No one ever really talked about that.

But she'd always been there, water rushing against the windows of my soul, shushing me to sleep. In one form or another, she'd flooded me with sound, like a waterfall that kept me safe in my own cave. A water shield that made me invisible, that let me do whatever I wanted. That hid the way I burned so freely inside myself.

And now I couldn't *hear* her.

The agony was like nothing I'd ever felt, but what was I supposed to do with it? Tears would sound too much like she had sounded. I couldn't even cry for her, or I'd never get up again, peel myself away from all this stone beneath my cheek.

I didn't actually remember having fallen down at all, but then there were hands picking me up. Had I been on the ground? Had I passed out? I must have, if there were coven daughters lifting me to my feet with strangely gentle hands. One of them still had a half-snout and fangs. "So you're the one who was baying," I said woozily to her. "Aren't you supposed to be rending me from stem to stern or something?"

"No one shall be rending anyone," a tripled voice rang out, and I turned. Mara was there, somehow slightly less like a charred, melted plastic doll in the starlit dark. "The worst is done; the damage is wrought. There will be no more evil wreaked. Not by us, at the very least."

"*Of course the worst is done!*" I shrieked at her. I hadn't meant to scream like that, but now it felt like the only sound I was likely to make for a while. "*Riss is gone gone gone, he took her away! I need her back! Give her back to me!*"

"We *all* need her back, child," she said, again in those calm but ravaged tones. It was so strange I bothered to listen below it, just for a second. Beneath she sounded like a careful detonation, a building scheduled for demolition caving, controlled, unto itself. "We need her now because *he* is free. I have failed. My net has failed. I can feel him stir already under the fathoms."

"Fjolar?" I demanded. My voices were pure cacophony, a music box shattering under a hammer, all snapped cords and smashed-up gears. "Death, or whatever? Obviously he was free before, at least free enough to stalk Riss and then *take* her. And so what, you don't have him trapped, so now you don't get to live forever anymore, you miserable hag?" I tossed my head back and hawked thickly, spitting in her face. *"Do you think I care what happens to you now?"*

She wiped it away calmly, no trace of anger anywhere on her, nowhere in her sound. Nothing but devastation, and that buckling iron chassis of control. "It's not about what happens to me, child. And my feckless boy—my death-son made of the flesh I lent him—is not what we should fear."

I flinched away from her, but she caught me in an iron grip, made me meet her gaze. She stroked lightly at the edges of my face, and for the first time I saw the dead weight in her eyes, thousands of years of exhaustion floodlit by the moonlight. "It's what happens to you, and this whole unready world, when a king of demons walks its face again."

ACKNOWLEDGMENTS

I owe so many thanks that simply being in a position to give them feels like the most wonderful daydream. First of all, my eternal gratitude to Melissa Miller for her dazzling editorial genius; she took an ember of a book and fanned it (very vigorously) into something so much bigger, more elaborate, and more intensely glittery than I could ever have accomplished on my own. I am forever indebted to her vision and her trust that I could pull this off. One day, she will know exactly how many all-nighters and 3 a.m. spring rolls went into the making of this book.

Many thanks, too, to Claudia Gabel for taking on me and the twins with such open, gracious warmth, as well as to Kelsey Horton, Rebecca Aronson, and the rest of the magnificent team at Katherine Tegen Books and HarperCollins. Tremendous thanks to the foremost lady, Katherine Tegen herself, for welcoming me into her fold and allowing me to keep almost all the scandalous bits. And to Lisa Perrin, for the cover of my dreams.

Many thanks to everyone at Waxman-Leavell, especially Holly Root, aka Publishing Galadriel.

So many, many thanks to Taylor Haggerty, queen of inside jokes, and a finer, fiercer agent and dear friend than I could have dreamed up for myself. Thank you for your lovely mind, kindest heart, and murderously funny wit—and for believing in me since the beginning. See you at the green dot, T, and here's to many more so-shots.

I'm beyond grateful to the brilliant Kayla Olson, Natasha Ngan, Siân Gaetano, and Alyssa for being lovely enough to read for me, and for their invaluable feedback and critique. And to the effervescent (no other word does her justice) Jilly Gagnon for sitting by my side when everything seemed so terribly hard, and for plying me with her inimitable brand of comedy, mostly to do with mossy grottos. Girl, you are a treasure beyond compare. Never leave me lest I wither pitifully on the vine.

I'd never be here without the friends who still love me—who somehow always manage to love me, sometimes to superhuman extremes—even when I disappear into the writing cave for days and/or weeks. You know who you are, and rest assured that I will buy you all the wines. I'm beyond lucky to have you.

Thank you to bat, for turning my blood to glitter in the best way. Apparently there is such a thing, and apparently it's awesome.

All my thanks to my wonderful family and kin—first and foremost to my tireless, scarily smart, and endlessly benevolent parents, to whom this book is dedicated, for nurturing such a weird and witchy child. I'm particularly indebted to Lidija Popović, mother of mothers, queen of the universe, for reading everything I've ever written, loving it effusively, and only looking at me funny every once in a while; and to Momir Popović for shouting about my writing from the rooftops until my ears burned. Thanks to my younger brother, Marko, for driving me to books as a child and to drink as an adult—just kidding, I couldn't be more proud to be your sister. To my grandmothers, Djuja Crnković and Kosa Popović, who let me roam around making up stories and creeping out the neighbors, and who always made me feel so beloved. To my grandfathers, Milisav Popović and Anton Crnković, may you rest in peace and I so hope I made you proud.

And finally, most importantly, thank you to Montenegro, particularly Kotor (Cattaro) and Žabljak, for being the cradle of (half) my bloodline, and for lending me the backdrops for this book. Any geographical mistakes and tweaks are mine, and please forgive the liberties I took with local stories and legends.